MOUNTAIN BIKING THE DEEP SOUTH

Dennis Coello's America by Mountain Bike Series

MOUNTAIN BIKING
THE DEEP SOUTH

*Dennis Coello's America by
Mountain Bike Series*

Louisiana
Mississippi
Alabama
Georgia

Steve Jones

Foreword, Introduction, and Afterword
by Dennis Coello, Series Editor

MENASHA
RIDGE
PRESS

FALCON™

Library of Congress Cataloging-in-Publication Data:

Jones, Steve, 1954-
    Mountain biking the Deep South : Louisiana, Mississippi, Alabama,
    Georgia / Steve Jones ; foreword, introduction, and afterword by
    Dennis Coello. — 1st ed.
        p.   cm. — (Dennis Coello's America by mountain bike series)
    ISBN 1-56044-455-X
    1. All terrain cycling—Southern States—Guidebooks. 2. Bicycle
trails—Southern States—Guidebooks. 3. Southern States—
Guidebooks. I. Title. II. Series: America by mountain bike
series.
GV1045.5.S67J65   1996
796.6'4'0975—dc20   96-18395
                                                              CIP
Photos by the author unless otherwise credited
Maps by Tim Krasnansky and Brian Taylor at RapiDesign
Cover photo by Karl Weatherly

Menasha Ridge Press
3169 Cahaba Heights Road
Birmingham, Alabama 35243

Falcon Press
P.O. Box 1718
Helena, Montana 59624

♲ Text pages printed on recycled paper

CAUTION
Outdoor recreation activities are by their very nature potentially hazardous. All participants in such activities must assume the responsibility for their own actions and
safety. The information contained in this guidebook cannot replace sound judgment
and good decision-making skills, which help reduce risk exposure, nor does the scope
of this book allow for disclosure of all the potential hazards and risks involved in such
activities.
    Learn as much as possible about the outdoor recreation activities you participate in,
prepare for the unexpected, and be safe and cautious. The reward will be a safer and
more enjoyable experience.

Table of Contents

AMERICA BY MOUNTAIN BIKE *MAP LEGEND*

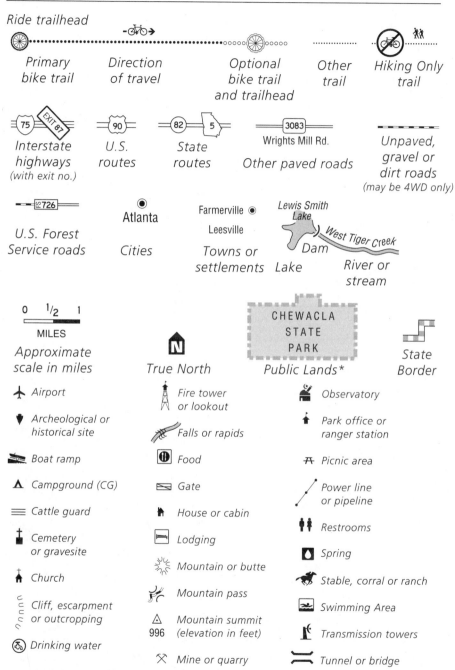

Ride trailhead

Primary bike trail	Direction of travel	Optional bike trail and trailhead	Other trail	Hiking Only trail

Interstate highways (with exit no.)	U.S. routes	State routes	Wrights Mill Rd. Other paved roads	Unpaved, gravel or dirt roads (may be 4WD only)

U.S. Forest Service roads	Atlanta Cities	Farmerville ⊙ Leesville Towns or settlements	Lewis Smith Lake / West Tiger Creek Dam Lake River or stream

0 ½ 1
MILES

Approximate scale in miles

N True North

CHEWACLA STATE PARK
Public Lands*

State Border

- ✈ Airport
- ♦ Archeological or historical site
- Boat ramp
- ▲ Campground (CG)
- ☰ Cattle guard
- ✝ Cemetery or gravesite
- ♦ Church
- Cliff, escarpment or outcropping
- ♿ Drinking water

- Fire tower or lookout
- Falls or rapids
- 🍴 Food
- Gate
- ♠ House or cabin
- 🛏 Lodging
- Mountain or butte
- Mountain pass
- △ 996 Mountain summit (elevation in feet)
- ✕ Mine or quarry

- Observatory
- Park office or ranger station
- ⅜ Picnic area
- Power line or pipeline
- 👫 Restrooms
- Spring
- 🐎 Stable, corral or ranch
- Swimming Area
- Transmission towers
- Tunnel or bridge

Remember, private property exists in and around our National Forests.

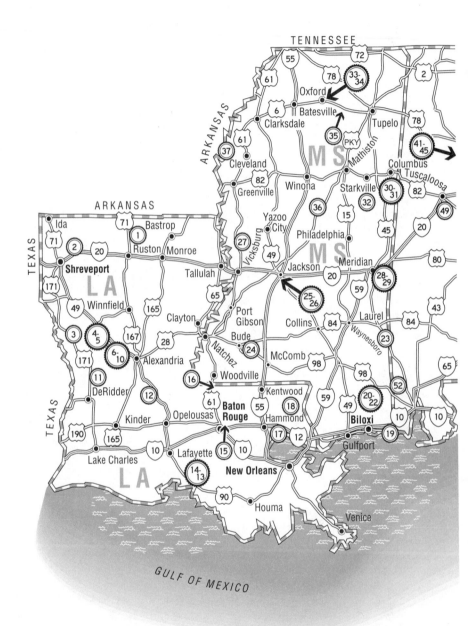

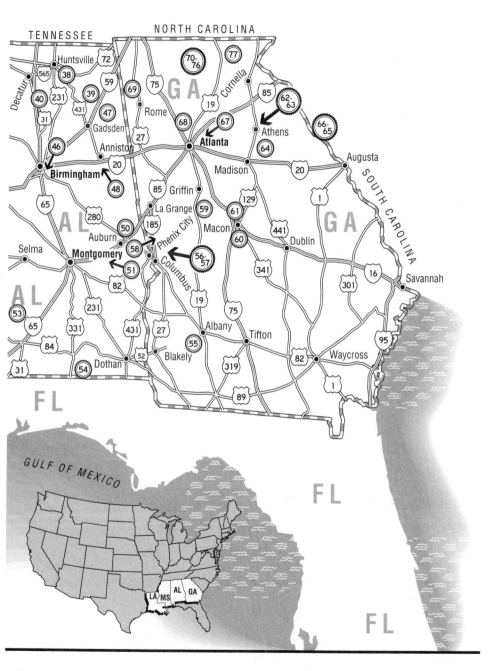

List of Maps

Acknowledgments

The research for this book put me in the saddle for nearly a thousand miles of mountain bike trails in the Deep South. Although I had to ride many of these miles alone ("You're going where? Mississippi? Uh, no thanks.") and was often guided by little more than a fiber optic phone line, I never felt lonely. I always kept in my head conversations with those who have helped me.

To my friend Brian, whose excited reports of wonderful times out on the trail convinced me to get my own mountain bike, thank you. To my wife and best friend, Pam, who has always understood my need to create and recreate, this book is as much yours as it is mine. The snacks you packed in my supplies answered the question, "Can man live on trail mix alone?" To my son, Jared, who had to stay behind and take care of the house and the women when you wanted to go out pedaling with pop ("I want to go to Mississippi!"), it was a great day when you came into my life. And to the rest of my family—my moms, my dads, my brothers and sisters—thanks.

Someone once told me, "A good editor is worth his weight in gold." To Dennis Coello, who set my free wheel spinning and kept it going in the right direction, you've been my Fort Knox. Thanks to all the great folks at Menasha and Falcon who have gambled on folks like me to bring in the best outdoors books available.

Mountain biking is many things to many people. Some hop on the saddle just to be included. Others search out the lonely and isolated tracks. Some like the slop and goo of a perpetual bayou. Others become uncontrollably giddy sliding about in the sand. There are some who can't find enough rocks, and others who consider anything bumpier than asphalt out of the question. Roots, river crossings, and rocks all go in the category as desirable by some. I met bikers who only feel fulfilled when they can ride a trail without having to get off; others say, "If you aren't hiking, you aren't biking!"

And yet we're all out there using the world's greatest invention to investigate those outer and inner sanctums of body and spirit. My biggest thanks goes to you, the mountain bikers who pointed me to where you get your thrills and told me, "We can't get enough of any of it!" I hope you use this book to your health.

Steve Jones

Foreword

Welcome to *America by Mountain Bike,* a 20-plus-book series designed to provide all-terrain bikers with the information they need to find and ride the very best trails everywhere in the mainland United States. Whether you're new to the sport and don't know where to pedal, or an experienced mountain biker who wants to learn the classic trails in another region, this series is for you. Drop a few bucks for the book, spend an hour with the detailed maps and route descriptions, and you're prepared for the finest in off-road cycling.

My role as editor of this series was simple: First, find a mountain biker who knows the area and loves to ride. Second, ask that person to spend a year researching the most popular and very best rides around. And third, have that rider describe each trail in terms of difficulty, scenery, condition, elevation change, and all other categories of information that are important to trail riders. "Pretend you've just completed a ride and met up with fellow mountain bikers at the trailhead," I told each author. "Imagine their questions, be clear in your answers."

As I said, the *editorial* process—that of sending out riders and reading the submitted chapters—is a snap. But the work involved in finding, riding, and writing about each trail is enormous. In some instances our authors' tasks are made easier by the information contributed by local bike shops or cycling clubs, or even by the writers of local "where-to" guides. Credit for these contributions is provided, when appropriate, in each chapter, and our sincere thanks goes to all who have helped.

But the overwhelming majority of trails are discovered and pedaled by our authors themselves, then compared with dozens of other routes to determine if they qualify as "classic"—that area's best in scenery and cycling fun. If you've ever had the experience of pioneering a route from outdated topographic maps, or entering a bike shop to request information from local riders who would much prefer to keep their favorite trails secret, or know how it is to double- and triple-check data to be positive your trail info is correct, then you have an idea of how each of our authors has labored to bring about these books. You and I, and all the mountain bikers of America, are the richer for their efforts.

You'll get more out of this book if you take a moment to read the Introduction explaining how to read the trail listings. The "Topographic Maps" section will help you understand how useful topos will be on a ride, and will also tell you where to get them. And though this is a "where-to," not a "how-to" guide, those of you who have not traveled the backcountry might find "Hitting the Trail" of particular value.

In addition to the material above, newcomers to mountain biking might want to spend a minute with the glossary, page 317, so that terms like *hard-pack, single-track,* and *water bars* won't throw you when you come across them in the text.

Finally, the tips in the Afterword on mountain biking etiquette and the land-use controversy might help us all enjoy the trails a little more.

All the best.

Dennis Coello
St. Louis

Preface

Mention the Deep South to most people who don't live there, and they immediately break out in a sweat imagining endless rows of cotton fields plowed by a mule and baked by an equatorial sun. Or they might give an involuntary shudder as they recall Burt Reynolds with a bow and arrow on the banks of a wild north Georgia river. It's that kind of place. Full of mystery. Misunderstood.

To get an idea of just how misunderstood it is, mention mountain biking in Mississippi or Louisiana. You get some of the strangest looks, as if you had been dabbling in Granny's cold medicine a little too long. And these are looks from the people who live there. But I got over people looking at me strange after I put on my first biking helmet and tight black shorts. It's a small price to pay for the feeling of being young again and on a bike, exploring wherever and however you want.

So, repeat the phrase "mountain biking in the Deep South" a few times before we get started. Make yourself a mint julep if you need to. Before you can say "fiddle-dee-dee," you'll get a hankering to take your bike out and roll on some of the best trails anywhere, here in the Deep South. Come on, I'll show you what I mean.

SOUTHERNERS

The original Southerners reportedly crossed the Iberian Peninsula long ago in search of more hospitable conditions. The Choctaw, Cherokee, and other indigenous tribes De Soto found living in the river valleys in the early sixteenth century left behind a long legacy. Many of the names, although Anglicized, remain in our vocabulary to describe what cannot be said accurately in any other language: Amicalola, Cheaha, Chehaw, Tallapoosa, Talladega, Coosa, Chattahoochee, Mississippi, Etowah, and Kisatchie. The list goes on although the people who spoke them originally have nearly reached cultural extinction, replaced by opportunists who brought with them an incurable fever for gold.

The demand for laborers in the largely agrarian antebellum society created by the South's long growing season did more to bring about the Civil War than any wishes to dominate a race. In any event, the great rift between northern industry and southern farms took place largely on the plantations. As a result, the Southern psyche became shaped by being the only site in America since independence where sustained sieges of warfare have ever taken place. Perhaps

Mountain biking is great even when there are no mountains.

this has created what the rest of America has watched develop: Southern culture.

The idea of Southern hospitality is no mistake. People born and raised in the South are among the nicest and kindest people anywhere, despite the undying reputation of its being home to the original rednecks. Oh sure, occasionally evidence can be sighted of backward ways—ball caps emblazoned with a Confederate snarling the words: "Don't get mad, get even," or jalopies bearing a front license plate decorated with the Confederate battle flag and the sentiment: "Hell no I won't forget." As my mama always told me when someone did something tacky, "Just consider the source."

More examples than a coon dog has fleas point to the Southerner's prolific creativity in the areas of the arts, especially music. Along with the more widely known form of rock 'n' roll, the origins of country, blues, jazz, bluegrass, and zydeco can all be traced to points in the Deep South. A friend of mine wondered out loud one day when we were discussing this phenomenon, "What was the rest of the country doing while all this was happening?" They were either listening to talk about it or reading about it.

The art of spinning a good yarn is also a Southern trait, a holdover from cotton-picking days or times spent snapping beans on the front porch. A good story just made the unbearable bearable. Along with heavyweights like William Faulkner and Tennessee Williams, a list longer than a Louisiana bayou can be made of other significant Southern writers. Some of these include Flannery O'Connor, Joel Chandler Harris, Alice Walker, Erskine Caldwell, Harper Lee, John Grisham, Lewis Grizzard, Margaret Mitchell, and Sidney Lanier. It must be the water. Or the heat.

Painting, sculpting, weaving, pottery, basket-making, you name it—if the craft involves using hands, Southerners actively pursue it. Which reminds me, the kitchen is one of my favorite destinations. What with all the fried chicken, biscuits, gravy, creamed corn, fried okra, pork chops, grits (yes, grits), and boiled peanuts—why, it's a wonder I can waddle off to my mountain bike and climb onto the saddle at all.

I haven't done it yet, but one day I just might find me a ball cap that I saw someone wearing not too long ago. It had a saying on it that captures much of what it means to be a part of this land: "American by Birth—Southern by the Grace of God." Y'know whadda mean?

THE LAND

Some people snicker at the thought of mountains in the South, but these folks are apparently unfamiliar with the topography of any ground east of the Mississippi and south of the Mason-Dixon line. In this area mountains provide trails and scenery unsurpassed in any region of the lower 48. Although it lies outside of what this book refers to as the Deep South, North Carolina boasts the highest peak east of the Mississippi at Mount Mitchell (6,684 feet).

The mountainous regions do, however, fall off considerably the farther west and south you go from that point. Georgia's Brasstown Bald (4,784 feet) and Alabama's Cheaha Mountain (2,405 feet) loom considerably taller than Mississippi's highest point, Woodall Mountain (806 feet) and Louisiana's Driskell Mountain (535 feet). Hills, mountains—there's not a whole lot of difference when you get down to it. Look it up. A mountain is defined as elevation taller than a hill, and a hill gets described as land lower than a mountain. See what I mean? The experts don't even know the difference. Anyway, one person's floor is another's ceiling.

The richness of the mountain biker's experience, though, does not come simply from riding steep trails. The coastal trails snake through marshes and swamps that change character throughout the year as much as the inland peaks do. Trips along the eastern banks of the Mississippi give glimpses of hardwood swamps where you're just as likely to see an alligator or armadillo as you are a wood duck. Pine belts, coastal plains, steep mountains—with just about every variation in between—await the adventuresome cyclist who knows where to go in the Deep South. And now you do. Pick the trail to fit your mood and celebrate the fact your two good legs and tires can bring it right up under you. I feel better already.

ANIMALS

Mountain biking is for many an extension of a fascination with the natural wonders around them. Few other modes allow such primitive territory to be covered as quickly and relatively unobtrusively as the off-road bicycle. Almost immediately after I began to roll in the woods, I started spying the Deep South's rich wildlife like never before.

I could have counted on one handlebar the number of wild turkeys I had seen before riding the back trails. On one of my earliest trips, I topped a rise and startled a flock, which immediately took off. The sky turned black with their big wings beating in a crescendo of air against feather. It still amazes me when I see such an ungainly looking bird suddenly take on such beauty and grace in flight. A bike ride when I see one of these, even if it just scoots off into the underbrush a-la-roadrunner, is still special.

Grouse, quail, bobwhites, hawks, owls, and eagles are seen less often, but are no less spectacular. Even the much maligned vulture moves magically on slips of jetstream as it heads toward its roost. A flock of 50–75 of these silent gliders circling their way to land in a tall, dead white pine will imprint an image not easily erased. In late spring, a pair of mating hawks may be discovered as they perform a gyre of ascent hundreds of feet high before folding back their wings and diving into the valley.

Southern songbirds fill the morning air with such tunes and variety that it seems impossible such a diverse collection exists anywhere else on earth. Wrens warble and cardinals chirp after first allowing the morning's most spectacular bird, the wood thrush, to awaken them. Some stick around for the entire year while others come and go with the seasons. A sure sign of spring around our house is hearing the first whippoorwill sing its seemingly all-night song.

Other sounds fill the air at different times during the year. Insects whir and buzz beginning in late February in the northern region of the Deep South and hardly stop at all down around the gulf coast. The long growing season which enables such crops as the sweet potato and peanut to mature also provides a favorable place for an exotic array of six-legged life to raise families.

Many people imagine the southern climes to be an area overrun with mosquitoes, bees, and the like. At times, especially during hatches answering the call to procreate, the air becomes so filled with the winged wonders it is hard to see the space in between them. Some think the answer is to retreat to the air-conditioned climate of the den until the bugs go away, but natural controls quickly bring the insects to a manageable population. Still, it is a good idea to carry along a bottle of fly-flap spray for times when a dose of deet is the lesser of two evils.

"The race is on! Last one to the Deep South is a rotten egg!"

Less troublesome for most, and just as interesting, are the furry additions to the animal kingdom. Squirrels and chipmunks seem almost constant companions to cycling along trails down south, barking and scurrying off to safety. Another nut-hunter, the deer, is seen nearly as often, and sometimes snorts its displeasure at having its daily routine interrupted. Occasionally, you may have a close encounter of the antlered kind when one of the fleet-hooved ruminants jumps across the trail ahead of you . . . or over you.

Slower, and less frequently spotted, opossums, armadillos, skunks, bears, bobcats, minks, otters, beavers, ground hogs, coyotes, foxes, wild hogs, and raccoons roam the animal trails you will see on your way through the more secluded sections of forest. However, the possibility of coming across one of these on any given day lends an expectant air to the ride. Sometimes, as in the case of a skunk sighting, the air may be one you want to avoid.

Lower on the list of critters you might meet up with are the reptiles and amphibians. Most people would just as soon not see the slithering of a snake, but the silence of your two wheels makes this a possibility, especially if one crosses the trail about the same time you do. Turtles are likely to be found crawling on their way to another snack during the summer months. Skinks and lizards may be seen, but more often are heard rattling under leaf litter. You may even be privileged enough to catch an alligator basking on the bank. Frogs and toads seldom give their location away during daylight, but when the dark comes, croaks of all sorts float through the muggy air. You may feel tempted to join in.

Wintertime sounds of animals on the hunt for prey and companionship are much less common. Instead, the sound of water falling on rocks is far more likely to ride over the whoosh of wind through tree branches. But if you're quiet—and lucky—you might catch the sound of a honking woodcock down by the creek looking for a midday meal of worms. One thing is for sure, though; the alert mountain biker will be rewarded by sightings of many animals, enriching the ride.

WEATHER

Although the insects and other critters have their own season, and appropriate plans can be made to avoid their inconveniences, weather and climate in the Deep South can be brutal at any time of the year—in either extreme. Most people associate the South with sweltering summers so humid it creates drag on the trail. This is indeed the rule from early June to mid-September, and early morning or late evening rides tend to be more enjoyable.

There are, however, incredibly wonderful exceptions to this rule. One night in middle Mississippi in mid-July, the temperatures dropped into the 50s, the bugs disappeared, and the haze blew off, revealing a wonderfully clear night sky. The campfire felt especially good that night, and the next morning's ride reminded me of early fall.

Although snowstorms and icy conditions are little threat to occur even in the winter, there are stories and records of wintry conditions visiting the Deep South in the middle of summer. You may have heard the report of soldiers who died from hypothermia after slogging around in the Florida swamps and getting caught in a chilly rain. So plan to pack along a rain jacket any time you're headed out for an extended ride.

Although it is unusual, wintertime in the Deep South can be as bitterly cold and windy and snowy as anywhere. The late spring blizzard of 1993 was the most destructive storm in recent memory; its evidence can be seen along trails in northern Georgia, especially. Another snowstorm struck middle and south Georgia in early February 1973: it started snowing on a Friday morning and snowed until the following morning, dumping over 12 inches of thick, wet snow.

Big winds are different. The Deep South has great potential to produce deadly tornadoes from March to November; the transitional seasons—spring and fall—are good times to keep an especially alert eye on the sky. All reports of tornadoes in our area have stated that an unnaturally green cast to the sky precedes the touchdown of a funnel cloud. I used to think mountains provided protection from tornadoes. But in November of 1992, a tornado destroyed a large section of forest north of Dahlonega, Georgia. In the spring of 1994, a tornado again tore through the north Georgia mountains, hugging the steep contours as it traveled over 45 miles without breaking contact with the ground. And for those of you who believe that tornadoes—like lightning—never strike the same place twice, another followed almost the same path on that Palm Sunday—45 minutes later!

Lightning strikes are much more commonly seen than tornadoes, and they cause more fatalities than any other outdoor threat. The southern climes can generate thunderstorms at any time of the year. Granted, they are much more common from March to November, but just this past January a thunderstorm exploded that was as ferocious as those in the summer, despite the fact it was 32 degrees.

There is no such thing as a rainy season in the Deep South. I've seen summers when there hasn't been a drop of rain from Memorial Day to Labor Day. These same months can likewise produce over 40 inches of rain. Generally, the best times to enjoy the trails of the Deep South are the months outside of July, August, and early September. But with some caution, plenty of drinking water, and early morning or late afternoon departures, even these months hold their own special experiences.

Steve Jones

MOUNTAIN BIKING THE GREAT PLAINS

Dennis Coello's America by Mountain Bike Series

Introduction

TRAIL DESCRIPTION OUTLINE

Information on each trail in this book begins with a general description that includes length, configuration, scenery, highlights, trail conditions, and difficulty. Additional description is contained in eleven individual categories. The following will help you understand all of the information provided.

Trail name: Trail names are as designated on United States Geological Survey (USGS) or Forest Service or other maps, and/or by local custom.

Note: Information contained in the next six headings is included in the introductory paragraphs to each ride.

Length: The overall length of a trail is described in miles, unless stated otherwise.

Configuration: This is a description of the shape of each trail—whether the trail is a loop, out-and-back (that is, along the same route), figure eight, trapezoid, isosceles triangle, or if it connects with another trail described in the book.

Difficulty: This provides at a glance a description of the degree of physical exertion required to complete the ride, and the technical skill required to pedal it. Authors were asked to keep in mind the fact that all riders are not equal, and thus to gauge the trail in terms of how the middle-of-the-road rider—someone between the newcomer and Ned Overend—could handle the route. Comments about the trail's length, condition, and elevation change will also assist you in determining the difficulty of any trail relative to your own abilities.

Condition: Trails are described in terms of being paved, unpaved, sandy, hardpacked, washboarded, two- or four-wheel-drive, single-track or double-track. All terms that might be unfamiliar to the first-time mountain biker are defined in the Glossary.

Scenery: Here you will find a general description of the natural surroundings during the seasons most riders pedal the trail, and a suggestion of what is to be found at special times (like great fall foliage or cactus in bloom).

Highlights: Towns, major water crossings, historical sites, etc., are listed.

General location: This category describes where the trail is located in reference to a nearby town or other landmark.

Elevation change: Unless stated otherwise, the figure provided is the total gain and loss of elevation along the trail. In regions where the elevation variation is not extreme, the route is simply described as flat, rolling, or possessing short steep climbs or descents.

Season: This is the best time of year to pedal the route, taking into account trail condition (for example, when it will not be muddy), riding comfort (when the weather is too hot, cold, or wet), and local hunting seasons.

Note: Because the exact opening and closing dates of deer, elk, moose, and antelope seasons often change from year to year, riders should check with the local Fish and Game department or call a sporting goods store (or any place that sells hunting licenses) in a nearby town before heading out. Wear bright clothes in fall, and don't wear suede jackets while in the saddle. Hunter's-orange tape on the helmet is also a good idea.

Services: This category is of primary importance in guides for paved-road tourers, but is far less crucial to most mountain bike trail descriptions because there are usually no services whatsoever to be found. Authors have noted when water is available on desert or long mountain routes and have listed the availability of food, lodging, campgrounds, and bike shops. If all these services are present, you will find only the words "All services available in . . ."

Hazards: Special hazards like steep cliffs, great amounts of deadfall, or barbed-wire fences very close to the trail are noted here.

Rescue index: Determining how far one is from help on any particular trail can be difficult due to the backcountry nature of most mountain bike rides. Authors therefore state the proximity of homes or Forest Service outposts, nearby roads where one might hitch a ride, or the likelihood of other bikers being encountered on the trail. Phone numbers of local sheriff departments or hospitals have not been provided because phones are almost never available. If you are able to reach a phone, the local operator will connect you with emergency services.

Land status: This category provides information regarding whether the trail crosses land operated by the Forest Service, Bureau of Land Management, a city, state, or national park, whether it crosses private land whose owner (at the time the author did the research) has allowed mountain bikers right of passage, and so on.

Note: Authors have been extremely careful to offer only those routes that are open to bikers and are legal to ride. However, because land ownership changes over time, and because the land-use controversy created by mountain bikes still has not completely subsided, it is the duty of each cyclist to look for and to heed signs warning against trail use. Don't expect this book to get you off the hook when you're facing some small-town judge for pedaling past a "Biking Prohibited" sign erected the day before. Look for these signs, read them, and heed the advice. And remember there's always another trail.

Maps: The maps in this book have been produced with great care, and, in conjunction with the trail-following suggestions, will help you stay on course.

But as every experienced mountain biker knows, things can get tricky in the backcountry. It is therefore strongly suggested that you avail yourself of the detailed information found in the 7.5 minute series USGS (United States Geological Survey) topographic maps. In some cases, authors have found that specific Forest Service or other maps may be more useful than the USGS quads, and tell how to obtain them.

Finding the trail: Detailed information on how to reach the trailhead and where to park your car is provided here.

Sources of additional information: Here you will find the address and/or phone number of a bike shop, governmental agency, or other source from which trail information can be obtained.

Notes on the trail: This is where you are guided carefully through any portions of the trail that are particularly difficult to follow. The author also may add information about the route that does not fit easily in the other categories. This category will not be present for those rides where the route is easy to follow.

ABBREVIATIONS

The following road-designation abbreviations are used in the *America by Mountain Bike* series:

CR	County Road
FR	Farm Route
FS	Forest Service road
I-	Interstate
IR	Indian Route
US	United States highway

State highways are designated with the appropriate two-letter state abbreviation, followed by the road number. *Example:* LA 10 = Louisiana State Highway 10.

Postal Service two-letter state codes:

AL	Alabama	FL	Florida
AK	Alaska	GA	Georgia
AZ	Arizona	HI	Hawaii
AR	Arkansas	ID	Idaho
CA	California	IL	Illinois
CO	Colorado	IN	Indiana
CT	Connecticut	IA	Iowa
DE	Delaware	KS	Kansas
DC	District of Columbia	KY	Kentucky

LA	Louisiana	OH	Ohio
ME	Maine	OK	Oklahoma
MD	Maryland	OR	Oregon
MA	Massachusetts	PA	Pennsylvania
MI	Michigan	RI	Rhode Island
MN	Minnesota	SC	South Carolina
MS	Mississippi	SD	South Dakota
MO	Missouri	TN	Tennessee
MT	Montana	TX	Texas
NE	Nebraska	UT	Utah
NV	Nevada	VT	Vermont
NH	New Hampshire	VA	Virginia
NJ	New Jersey	WA	Washington
NM	New Mexico	WV	West Virginia
NY	New York	WI	Wisconsin
NC	North Carolina	WY	Wyoming
ND	North Dakota		

TOPOGRAPHIC MAPS

The maps in this book, when used in conjunction with the route directions present in each chapter, will in most instances be sufficient to get you to the trail and keep you on it. However, you will find superior detail and valuable information in the 7.5 minute series United States Geological Survey (USGS) topographic maps. Recognizing how indispensable these are to bikers and hikers alike, many bike shops and sporting goods stores now carry topos of the local area.

But if you're brand new to mountain biking you might be wondering, "What's a topographic map?" In short, these differ from standard "flat" maps in that they indicate not only linear distance, but elevation as well. One glance at a "topo" will show you the difference, for "contour lines" are spread across the map like dozens of intricate spider webs. Each contour line represents a particular elevation, and at the base of each topo a particular "contour interval" designation is given. Yes, it sounds confusing if you're new to the lingo, but it truly is a simple and wonderfully helpful system. Keep reading.

Let's assume that the 7.5 minute series topo before us says "Contour Interval 40 feet," that the short trail we'll be pedaling is two inches in length on the map, and that it crosses five contour lines from its beginning to end. What do we know? Well, because the linear scale of this series is 2,000 feet to the inch (roughly 2 ¾ inches representing 1 mile), we know our trail is approximately ⅘ of a mile long (2 inches × 2,000 feet). But we also know we'll be climbing or descending 200 vertical feet (5 contour lines × 40 feet each) over that distance. And the elevation designations written on occasional contour lines will tell us if we're heading up or down.

The authors of this series warn their readers of upcoming terrain, but only a detailed topo gives you the information you need to pinpoint your position exactly on a map, steer yourself toward optional trails and roads nearby, plus let you know at a glance if you'll be pedaling hard to take them. It's a lot of information for a very low cost. In fact, the only drawback with topos is their size—several feet square. I've tried rolling them into tubes, folding them carefully, even cutting them into blocks and photocopying the pieces. Any of these systems is a pain, but no matter how you pack the maps you'll be happy they're along. And you'll be even happier if you pack a compass as well.

In addition to local bike shops and sporting goods stores, you'll find topos at major universities and some public libraries, where you might try photocopying the ones you need to avoid the cost of buying them. But if you want your own and can't find them locally, write to:

USGS Map Sales
Box 25286
Denver, CO 80225

Ask for an index while you're at it, plus a price list and a copy of the booklet *Topographic Maps*. In minutes you'll be reading them like a pro.

A second excellent series of maps available to mountain bikers is that put out by the United States Forest Service. If your trail runs through an area designated as a national forest, look in the phone book (white pages) under the United States Government listings, find the Department of Agriculture heading, and then run your finger down that section until you find the Forest Service. Give them a call and they'll provide the address of the regional Forest Service office, from which you can obtain the appropriate map.

TRAIL ETIQUETTE

Pick up almost any mountain bike magazine these days and you'll find articles and letters to the editor about trail conflict. For example, you'll find hikers' tales of being blindsided by speeding mountain bikers, complaints from mountain bikers about being blamed for trail damage that was really caused by horse or cattle traffic, and cries from bikers about those "kamikaze" riders who through their antics threaten to close even more trails to all of us.

The authors of this series have been very careful to guide you to only those trails that are open to mountain biking (or at least were open at the time of their research), and without exception have warned of the damage done to our sport through injudicious riding. My personal views on this matter appear in the Afterword, but all of us can benefit from glancing over the following International Mountain Bicycling Association (IMBA) Rules of the Trail before saddling up.

1. *Ride on open trails only.* Respect trail and road closures (ask if not sure), avoid possible trespass on private land, obtain permits and authorization as may be required. Federal and State wilderness areas are closed to cycling.

2. *Leave no trace.* Be sensitive to the dirt beneath you. Even on open trails, you should not ride under conditions where you will leave evidence of your passing, such as on certain soils shortly after rain. Observe the different types of soils and trail construction; practice low-impact cycling. This also means staying on the trail and not creating any new ones. Be sure to pack out at least as much as you pack in.

3. *Control your bicycle!* Inattention for even a second can cause disaster. Excessive speed can maim and threaten people; there is no excuse for it!

4. *Always yield the trail.* Make known your approach well in advance. A friendly greeting (or a bell) is considerate and works well; startling someone may cause loss of trail access. Show your respect when passing others by slowing to a walk or even stopping. Anticipate that other trail users may be around corners or in blind spots.

5. *Never spook animals.* All animals are startled by an unannounced approach, a sudden movement, or a loud noise. This can be dangerous for you, for others, and for the animals. Give animals extra room and time to adjust to you. In passing, use special care and follow the directions of horseback riders (ask if uncertain). Running cattle and disturbing wild animals is a serious offense. Leave gates as you found them, or as marked.

6. *Plan ahead.* Know your equipment, your ability, and the area in which you are riding—and prepare accordingly. Be self-sufficient at all times. Wear a helmet, keep your machine in good condition, and carry necessary supplies for changes in weather or other conditions. A well-executed trip is a satisfaction to you and not a burden or offense to others.

For more information, contact IMBA, P.O. Box 412043, Los Angeles, CA 90041, (818) 792-8830.

HITTING THE TRAIL

Once again, because this is a "where-to," not a "how-to" guide, the following will be brief. If you're a veteran trail rider these suggestions might serve to remind you of something you've forgotten to pack. If you're a newcomer, they might convince you to think twice before hitting the backcountry unprepared.

Water: I've heard the questions dozens of times. "How much is enough? One bottle? Two? Three?! But think of all that extra weight!" Well, one simple physiological fact should convince you to err on the side of excess when it comes to deciding how much water to pack: a human working hard in 90-degree temperature needs approximately ten quarts of fluids every day. Ten quarts. That's two and a half gallons—12 large water bottles, or 16 small ones. And, with water weighing in at approximately 8 pounds per gallon, a one-day supply comes to a whopping 20 pounds.

In other words, pack along two or three bottles even for short rides. And make sure you can purify the water found along the trail on longer routes. When writing of those routes where this could be of critical importance, each author has provided information on where water can be found near the trail— if it can be found at all. But drink it untreated and you run the risk of disease. (See *Giardia* in the Glossary.)

One sure way to kill both the bacteria and viruses in water is to bring it to a "furious boil." Right. That's just how you want to spend your time on a bike ride. Besides, who wants to carry a stove, or denude the countryside stoking bonfires to boil water?

Luckily, there is a better way. Many riders pack along the effective, inexpensive, and only slightly distasteful tetraglycine hydroperiodide tablets (sold under the names Potable Aqua, Globaline, and Coughlan's, among others). Some invest in portable, lightweight purifiers that filter out the crud. Yes, purifying water with tablets or filters is a bother. But catch a case of Giardia sometime and you'll understand why it's worth the trouble.

Tools: Ever since my first cross-country tour in 1965 I've been kidded about the number of tools I pack on the trail. And so I will exit entirely from this discussion by providing a list compiled by two mechanic (and mountain biker) friends of mine. After all, since they make their livings fixing bikes, and get their kicks by riding them, who could be a better source?

These two suggest the following as an absolute minimum:

tire levers
spare tube and patch kit
air pump
allen wrenches (3, 4, 5, and 6 mm)

six-inch crescent (adjustable-end) wrench
small flat-blade screwdriver
chain rivet tool
spoke wrench

But, while they're on the trail, their personal tool pouches contain these additional items:

channel locks (small)
air gauge
tire valve cap (the metal kind, with a valve-stem remover)
baling wire (ten or so inches, for temporary repairs)
duct tape (small roll for temporary repairs or tire boot)
boot material (small piece of old tire or a large tube patch)
spare chain link
rear derailleur pulley
spare nuts and bolts
paper towel and tube of waterless hand cleaner

First-Aid Kit: My personal kit contains the following, sealed inside double Ziploc bags:

sunscreen
aspirin
butterfly-closure bandages
Band-Aids
gauze compress pads (a half-dozen 4" × 4")
gauze (one roll)
ace bandages or Spenco joint wraps
Benadryl (an antihistamine, in case of allergic reactions)
water purification tablets
Moleskin/Spenco "Second Skin"
hydrogen peroxide, iodine, or Mercurochrome (some kind of antiseptic)
snakebite kit

Final Considerations: The authors of this series have done a good job in suggesting that specific items be packed for certain trails—raingear in particular seasons, a hat and gloves for mountain passes, or shades for desert jaunts. Heed their warnings, and think ahead. Good luck.

Dennis Coello

LOUISIANA

Incredible as it may seem to those who have never visited the Pelican State, mountain biking is as common here as crawfish in the Atchafalaya Swamp. Forget about the mud, the bugs, and the heat. You're in Louisiana now, and all things have a different scale of reference. One thing you can count on, however, is diversity: in trails, people, plants, animals, food, speech, and entertainment. I have searched all over and found the flame beneath the great melting pot we call America. It is here in Louisiana.

From the beginning, before De Soto slogged through looking for gold and springs of eternal youth, before the Chitimacha Indians made this their home and befriended the Acadians (who had been forcibly removed from Canada by the British in 1755 and became Cajuns), the land in Louisiana was controlled and shaped by the Father of Waters, the mighty Mississippi. From the Rockies to the Appalachians, the great river pulls the land to its lap, building one year and destroying the next. Despite the levees, canals, and prayers, water is still the undeniable natural force of the land.

The week before I traveled to Louisiana, seven inches of rain fell in seven days. My boots did not dry the entire time I was there. After I left, New Orleans was flooded by several feet of water. Therefore, when you read or hear the term "wet" used to describe Louisiana trail conditions, consider the source: if it is a native telling you it's wet, take your water wings and paddle. (By the way, the perfect complement to a day on the bayou backroads would be to shift over into the bayous themselves and float a canoe or wet a line. Nearly every trailhead is within a short distance of some body of water.)

But this is not to say there is no high and dry land to ride on. For the skeptics out there, Driskell Mountain in Bienville Parish towers 535 feet above sea level. Granted, this type of elevation change will not cause you to go out and purchase a topo map to find a recovery plateau, but surprisingly few Louisiana trails can be ridden without your having to get onto the small ring and hammer hard. And the trail in Lincoln Parish Park, slightly to the northeast of Driskell Mountain, features enough elevation change and challenge to give it a reputation as one of the best locations for mountain biking anywhere.

The Kisatchie National Forest offers as rugged a trail as you will want to try. It's certainly not for everyone. But a little farther south near Kincaid Reservoir, trails do abound for everyone: hilly slopes, bog crossings, forest service roads. The Kincaid Recreational Area has approximately 75 miles of trail that can be conveniently reached in less than 30 minutes by car from the central parking spot at the entrance.

The hills become more scattered farther south. West of the Mississippi, marshes, swamps, bay-galls, bayous, creeks, ponds, lakes, sloughs, and rivers make this land more fluid than solid. East of the great river, however, the loess bluffs come into play, providing ups and downs to keep the pulse pounding.

Baton Rouge's Hooper Road Park and the Tunica Hills trails have been carved through prime examples of this unusual landscape.

After leaving the loess behind, the trails to the east flatten out again and show why this land was heavily farmed in cotton, soybeans, cattle, and, of course, sugar. The process used to granulate sugar was first developed here in this land of many moods, and it helped finance the many extravagant mansions seen along the area's roads.

South of Lafayette and New Orleans, expect to find consistently dry ground only on top of levees. Hundreds of miles of these manmade mudwalls, topped with gravel, run from Baton Rouge to New Orleans and Simmesport to Morgan City. They're not exactly mountains, but compared to the rest of the landscape along these embankments, they will seem to be.

The sweetest thing about Louisiana for the mountain biker, however, is the sense of adventure permeating the trails. All the while I was riding here, I couldn't get over the feeling that the land had stopped moving just long enough for me to make my way through on rubber tires. But that's for you to decide. Enjoy your trip.

Monroe Area Rides

If I said, "Biedenharn" to you, what would you think? It's not exactly a house-hold name, but the product first bottled by this man certainly is. As you head through the Monroe area on your way to a bike trail, leave enough time to stop by and visit the home built by the creator of "the real thing" back in the days when it contained considerably more kick than today.

Kicking is something they do quite a bit of in northern Louisiana. Besides having to employ a hard kick to make the mountainous climbs on a bike, two colleges—Louisiana Tech and Grambling—spice up the fall with football like it's played nowhere else. Even though I never played on an organized football team, the legend of Eddie Robinson and his reputation for fielding winning teams with the Grambling Tigers did not escape me. I did, however, march in my high school's band as one of the drummers, and it was the moves of the Grambling University marching band that we tried to imitate. If this seems like a strange recollection, it won't after you've had to shimmy and shake your way through the tight turns on the trail at Lincoln Parish. Ready? Break!

For more information:

Outfitters Unlimited
3027 Breard
Monroe, LA 71201
(318) 322-8153

Bicycle and Fitness Center
111 North Trenton
Ruston, LA 71273
(318) 255-3009

Monroe/West Monroe Convention and Visitors Bureau
1333 State Farm Drive
Monroe, LA 71202
(800) 843-1872

RIDE 1   LINCOLN PARISH PARK

No counties were drawn up in Louisiana; instead, parishes take their place—64 of them, and none more welcome to the mountain biker than Lincoln Parish. In fact, this ten-mile loop of single-track, double-track, gravel and asphalt roads, designed by Lloyd Brick in 1993 inside the 260-acre park, is

RIDE 1 *LINCOLN PARISH PARK*

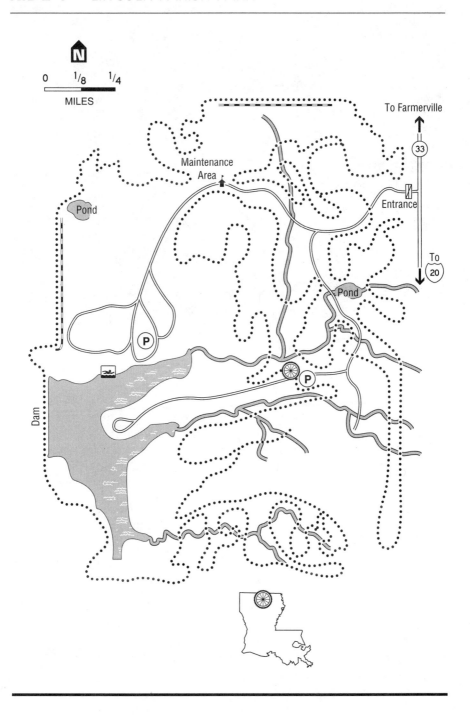

Lincoln Parish Park—one of the best trails anywhere—a Lloyd Brick Original.

regarded by mountain bikers as one of the top 25 trails in the nation. I found nothing to disprove its high rank.

Seldom does the single-track widen up more than to allow handlebars and slightly akimbo knees. Don't expect many straight sections on this course either, unless they're like the 25-foot shot straight down the side of a creek bank. Expert riders will find that many skilled maneuvers are required in order to finish the loop without doing some hiking or a strategic dab.

The intensity of concentration demanded to wiggle or power through many areas doesn't allow for much daydreaming. Still, you can catch quick looks at the fairly mature upland forest of oaks and gums shading the way through what the man at the entrance told me is "the perfect place for a park."

General location: Located just north of Ruston, Louisiana, off Highway 33 to Farmerville.
Elevation change: The classic, long climbs are not here, but plenty of sufficiently sustained steep hills keep the pulse pounding.
Season: Wet takes on a different meaning in Louisiana. Conditions considered too wet farther east are just about as good as they come in some parts of this low-lying region. However, in places this trail shows clay, which can become treacherous when wet.

Services: All services can be found in nearby Ruston.

Hazards: This trail is not for the beginner. Although the condition of the trail is well maintained with few roots and holes, maneuvers requiring high bike control are called for in places; failure to execute properly could have some inconvenient consequences.

Rescue index: A whistle shrilly blown would bring someone to your aid fairly quickly in this popular park.

Land status: This is property owned by the Lincoln Parish government.

Maps: Maps may be—if you're lucky—obtained at the entrance to the park, but I was unable to get one the day I showed up. But a map can be found at Bicycle and Fitness Center in Ruston. Just ask for the Lincoln Parish Park Bike Trail Map.

Finding the trail: Take the exit to Highway 33 off I-20 just east of Ruston and turn north. Look for the brown-and-white park sign down about 3.5 miles on the left. Pay your entrance fee at the gate and take the first left; you will cross a bridge and curve around to the right before coming to the parking area on the left. The trail comes across the parking area at the top, but I began riding at the entrance down on the left past the big tree and behind the picnic table.

Sources of additional information:

Lincoln Parish Park
LA Highway 33
Ruston, LA 71273
(318) 251-5156

Bicycle and Fitness Center
111 North Trenton
Ruston, LA 71273
(318) 255-3009

Ruston/Lincoln Convention and Visitor's Bureau
900 North Trenton
Ruston, LA 71270
(318) 255-2031

Notes on the trail: This trail has hosted Louisiana NORBA championship races; its popularity is widespread, drawing riders from all over the Deep South, including Arkansas and Texas. The trail is adequately marked with orange surveyor's tape, and by following bike tracks and your basic instincts about where a good trail would go next, you should have no trouble doing most of the loop. After coming out at the concession stand for the second time from a different direction, I saw storm clouds gathering and headed back to the trailhead on the paved park road. I wound up a mile shy of riding the entire 10.4 length.

RIDE 2 SUGAR CANE TRAIL

This National Recreational Trail, formerly used for little foot travel only, was converted to a bike trail at least nine years ago when area riders began to take pirate rides (also known as "shotgun rides" for what you might have to contend with if you're caught) on this easy five-mile loop around Caney Lake. This lake has two sections: one is for boating, and the other is for fishing and was referred to reverently by an old angler and his buddy as "Ole Caney."

Don Hunter, a long-time mountain biker from Minden, Louisiana, got together with Alma Tippins, the Caney Lakes Ranger, and proposed the addition of more single-track to loop around Lower Caney Lake. Another ranger (and biker), Chris Sporl from the National Forest Office in Alexandria helped lay out some "true small-ring trail."

While the newest addition of four miles makes the entire single-track at Caney Lakes over ten miles long, Hunter promises to keep adding sections wherever he can. "It's likely we'll have nearly 15 miles of single-track located here shortly."

After experiencing the magnificent longleaf pines growing over ferns, mosses, and more yaupon than you can count, you'll be wondering why you haven't ridden this trail before. The woods are rich with wildlife: songbirds and great blue herons nest along the lake banks. Deer, squirrel, and turkeys browse among . . . the armadillo.

It is also here in these woods where the rider unfamiliar with a peculiar Deep South phenomenon, Armadillo Suicide Spasms, has a chance of joining a large club of vehicle operators: Those Who Have Hit an Armadillo on the Highway (TWHHAH!). An armadillo presents a hazard to any who travel any road or open throughway, including a mountain bike trail. Hitting one of these "possums on the half-shell" while bike-borne can wreak marsupial havoc with tire rim. So be careful. On one single lap around the lake, I had to avoid three armadillos that threw themselves in front of my tire.

General location: Just north of Minden, Louisiana, off Highway 159; recently placed signs will lead you to the fee station.
Elevation change: Even the most significant changes here seldom require using the small crank ring, much to the surprise of people wondering where Louisiana gets hills like these.
Season: Summer's humid heat, attendant clouds of insects, and, yes, snakes aplenty make this the least preferred time to ride.
Services: Shreveport provides all the necessary services; closer by, Minden will meet most basic needs.

RIDE 2 *SUGAR CANE TRAIL*

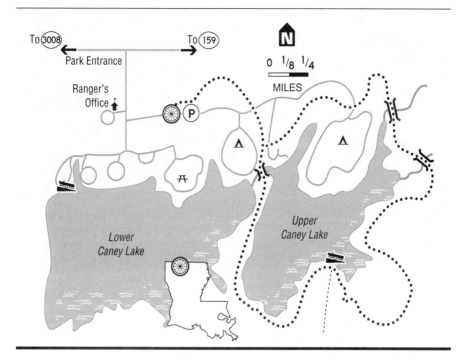

Hazards: The trail itself presents few obstacles to safe travel; bridges and boardwalks have been built where necessary. However, hunters do hunt in the area where it opens up and crosses the two bridges, though they are prohibited from hunting anywhere else. Care should be exercised to signal your presence during hunting season in this part of the loop. Definitely do not put antlers on your helmet or ride with a white saddle. Two people fishing in a boat heard me coming down the trail and thought I was a deer. They looked thoroughly disappointed when they discovered I was "just an old mountain biker."

Rescue index: The open waters of Caney Lakes will quickly carry a call for help.

Land status: This is part of the Kisatchie National Forest.

Maps: Ask for the Caney Lakes Recreational Area and Sugar Cane Trail map at the ranger's office on your right as you come to the pay station.

Finding the trail: Take the first left after paying the user fee. The small parking area is on the left where the sign for this National Recreation Trail points the way to the loop.

Sturdy bridge joins two lakes near Sugar Cane Trail.

Sources of additional information:

Sugar Cane District Ranger
P.O. Box 479
Homer, LA 71040
(318) 927-2061

Forest Supervisor
National Forests
2500 Shreveport Highway
Alexandria, LA 71360
(318) 473-7160

Notes on the trail: The .75-mile trail spur at the trailhead leads to a fork in the trail that starts and finishes the 5-mile loop around the lake. The terrain and ease of the trail make for a leisurely cruise through the dense underbrush, where many critters can be spotted going about their business. A few spots— like one bridge crossing—will probably require getting off and walking just for safety's sake, that is, unless your trials skills are expert.

The newest trail—along Lower Caney Lake—is found by continuing south across the dam between the two lakes. The eastern trail forks off to the left for the easier part; continuing straight puts you on the more technical route. Whichever way you choose, hours of riding pleasure await at Caney Lakes.

Shreveport Area Ride

This northwestern Louisiana city hugs one bank of the Red River while its twin, Bossier City, lies on the opposite side of the nation's largest neon-lit bridge. Road signs announce you're in an area known as Ark-La-Tex, where cultures swirl together like the river eddies that brought the people together in the first place.

Riverboat casinos, thoroughbred racing, professional sports teams, rose gardens, military and natural history museums, parks, and wildlife management areas are just some of the other places you can visit when off the saddle. Festivals as diverse as Bonnie and Clyde Days to the Oil Patch Festival (where the Miss Oil Patch Pageant anoints a new winner each year) draw visitors to towns with names that easily roll off the tongue: Shongaloo, Mira, Caspiana, and Dubberly.

Lake Bistineau State Park, where cypress trees and their knees provide habitat for great blue herons, frogs, songbirds, and the lunker lurking in cutout banks, plans to develop hiking trails which will also allow mountain bikes. The Bodcau Wildlife Management Area, owned by the U.S. Army Corps of Engineers, serves all kinds of outdoor enthusiasts: hunters, hikers, boaters, campers, birders, and bikers. Even though the WMAs don't actively cater to the mountain biker, all roads and trails not posted are open to bikes.

For more information:

Shreve Island Bicycle Center
2415 East 70th Street
Shreveport, LA 71105
(318) 797-9500

Shreveport-Bossier Convention and Tourist Bureau
P.O. Box 1761
Shreveport , LA 71166
(318) 222-9391 and (800) 551-8682

Lake Bistineau State Park
P.O. Box 589
Doyline, LA 71023
(318) 745-3503

Louisiana Department of Wildlife and Fisheries
P.O. Box 915
Minden, LA 71055
(318) 371-3050

RIDE 3   *HODGES GARDENS TRAILS*

The striking sandstone outcrops—leftovers from the quarry producing jetty stone bound for Port Arthur, Texas—form the backdrop to the ride at Hodges Gardens in Many, Louisiana. Two separate, easy, off-road hiking and biking trails can be ridden for approximately two miles: three-quarter mile in the western area loop and slightly more than a mile in the eastern trail loop near the bison pasture.

The road running through the park was once known as The King's Highway in the days when early explorers made their way to Mexico City and Texas from the east. Once you've ridden the trail near the entrance, you'll be strongly tempted to continue the trip along the asphalt to make the most of the $6.50 per person admission fee. And continuing is worth it. A large lake has a fountain near a gazebo where you can sit and watch the 30-foot tall plumes splash rhythmically back into the lake. Above the lake, gardens of daylilies and azaleas have been planted among the jutting faces of sandstone. A man-made waterfall cascades through ponds where aquatic plants like the American Lotus and water lilies bloom.

By the time you reach the other trailhead off the road to the greenhouses, longer and more technical paths sweep along a creek ridge. In this section evidence can be found of an extension used in a recent biking event. The trail intersects with the yellow-blazed main trail, and remains open for about a half mile, maybe less, before it funnels away. I had a close call with disorientation in these woods, so make sure you take bearings often.

General location: The entrance to Hodges Gardens is found directly off Highway 171, south of Many, Louisiana.

Elevation change: Significant elevation changes occur infrequently.

Season: The admission fee keeps use low and, therefore, the trail remains in pretty good shape year-round. Periods of high water can wash out the bridges across the small bayous. Hodges Gardens is open from 8 A.M. until sunset every day except Christmas Eve, Christmas Day, and New Year's Day.

Services: You can depend on Many to provide you with the basics, but a trip to Natchitoches, the oldest city in the Louisiana Purchase Territory, may be needed to get specialty items.

Hazards: Remember, there will be other vehicles on the road if you choose to ride your knobbies on the more than 5 miles of pavement within the park. Some bridges may be washed out, and stair steps need to be taken in a few places.

Rescue index: It is an easily accessible area with frequent, but not heavy, traffic. A bell or whistle would attract lots of attention.

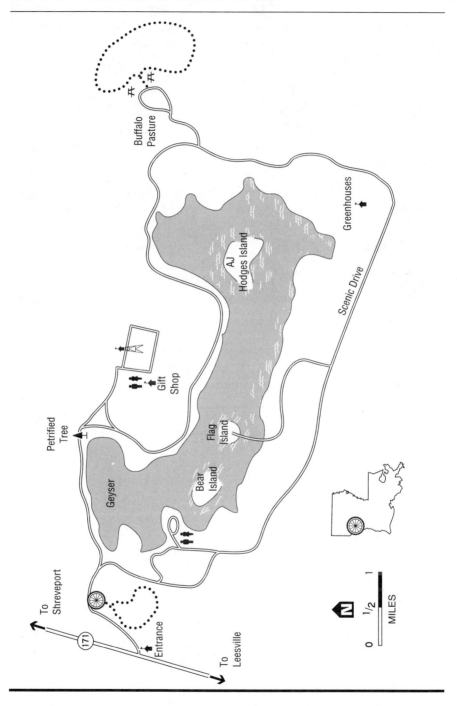

Biking along the abandoned roadbed of former jettystone quarry.

Land status: This self-sufficient operation by the A.J. and Nona Trigg Hodges Foundation owns all the fenced acreage in and around the trails and roads.

Maps: The front office has a complete map of the entire park, showing trailheads, trails, and major roads.

Finding the trail: The first trailhead is .25-mile or so inside on the right. A sign has been placed at the edge of the forest where single-track enters the understory. Another trail can be found by following the signs to the greenhouses and crossing the cattle guard at the corner of the bison pasture. Turn left at the sign. You may be able to ride down the steps—or to the side of them—to where the eastern loop begins.

Sources of additional information:

Hodges Gardens
P.O. Box 900
Many, LA 71449
(318) 586-3523

Notes on the trail: This trail ranks as one of the most colorful in the Deep South. The groundskeepers ensure some group of plants is always in bloom in the cultivated areas, and the outlying forest has its own special complement of traditional Louisiana flora blossoming among the mixed hardwoods and loblolly pines.

These trails, clearly marked and blazed, won't be in demand by the biker looking for a lengthy workout, but it is a good destination in the fall or spring. You can spend all day in the various gardens and trails and enjoy a picnic lunch overlooking the 225-acre lake with its impressive geyser and petrified tree.

Alexandria Area Rides

With its central location and reputation for being a crossroads, it's a wonder this city did not wind up as the state's capitol. Mountain bikers, though, have christened it as the unchallenged hub of two-wheeled activity. By riding trails and Forest Service roads in Dry Prong, Camp Claiborne, the Kisatchie National Forest, Kincaid Reservoir, and the Wild Azalea Trail, a mountain biking vacation could easily last for weeks.

The Red River continues its state-long flow through Alexandria. After heading south for about 20 miles, it changes course and goes north and east until a scant five miles from the Mississippi, when it turns right on its way to the Atchafalaya Swamp. As you would guess, spring rains sog low-lying trails in the area. In addition, many "wet weather springs" spread out on tops of trails. Mountain biking through these seasonally wet areas at too high a speed can be extremely hazardous.

Alexandria marks the spot where Louisiana has a definite shift in culture. As a holdover from the early days of Cajun settlements and French influence, the area north of Alexandria has a concentration of Protestant churches, while the southern sections see more Catholic predominance. One older Cajun gentleman also expressed amusement and incredulity at the fact there were restaurants as far north as Alexandria "specializing in crawfish cuisine. Haw!"

Whatever the prejudices, the cultural atmospheres north and south of Alexandria are unmistakably different. Despite these local variations in custom, the mountain biker can sample some of the best riding in the state by going a short distance in all directions from Alexandria.

For more information:

Red River Cyclery
3752 MacArthur Drive
Alexandria, LA 71306
(318) 473-4256

Alexandria/Pineville Convention and Visitors Bureau
P.O. Box 8110
Alexandria, LA 71306
(800) 742-7049 or (318) 443-7049

Kisatchie National Forest, Evangeline District
3727 Government Street
Alexandria, LA 71302
(318) 445-9396

or 3362 Lake Charles Highway
Leesville, LA 71446
(318) 239-6576

RIDE 4 *CAROLINE DORMAN TRAIL*

The trail—named for the woman who helped pass legislation protecting much of what is the Kisatchie Hills Wilderness Area—is just that . . . wild! It is unlike any other land formation in Louisiana, with long, rocky elevation changes of over 200 feet in one direction along its 12-mile out-and-back length (24 miles total).

This is one of those trails that seems better suited to other forms of designated travel: feet and hooves. But you should take your bike, especially if you enjoy highly technical turns, drops, and climbs. Large chunks of dislodged rock guard narrow pathways sometimes only wide enough to accommodate the thickness of a knobby.

Springs ooze out to form wide, soft, muddy areas requiring a deft combination of strength and balance in order to make it through without walking. These springs eventually flow into the creeks filling the Kisatchie Bayou, a body of water rushing more with a mountain river's cadence than the languid meander of most Louisiana streams.

General location: This trail is located southwest of Natchitoches off the Longleaf Trail, a paved road cutting through the Kisatchie Hills Wilderness.
Elevation change: Some changes are so radical, "Foot Travel Only" may be the safest choice. Taking the trail one-way from the trailhead where the Longleaf Trail joins Forest Service Road 329 down to the Kisatchie Bayou Recreational Area will give a generally downhill ride.
Season: Times of rains and high water will make muddy potholes more trouble than they're worth for many bikers. The presence of summertime's heat and biting insects may tip the scales toward reserving this ride for the cooler months.
Services: Northeast in Natchitoches, about 45 minutes away, you can get most items replenished. Water can be obtained at Lotus Camp or Red Bluff Camp, just off the Longleaf Scenic Trail.
Hazards: The extremely rugged terrain can be a struggle to get over without hiking occasionally. The wildlife, especially snakes using rock crevices or creek crossings as hunting spots, can significantly impede travel.
Rescue index: Few places in the Deep South put you in a more remote environment. Take care here; getting to you could be long and difficult.

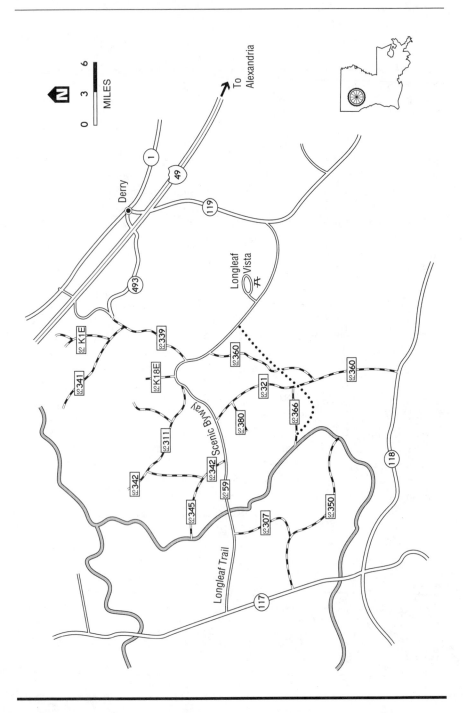

Land status: This is land owned by the National Forest Service and organized as the Kisatchie District of the Kisatchie National Forest.

Maps: You need to request the map of the Caroline Dorman Trail in the Kisatchie National Forest. Sandstone Trail (38 miles and blazed with green), to connect eventually with Caroline Dorman Trail, has a separate map which can be obtained from the National Forest Service District Ranger Office in Natchitoches. Topo maps (7.5 minute series), Bellwood, Kisatchie, Flora, Bayou L'Ivrogne, and Gorum, will give detailed insight into the many interesting features found here.

Finding the trail: Exit Interstate 49 onto LA 119 going south. Turn right onto Longleaf Trail Scenic Byway. One trailhead is across from where Backbone Trail begins at Longleaf Byway's junction with FS 329; the other trailhead is found along the banks of the Kisatchie Bayou at the Kisatchie Bayou Recreational Area. Find it by turning left onto FS 321 and then taking the third signed road to the right, FS 366.

Sources of additional information:

Natchitoches District Ranger
National Forest Service
P.O. Box 2120 (Highway 6 West)
Natchitoches, LA 71457
(318) 352-2568

Notes on the trail: The trail winds along above the Kisatchie Bayou's shores for a mile or so outside the recreational area (no charge for camping!). In fact, a good way to complete the nearly 12 rugged miles (one-way) would be to start out where the trail intersects with FS 329 and the Longleaf Trail. Take advantage of the general loss of elevation and ride down to where you set the shuttle at the recreation area.

Three other trail intersections (2 occur on FS 360 and 1 on FS 321) make it possible to use these roads to finish a loop of various lengths. This 24-mile-total trail length, there-and-back (unless you set a shuttle) will make more than a good day's travel. Consider the shuttle or riding one of the smaller loops before committing yourself to riding the entire length and back. Despite its many challenges, this remains a rewarding ride through an unusual section of forest. But it's not for someone looking for paved paths and shaved ice stands along the way.

RIDE 5   *SANDSTONE TRAIL*

If you enjoy the rugged challenge offered by the Caroline Dorman Trail, stay in the area and explore the even wilder side of the Kisatchie Hills. After the Caroline Dorman Trail, the trails become more difficult to negotiate. If you

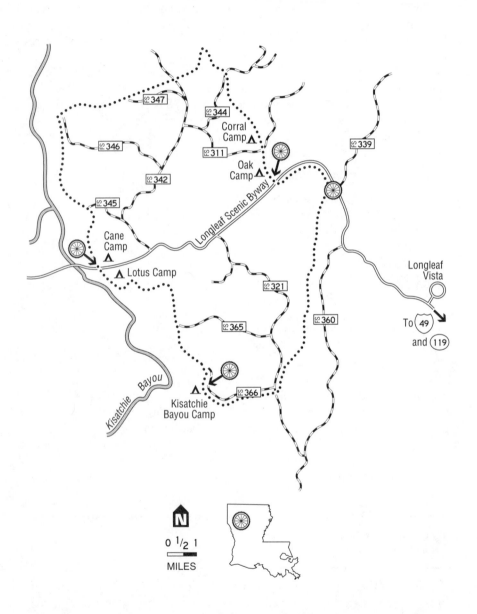

want to try a larger dose of true wilderness, take on a piece of the Sandstone Trail—a 38-mile loop of single-track and gravel road. Of course, if you're able, ride the entire length in one day . . . but pack plenty of trail mix.

Better yet, use The Sandstone as a bike-camp trail . . . but only from May 1 to September 30. During the other months—when hunters abound and you're likely to be mistaken for a whitetail—you can pitch a tent at Oak, Cane, Corral, Coyote, and Custis primitive camps only.

Whatever you decide, allow plenty of time to enjoy this unique and lovely landscape.

General location: You'll find these trails tucked into the wild and woolly region of the National Red Dirt Management Preserve in the Kisatchie National Forest.

Elevation change: As with the Caroline Dorman Trail, you'll be contending with steep terrain; you'll also get a taste of upland Louisiana swamps. Make sure your small crank ring works.

Season: If you insist on riding this trail during hunting season, wear bright orange and make a lot of noise. Also, as in other areas of Louisiana, the hot and humid months are favored more by serpents and insects than mountain bikers. Other than those considerations, it is open and available year-round.

Services: Bring all your water, or stop by Lotus Camp or Cane Camp off Longleaf Trail to get more. Other services can be found in Natchitoches. Don't forget to find Lasyone's and sample a meat pie or two; they also keep well on the trail.

Hazards: Along with all the other expected hazards of exposed roots, rocky descents, muddy spots, and horses, the most memorable hazard of my entire trip reared its head here. As I was making a very tentative creek crossing—on foot—I spied a swirling coil of black out of my left eye. I stopped, turned, and came face-to-jaw with a water moccasin. Despite the many times I've been out in the woods, this was my first confrontation with a cottonmouth. The snake faced me and displayed a gaping maw of white. Its tail vibrated back and forth like a rattlesnake's. As I made my way across the creek—keeping my bike between us—it changed its position in the water to keep its jaw facing me.

At the next creek crossing, my senses on alert for snakes, I searched but couldn't find any suggestion of serpent. Yet at the following creek, I saw another, less aggressive cottonmouth that, after showing me its white throat, slithered away under the creek bank. My senses remained alert during the rest of the trail, for the broken rocks, prime habitat for pygmy rattlers, looked exactly like the broken pattern on the backs of these rattlesnakes.

Although I saw no pygmies, I did see my first coral snake in the flesh. This beautifully colored and shy reptile carries a powerful neurotoxin in its venom sacks. As Howard down on the Kisatchie's banks told me later that day, "Coral snakes got to bite you right here." He held his middle and forefinger of one hand in between his thumb and forefinger of the other. "They have really short fangs, but if they bite you," he advised, "cut your arm off."

Rescue index: This is another remotely situated trail; be especially cautious.
Land status: Kisatchie National Forest.
Maps: Topo maps in the 7.5 minute series, Bellwood, Flora, Kisatchie, and Bayou L'Ivrogne, provide the information for the Kisatchie Hills Wilderness. Request the Sandstone Trail map from the U.S. ranger office in Natchitoches for the basic information, but obtain the Kisatchie National Forest map for more details.
Finding the trail: Exit Interstate 49 onto LA 119 going south. Turn right onto Longleaf Trail Scenic Byway. Just past Longleaf Vista Recreational Area, look for a sign on the left for Lotus Campground. You can park, set a shuttle, and replenish your water supply here.

Sources of additional information: If you see a man and his wife coming down the gravel road in a wagon equipped with automobile bucket seats and being pulled by two donkeys—Mary and BigHead—it'll probably be Howard and his wife. They told me about the spring on up the road and how people come "all the way from Alexandria just to fill gallon jugs" to take back home. Or maybe they will tell you how some of the trails and roads around here served as stagecoach routes and Pony Express trails.

Natchitoches District Ranger
National Forest Service
P.O. Box 2120 (Highway 6 West)
Natchitoches, LA 71457
(318) 352-2568

Natchitoches Parish Tourist Commission
P.O. Box 411
Natchitoches, LA 71458
(318) 352-8072

Notes on the trail: The Sandstone Trail incorporates part of the Caroline Dorman Trail in its 38-mile loop. Beginning at the trailhead at Lotus Camp on Forest Service Road 398, head north and clockwise just east of the head-waters of the Kisatchie Bayou. Continue north at the intersection with FS 345, crossing it and keeping a northerly direction until picking up a part of FS 346. Begin an eastern turn toward FS 342, which you cross before turning south toward Corral and Oak camp sites.

The first half of Sandstone ends with its junction with the paved Longleaf Trail Scenic Byway. The next couple of miles will head northeast and parallel this road just before FS 339 comes in on the left. Head down along Bayou L'Ivrogne until you cross it and join FS 321. Stay on this road until FS 366 turns off to the right. You'll ride this road all the way in to Kisatchie Bayou Camp. Lotus Camp—the end of the 38-mile loop—lies a hard up, up, and away toward Steep Middle Branch and Hill Creek. But you can do it because you brought along an extra meat pie from Lasyone's.

RIDE 6 *FOREST HILL/CAMP CLAIBORNE*

The 26-mile trail system on this former U.S. Army base was originally constructed for enduro competitions—which are still held there regularly—and has also been approved as a course for mountain bikes. How much you enjoy this trail network of various loop lengths depends on how much you enjoy riding rutted out, sandy swales. They don't make up the majority of miles, but enough of them exist to make them a consideration.

Part of the ride's technical nature comes from its past history as a military installation where a formerly well-used bombing zone still has "live ordnance." No trail, of course, crosses the zone, but it is close enough that officials have shut off access to some trailheads during ordnance retrieval (which still takes place, unlike the bombing). Forest Hill's explosiveness does not transfer to the trail's basic nature, however. It is an easily traveled trip. Tour groups from the Pack and Paddle in Lafayette usually plan a full day to cover the entire 26 miles at a moderate pace. The racer in you will knock it out in less than two hours.

You may want to wait until you get to Forest Hill to pick up plants or materials for that landscaping project you have planned. Over three million dollars a year are generated by the area's nurseries. One nursery is supplier to a huge discount market and grosses over a million dollars' business a year. For some reason, it seems this community got together and decided to build greenhouses and grow plants.

General location: This trail is found southwest of Alexandria, surrounded by national forest land.

Elevation change: There is no significant elevation change.

Season: Enduro races continue here, even in the middle of downpours. The trail's generally sandy nature makes it firmer when it's wet. But a Louisiana rule of thumb applies: it generally is too wet to ride in Louisiana only when water covers the trail too deep for too long.

Services: All services can be acquired in Alexandria.

Hazards: Motorized traffic can be frequent, especially during the weekends and holidays. Though highly unlikely, it is possible to somehow find your way onto the bombing range. Stay on the marked trails and roads.

Rescue index: Provided you stay away from bombs, your chances of survival —and a quick rescue should you need it—are pretty good. Eventually, the bombs will all be removed, but until then carry a map or good sense for where you are . . . and don't run through any fences with big signs on them.

Land status: This is, believe it or not, part of the Kisatchie National Forest.

Maps: I got one map, the one for the Loran Site, at the Forest Service office. The more detailed map—Forest Hill/Camp Claiborne map—came from Lafayette's Pack and Paddle, (800) 458-4560.

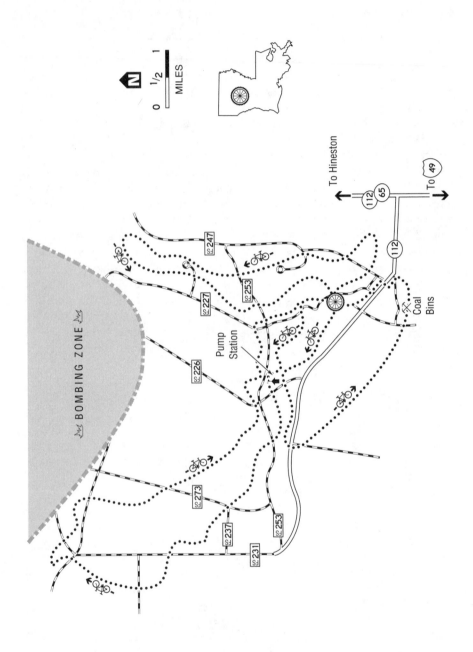

A wide spot in the trail beckons bikers to Forest Hill.

Finding the trail: Take the Forest Hill exit off Interstate 49 and head toward Forest Hill on Highway 112. Go through Forest Hill and take the right onto Highway 112/165; take the left following Highway 112 for 2 miles. Stay on the paved road until turning right onto the third gravel road on the right, Forest Service Road 258. Stay left on this road until you reach the open field. This is the camp from which you can launch 3 different independent loops, or the central point in a large loop of 26 miles of mostly single-track.

Sources of additional information:

National Forest Service
3727 Government Street
Alexandria, LA 71302
(318) 445-9396

Pack and Paddle
601 East Pinhook Drive
Lafayette, LA 70501
(800) 458-4560

Notes on the trail: What's nice about this trail system is, by being creative, all sorts of loops can give the sort of mileage you're looking for. From "The Camp," 3 different loops begin and end: 1 runs counterclockwise for a little over 6 miles southwest of The Camp; the longest makes a 14-mile loop clockwise northwest of The Camp; a final one leaves The Camp from the east and takes you 6 miles counterclockwise in between Forest Service 277 and FS 247. In addition to the existing 26 miles, 2 other trail systems are being planned for construction which will expand the total trail length (via a 3-leaf clover arrangement) to over 80 miles of off-road biking trails in the Camp Claiborne area.

RIDE 7 *WILD AZALEA TRAIL*

With the passing of the National Recreational Trails Act, construction began on a 31-mile hiking trail to link the Valentine Recreation Area in the Kisatchie National Forest with downtown Woodworth, Louisiana, 15 miles south of Alexandria. From its opening on June 7, 1978, until the fall of 1994, this trail was designated for "foot travel only."

After studying how the trail was used, and after seeing the low impact responsible mountain biking has on the treadway, the National Forest Service opened up this 31-mile one-way (62 miles total) of out-and back trail to off-road cyclists. Nearly everyone I talked to in Louisiana mentioned this trail, and for good reason. This is some of the prettiest country anywhere, offering routes successfully traveled by even the inexperienced biker.

The trail follows piney-top ridgelines down to the hardwood bottom-lands; open meadows and swamps funnel into upland forests of gum, oak, loblolly, and maple. Giant beech trees spread their leafy canopies over yaupon and Chinese privet. Songbirds and game birds, such as turkeys, quail, and bobwhites, chortle and cluck along the single-track; trailside greenery opens up into ferns and pines before closing around you with wisps of sapling branches and vines. It creates the feeling of riding inside a huge, green, leafy lung.

General location: This trail spans 31 miles (one-way) from Valentine Lake to Woodworth, Louisiana.
Elevation change: Some slopes make for brief, precarious descents and arduous climbs.
Season: The Deep South "Rule of Thumb" applies here: avoid extremes in heat, humidity, and nuisance animals, and you will enjoy riding this trail year-round.
Services: Woodworth can provide the basics, as can Gardner in the northwest. But for more specialized needs, go to Alexandria.
Hazards: Although there are enough exposed, slanting, wet roots, what always commanded my attention on this trail were the wet spots. Just when

The trail hugs the shore at Lake Kincaid.

I thought I could tell when it was safe to go over unprepared for a sudden sink into a bog, I would be sucked under, front-tire-first. This maneuver was generally finished with a leapfrog over the handlebars. I left my telltale deep footprints in more than one spot, and in one area, I landed with such force I was buried up to my knees. If it hadn't been for that passing armadillo whose tail I held onto as a tow line, I might be there yet.

Rescue index: The way the intersecting roads come into the Wild Azalea Trail, any help you may need can be fairly easily acquired.

Land status: This is another addition to the large repository of off-road choices in the Evangeline District of the Kisatchie National Forest.

Maps: The Wild Azalea National Recreation Trail map provides all necessary information and can be obtained at the National Forest Service office in Alexandria. The Elmer and Woodworth East quads (7.5 minute series), which cover most of the Wild Azalea Trail, may be fun for you to use. Also, the Kisatchie National Forest map is a handy reference for those who will be exploring in this area.

Finding the trail: One terminus is found on the west side of the city hall in Woodworth, Louisiana, on Highway 165, 15 miles south of Alexandria. The other terminus is located west of the parking area inside the Valentine Recreation Area in the northwest section of the Evangeline District in the Kisatchie National Forest.

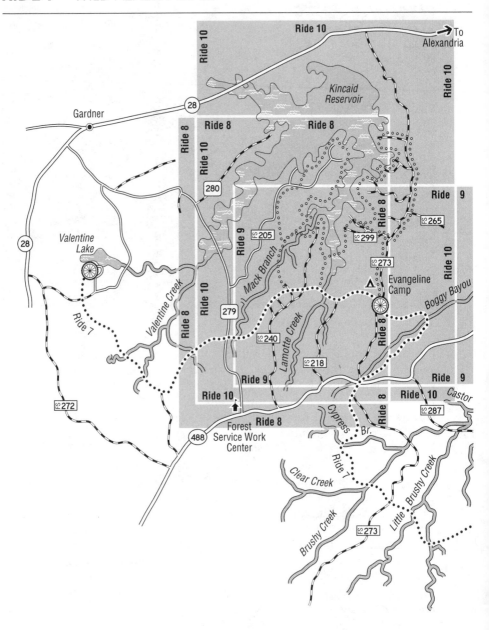

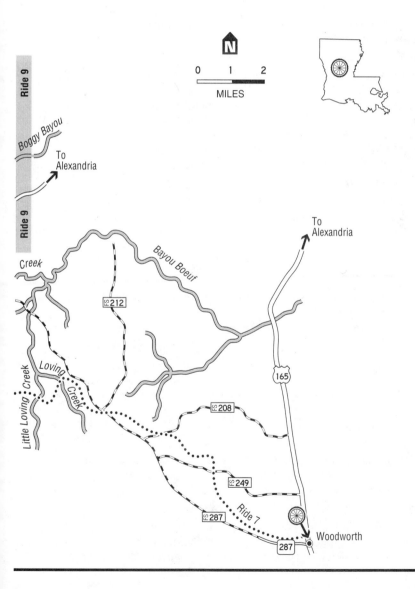

Sources of additional information:

Evangeline Ranger District
3727 Government Street
Alexandria, LA 71301
(318) 445-9396

Notes on the trail: There are 9 officially recognized points of trail access along the 31 miles (one-way) of mostly single-track. The two at Valentine Lake are situated within a mile of each other; the next one isn't until Forest Service Road 279, 5 miles away. This section offers many opportunities to cross the wet headlands of Valentine Creek.

The trail in between FS 279 and FS 273 connects to the routes leading up both sides of Kincaid Reservoir. In the next 3 miles the trail meets Boggy Bayou and borders it for the trip to FS 287. Castor Creek Scenic Area lies where 2 creeks—Clear and Brushy—come together to form Castor. On the other side of FS 273 (south of LA 488), Little Brushy, Little Loving, and Loving creeks are crossed on their way to Bayou Boeuf. The final (or first if you begin in Woodworth) 7 miles are the least remote portion.

The entire 31 miles (one-way, out-and-back) can be traveled in a very full day of biking, but a good choice may be to put on panniers and take along camping gear for a night or 2. Replenishing the water supply may take some careful planning. The water source at Evangeline Camp is not functioning. The water drawn from the well there has never tested pure enough to drink. The rangers—not the vandals—took the handle.

RIDE 8   *KINCAID LAKE CAMP LOOP*

The trails at Kincaid Lake draw riders from all over the United States to do some bayou biking. This 12-mile loop is one of four different rides—each over ten miles and offering challenges to bikers of all abilities—in the immediate area. The hundreds of acres of Kincaid Reservoir are home to many long, narrow waterways reaching far back into the quiet swamp. It is along the banks of one such area where the Kincaid Loop Trail connects to the 31-mile Wild Azalea National Recreational Trail.

The result is a place where mountain bikers can spend several days camped at either the recreational area at Kincaid Lake or the campground down the road at Valentine Lake and establish a home base from which several bike rides can be staged. The same quiet waterways offer the perfect "other sport" to try. After a morning ride, put a canoe or other boat in and explore the trails from the water. Many wading birds, songbirds, minks, turtles, countless frogs, and, of course, alligators inhabit this forest lake and banks. And don't forget the armadillos.

RIDE 8 *KINCAID LAKE CAMP LOOP*

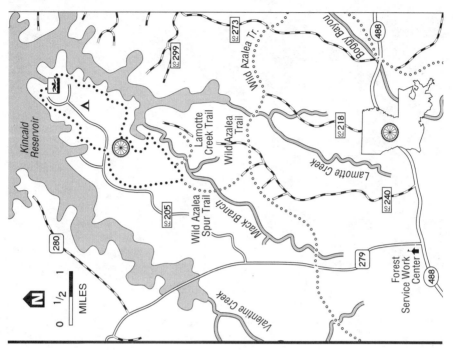

There are two things that any trail in Louisiana will be guaranteed to have: water and armadillos. It was on this trail where I bunny-hopped over an armadillo browsing among the yaupon one second, then standing frozen in the middle of the trail, the next. My entire body convulsed in an involuntary crash protection reflex, which is what I found out I do to bunny-hop. As I saw the armadillo pass under me, it squeaked, raised its tail, and went over to the other side of the trail . . . to plot an ambush for the next biker, no doubt. Be careful out there.

General location: This trail crawls along the banks of Kincaid Reservoir in the Kisatchie National Forest west of Alexandria, Louisiana.

Elevation change: Some changes require getting into your small front ring, but most can be achieved cranking your middle gear or higher.

Season: The drier times are generally from July to early spring. This is the best time to ride Kincaid relative to a wet trail, but hoping for a dry trail in Louisiana is like wishing for a lake in the Sahara.

Services: Alexandria has all services.

Hazards: There are numerous places where springs come to the surface and spread in a shallow wallow, causing cautious mountain bikers to question (a) "How soft is it?" and (b) "How deep is it?" and then adjust bike speed

Lamotte Creek flows into this lily-padded portion of Lake Kincaid.

accordingly. Some wallows have to be entered slowly to keep from flying and landing frog-like in the muck. Once committed, a good swift mud stomp or 2 in a bigger ring usually achieves a firmer purchase. Also, watch out for oncoming bikers doing the same thing.

Rescue index: You are fairly accessible despite getting the feeling that you are out in the middle of a Louisiana forest-swamp much of the time. By nearly circling the campground for approximately half of the loop, you're usually within earshot.

Land status: This land lies within the Kisatchie National Forest in the Evangeline Ranger District.

Maps: The campground host gave me my map to the Wild Azalea Trail, which has all area trails—including this one—marked on it. You can also call or write to the forest service office and request this map.

Finding the trail: This trail has many access points. For this particular loop you can park on the left after passing the entrance station and begin riding where the trail crosses Forest Service Road 205. Check your map and choose another junction if you'd like. There are at least 7 other junctions.

Sources of additional information:

National Forest Service
3727 Government Street
Alexandria, LA 71302
(318) 445-9396

Alexandria/Pineville Area Convention and Visitors Bureau
1470 MacArthur Drive
Alexandria, LA 71301
(800) 742-7049 or (318) 443-7049

Notes on the trail: This loop has well over half of its total length running between the camping area and the recreational area. By taking this loop in a clockwise direction—by no means mandatory—2 turns need to be taken for the loop to be completed. They are both right-hand turns. One is at the sign pointing to Lamotte Creek. (Taking this turn and the next 3 rights will bring you to a fork where you take the left to go to FS 205 or right, to where the Lamotte Creek sign stands, thereby completing a circle.) The other junction has a sign pointing left to the Wild Azalea Trail, .75 mile away. Take the right and cross FS 205 where the entrance building is; the trail continues to the Kincaid West Boat Ramp. Another section, blazed in yellow, winds its way down to the bridge, but the trail climbs the ridge and continues to the recreational area. Carefully ride the sidewalk until it goes back into a road on the north side of the parking lot; the trail has a sign—and a very muddy, wet spot—pointing to the Wild Azalea Trail and the camping areas.

After rounding the point, various spurs (some unsigned) will come into the trail from the right. Ignore these unless you want to go back to the camping area; instead, stay on the blue blazes to complete the loop. Other connections to the other Forest Service roads will come into the trail from the right if you're still going clockwise.

RIDE 9   *WILD AZALEA/LAKE KINCAID LOOP*

In 1994 the National Forest Service decided that the low number of hikers on the Wild Azalea Trail called for a move to give mountain bikers full access to this 31-mile one-way out-and-back (62 miles total) National Recreational Trail. What a gift! Use of this trail enables creative loops and excursions, from a scant few minutes to days on the trail. Although Forest Service roads have to be used in order to complete a loop, these roads normally see few vehicles, and a majority of those encountered haul logs out of the forest. One such loop of slightly more than ten miles of moderate single-track uses a portion of the Wild Azalea Trail and part of the Lake Kincaid Loop.

Ancient, moss-draped live oaks along the shore of Lake Kincaid give way to loblolly and slash pines farther inland. The understory among these trees is relatively open and provides long views of the gently rolling knolls. On top of one such hill I saw a pack of coyotes splayed out for a midday rest. The alpha dog, unsure of whether to bark or flee, roused the rest as I stopped, straddling the bar on my bike, and returned their stare. Finally, after figuring I was a threat, the leader gave a little yip and ran off with the others close behind.

RIDE 9 *WILD AZALEA / LAKE KINCAID LOOP*

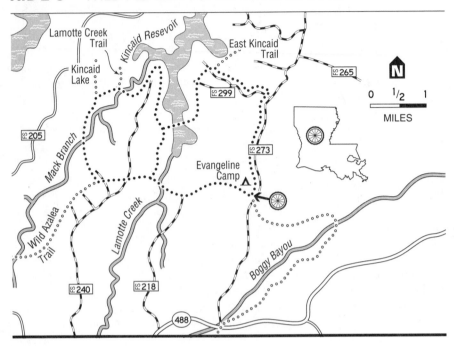

General location: This is another ride you can stage from Kincaid Recreational Area just west of Alexandria in the Kisatchie National Forest.

Elevation change: You'll be surprised at the degree of some of the elevation changes. Try not to be disappointed that the protruding roots in the single-track usually prevent successful ascents without walking.

Season: This is reported as an all-season trail. The generally sandy loam holds up well in wet times to the gentle use of knobbies. Summer riders need to be prepared for high heat and humidity and six-legged winged warriors seeking to spill some of your blood.

Services: Alexandria, some 10 miles east, is a good place to get what you need. Gardner, northwest of where you'll be riding, has a pay phone at the store where Forest Service Road 279 turns right onto the paved highway and makes a junction with LA 28 a hundred yards down on the left.

Hazards: Exposed roots can give you a very upsetting experience, as can some wet spots on the trail which will suck your front tire to a mucky halt.

Rescue index: You are not very far from help. Many people use this section of national forest land.

Land status: This is part of the Kisatchie National Forest, Evangeline District.

Maps: The map you want is called Wild Azalea National Recreation Trail. Call or write to the Evangeline District Ranger's office to get your copy. Also, the campground host usually has copies.

The trails in Louisiana open and close like a giant lung.

Finding the trail: Take Highway 165 and follow the signs. Take the right turn onto Forest Service Road 273; Evangeline Camp will be on the left. Park on the right in the space provided. The 3 miles of Wild Azalea Trail—heading first east, then south, along Boggy Bayou—cross LA 488 where you can loop back on FS 273 or take the trail back.

Sources of additional information: Mountain bikers have shown themselves to be the friendliest sources of information. If it's convenient, ask them how they ride this trail and what their favorite rides are. Additions to existing trails are being constructed at a fairly rapid pace. Creative trail architects arrange work parties of volunteers to build totally new mileage, carving single-track out of the brush and trunks, and voila!—a new venue.

Red River Cyclery
3752 MacArthur Drive
Alexandria, LA 71306
(318) 473-4256

Notes on the trail: Taken as a figure-8, this loop uses some gravel forest service roads to complete the circuit. Depending on when you would like to ride the gravel, first or last, determines the direction of start. Clockwise takes you to the trail first and the right turn toward Kincaid Reservoir. The next sign .5 mile away points the way to a northerly course up the lake on the Kincaid Lake Trail, marked by blue blazes; continuing straight (also on the Kincaid Lake Trail) carries you around a point and across Mack Branch.

Turn left. Shortly, another junction occurs. Turn left again. After crossing Mack Branch once more, the spur dead-ends into the Wild Azalea Trail with its yellow blazes. Take the next left and repeat the .5-mile section serving as the middle of the 8. This time take the right on Kincaid Lake Trail. At the junction with a gravel road (Oak Road), take a right past where Pine Road comes in from the left. Take the right on FS 273 back to the parking place. This ride can be a wet experience; 3 creeks are crossed and at least 2 muddy hillsides made me take hikes to the top. Another point where walking comes recommended is at "One Railing Bridge," a 3-foot-wide wooden structure spanning an inlet about 75 yards across.

RIDE 10 *KINCAID EAST LAKE LOOP*

Tour participants from Lafayette's Pack and Paddle usually ride down the scenic and occasionally difficult single-track on the east side of Kincaid Reservoir, beginning at the boat launch at the end of FS 273 and taking it until crossing the lake on "One Rail Bridge." Plenty of intersections with Forest Service roads occur, thereby making this loop (or an out-and-back, depending on whether or not Forest Service roads are ridden) a potential ride of anywhere from 2 to over 16 miles.

The shade found on the western section of the Kincaid Lake Trail is also a feature on this part of the path. The lake stays in sight for much of the way as small springs run off the hillsides and cross the trail. Most boaters stay out of the relatively narrow channels, but a few stray in looking for that special hiding place where a big bass lurks. I had stopped for a water break along the lakeside single-track when I saw a bass boat making its way slowly along the bank. The driver, and sole occupant, was directing the boat with a trolling motor as he stood in the bow and made casts underneath limbs. Just as the boat got in clear sight, I saw a bass hit the topwater lure. For approximately a minute, although it seemed longer, the man played the fish alongside the boat and scooped it into his net. It was hard to judge how much it weighed from where I sat, but as the man grabbed its lip and removed the lure, it hung down the length of his forearm. Big enough, as bassers say, to be termed a "hawg." The man looked at it admiringly a moment before gently releasing it back into the water.

General location: This route lies in the hardwood and pine forest on the east Kincaid Lake Trail in the Evangeline District of the Kisatchie National Forest.
Elevation change: Short, steep climbs can be ascended with timely gear changes and powerful, balanced explosions of pedaling.
Season: This comes as close to an all-season trail as you'll find in Louisiana. Proper training and preparation makes most days good for biking Kincaid

RIDE 10   *KINCAID EAST LAKE LOOP*

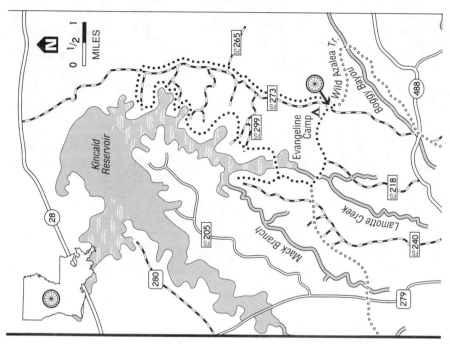

Lake. However, avoiding extremes in heat, humidity (moisture both in and below the air), and insects usually makes for a more enjoyable ride.

Services: Seek and you shall find in Alexandria.

Hazards: It is unlikely that you would run across an alligator, but it is more than possible. These large reptiles can achieve high land speeds. Should you inadvertently stray near a big mama's nest and see her charge, hammer down hard on the largest ring and get out of there as quickly as possible. Aggravated mama gators don't give but one chance. Roots on steep hillsides pose the other major obstacle to safe biking, but compared to an enraged gator, they barely merit mention.

Rescue index: This eastern section of trail lies in a more remote area than the western side. Prepare accordingly by carrying ample water. The walk out to FS 273 would not ever exceed 2 miles, provided you take the shortest route.

Land status: The Kisatchie National Forest stretches from north Louisiana near Minden to the Vernon Ranger District near Leesville and encompasses over 800,000 acres, including this trail section.

Maps: The Kisatchie National Forest map is a good one to help you find more possible trailheads, but the best single map to get for this loop is the Wild Azalea National Recreational Trail. The district office in Pineville and the campground hosts have these maps available for free. Pack and Paddle in

Pines mark an intersection on the Wild Azalea Trail.

Lafayette also offers a wide assortment of Louisiana mountain bike trail maps.

Finding the trail: Head south out of Alexandria on Highway 165; take the right at the light where Highway 488 comes into Highway 165. Turn right onto FS 273 and take it until it stops at the boat ramp. The trail begins on the left before you get to the end of the road.

Sources of additional information:

Pack and Paddle
601 East Pinhook Drive
Lafayette, LA 70501
(318) 232-5854

National Forest Service
3727 Government Street
Alexandria, LA 71302
(318) 445-9396

Notes on the trail: This trail allows an out-and-back of approximately 16 miles total by sticking to the single-track. Start at one of two locations: (1) The parking area approximately 2 miles down FS 273 on the right where the Wild Azalea Trail crosses and ride west on the Wild Azalea Trail and then north (a right turn a little over 2 miles from FS 273) on Lake Kincaid Trail to the boat launch at the end of FS 210. Or (2) park at the boat launch and ride south, turning left onto the Wild Azalea Trail and 2 miles more to FS 273. The slightly longer loop is completed in either direction by riding on FS 273.

RIDE 11 *WEST BAY WMA*

Depending on whether you talk to a leg-shaving racer or a novice mountain biker who falls over on level ground at slow speed (also known as an "Artie" for Artie Johnson who perfected this move), you'll receive different ideas about what makes up the classic trail: steep, flat, open, tight, long, short, wet, dry, single-track, roads, dirt, gravel, boulders. You name it, we search it out on the trail.

West Bay Wildlife Management Area's 62,115 acres of state-managed, privately owned land stretches across mostly flat pine plantations. Over 200 miles of gravel roads (which can be made into loops or out-and-backs of various lengths) open up into forests with hickory, red bay, and white bay growing among slash pines. Woodcocks nest over yaupon, smilax, and holly. Rabbits browse beneath dense stands of blackberries whose blooms turn these Deep South woods into a snowy wonderland.

"Bay-gall situations" (upland depressions that are permanently soaked and mushy) account for over a third of West Bay. Tupelos and black gums grow here along with buttonbush and other water-tolerant species. I asked a Louisiana Department of Wildlife and Fisheries officer why the words "bay-gall" are used to describe such a "situation." He didn't know, so I offer this explanation, which applies to mountain bikers attempting to ride through such a quagmire:

> Should you attempt to ride a "bay-gall"
> Sticking is a certainty.
> You'll no doubt kick, scream, wail, and bay
> as the mud delivers you gall.

General location: West Bay WMA is located in north-central Allen Parish near Elizabeth, Louisiana.

Elevation change: The elevation change experienced here is negligible.

Season: Because routes follow gravel and unimproved roads, riding can take place all year long. However, should you stray off into a bay-gall . . . well, we may just call you Artie.

Services: The basics can be obtained in Elizabeth. Leesville or Alexandria should offer most specialty items. There are 3 state-maintained camping areas inside the West Bay where camping is permitted. Water, but not electricity, is provided at all sites.

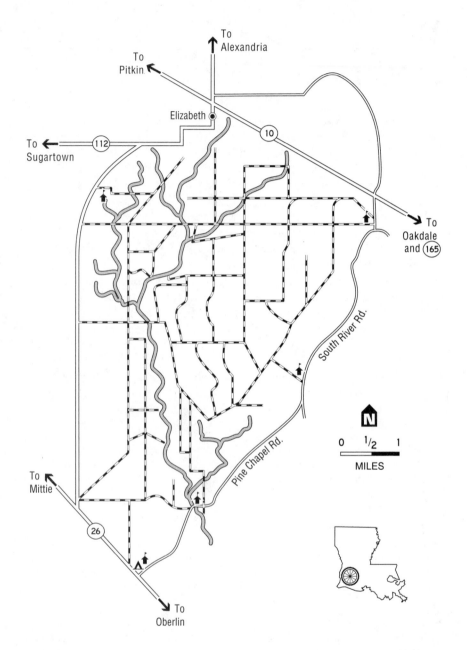

Note: *Gravel roads are trail routes.*

Hazards: As in all wildlife management areas, seasonal hunting occurs. If you must ride in areas known to be hunted (but this is not advised), be sure to properly adorn yourself with a fluorescent vest, hat, bike, shoes, tires—anything that can glow orange. Also, talk loudly, ring bells, and blow whistles. Be advised that this behavior will not endear you to any firearm-bearing citizen hoping to bag some game. Also, be on the alert for vehicular traffic.

Rescue index: There are many roads within this area; some may not be ridden regularly. If you were to venture down these and get in trouble, you probably wouldn't be seen for quite a while.

Land status: Not many areas have the status of being state-managed private land, but that's what this land is. A no-cost-to-the-state lease is given so that the state can manage the wildlife only. There are some isolated patches of land in the middle of the WMA that are private property, *not* part of the WMA.

Maps: A free guide to all of Louisiana's Wildlife Management Areas can be ordered from Louisiana Department of Wildlife and Fisheries, 1213 North Lakeshore Drive, Lake Charles, LA 70601. Their phone number is (318) 491-2575.

Finding the trail: Enter the WMA by turning onto Pine Chapel Road off LA 26 on the south border or turn onto River Road from LA 10 in the northern section.

Sources of additional information:

Louisiana Department of Wildlife and Fisheries
105 Avenue of the Acadians
Opelousas, LA 70570
(318) 948-0255

Notes on the trail: You can go to the center of the Wildlife Management Area, park, and bike your way out by taking roads that look promising. Loop until your heart's content. Do figure eights until your odometer reads 88. All roads are open for your use unless plainly posted as "Closed." This is a good place to come and let your mind wander as the scenery floats by.

Lafayette Area Rides

If you've been waiting patiently to satisfy your appetite for crawfish and Cajun cooking, not to mention zydeco rhythms, Lafayette is the place to let your free wheel spin a little more wildly. Although this is levee-land, there are a few trails you should not pass by when the water level's right.

One of the premier outdoor supply stores anywhere, The Pack and Paddle is the one-stop for anyone wanting the scoop on where to put down some tire tracks. In fact, they will arrange for you to accompany them on the road and trails as they direct one of their many tours of the Louisiana backroads and bayous. If you elect to go solo with your own group, they will provide you with maps of the trails from the Kisatchie National Forest to Chicot State Park.

Joan Williams also has a book of biking tours you will find to be an indispensable addition to your guidebook library called, *Backroad Tours of French Louisiana*. As of this writing, both Joan and her husband Dick have been involved in trying to get support for converting an old railbed into a multi-use trail. Despite the resounding success of the Tammany Trace conversion east of Baton Rouge, resistance to the idea still exists in Lafayette.

This area is rich in history of all sorts; nearby St. Martinville is the site where the Evangeline Oak, made famous by the poet Longfellow, spreads its moss-laden boughs. This and other attractions can be boned up on at the Jean Lafitte Acadian Cultural Center in Lafayette. I bypassed some interesting sites, such as the Lafayette Natural History Museum and Planetarium, in order to spend more time at Avery Island where Mr. McIlhenny's pepper sauce ferments three years in oak barrels before it spices my palate.

For more information:

Pack and Paddle
601 East Pinhook Drive
Lafayette, LA 70501
(800) 458-4560 or (318) 232-5854

Lafayette Convention and Visitors Commission
1400 Evangeline Thruway
Lafayette, LA 70501
(800) 346-1958

Acadian Cultural Center–Jean Lafitte National
Historical Park and Preserve
501 Fisher Road
Lafayette, LA 70508
(318) 232-0789

RIDE 12 *CHICOT STATE PARK*

The perfect complement to pedaling the seven-plus miles (14 total) of out-and-back mountain bike trail in Chicot State Park would be to paddle some of the 2,000 acres of water in Lake Chicot. Better yet, take along your fishing pole (and license) and try your hand at landing some of the monster crappie, bass, and bluegill. Hiking the trails inside the Louisiana State Arboretum can keep you entertained for at least another day, so a bike trip here should be planned to last for more than one day if time permits.

The single-track at Chicot varies from the tight, muddy path on the north end to the steeply rolling lakeside hilltops south of the bridge. The main trail has been blazed white; primitive camping area spurs lead off toward the lake in two places and have been blazed with blue paint. Bikers inexperienced with riding through mud and over exposed roots should exercise discretion before departing on this trail.

There is also a trail system set up on Lake Chicot. Buoys, colored and marked in ten different ways, signal approaches to landings and restricted, dangerous areas, as well as directing boaters to the cabins and Walker's Branch. Although I'm sure someone familiar with these waters could easily find the open, safe channels without getting lost, the cypress- and tupelo-lined banks look amazingly alike to the untrained eye.

General location: Chicot State Park is found west of Interstate 49 on County Road 3042, west of Ville Platte, Louisiana.

Elevation change: There are plenty of places where you can flex your thighs and calves for short distances.

Season: The wetter times certainly make this trail difficult to enjoy for those who don't like the slop. Other than that, if you can stand the heat and bugs, this trail accepts traffic year-round.

Services: Basic services can be found in Ville Platte; travel either south to Lafayette or north to Alexandria for your more special needs.

Hazards: Substantial, exposed roots cross the trail. In wetter times, some sections of the trail can be traveled only with great difficulty. Beginners might be daunted by some of the steeper sections.

Rescue index: Convenient pathways lead into and out of the park's more primitive areas. Should you need it, help can get to you with relative ease; the paved road remains a relatively short hike away.

Land status: Chicot State Park is managed by the state of Louisiana.

Maps: Maps of the State Park showing the existing trail system can be picked up at the entrance. Just ask for the Chicot State Park map.

Finding the trail: One end can be reached by looking for the sign on the right as you head north toward Chicot on CR 3042. Just after crossing the bridge

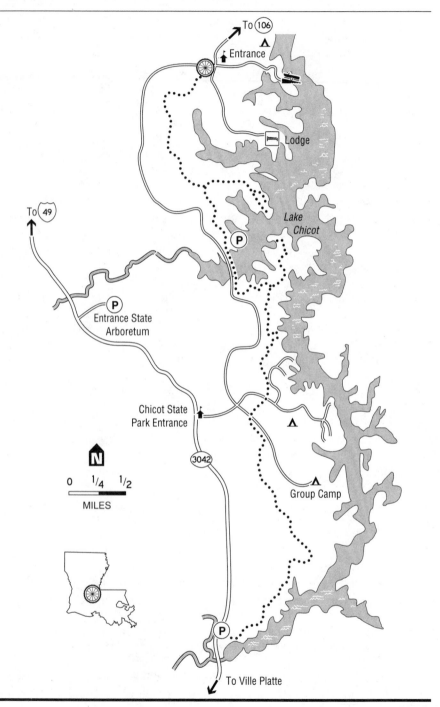

To 106

Entrance

Lodge

Lake
Chicot

To 49

P

P
Entrance State
Arboretum

Chicot State
Park Entrance

3042

N

0   1/4   1/2
MILES

Group Camp

P

To Ville Platte

Biking near bayous hints of the first exploration.

over Lake Chicot, look on your right where the trail begins. Inside the park you can pick up the trail by going straight or right at the first intersection after entering from CR 3042. Another place to begin your ride starts on either side of the bridge inside the park. Spaces are provided for parking on the north side of the bridge. The northernmost terminus is found catty-cornered from the entrance station off LA 106.

Sources of additional information:

> Chicot State Park
> Route 3 Box 494
> Ville Platte, LA 70586
> (318) 363-2403

> Louisiana Office of State Parks
> P.O. Box 44426
> Baton Rouge, LA 70804
> (318) 342-8111

Notes on the trail: By riding this trail as an out-and-back, and taking every spur back and forth, up to 18 miles can be routed along the shore and ridges of Lake Chicot. While this is in line with mileage many like to ride in one day, this trail's original users—hikers with camping on their mind—established (and the state has maintained) several primitive camping areas. These sites can be used by mountain bikers who obtain a written backcountry permit and set a trip plan giving the expected area of camping, route of travel, and dates for departure and return. A creative camper who brings along both bike and boat could park at one site, bike, then boat back to the vehicle.

RIDE 13 *LAKE FAUSSE POINTE STATE PARK TRAIL*

My trip down to this southernmost Louisiana loop in the Atchafalaya Basin was initially set up after series editor Dennis Coello returned from a Louisiana photo shoot. Despite "the unfortunately short [a ¾ mile route and a 1 ¾ mile one] and flat trails," scenery alone would be enough to qualify these trails as classic rides. Dennis did not mention that I needed to check with Captain Cleve at the park store to make sure the basin's water level was reading less than ten feet before setting out on the trail. Otherwise, expect to do some shin-sloshing where the Atchafalaya intrudes on trail.

I arrived too late to check in before the Louisiana State Park closed its gates at 8 P.M. (CST). I set up my tent alongside the road where—to my surprise— no sign prohibiting camping was seen. After hearing something big and heavy splashing through the water near me, I caught only a glimpse of shining green eyes disappearing into the swamp.

I was awakened once to the distinct snuffling of my tent flap. When I sat up and shined my flashlight toward the sound, I saw that a thick cloak of fog had completely enshrouded my tent. Even though I heard the unmistakable pitty-pat of armadillo legs running through the grass, I could see no farther than five feet. Louisiana fog shuffles in on armadillo snouts.

As I lay listening to the other night sounds trying to reclaim sleep, I counted five different, distinct frog noises. These croaked me off to a short snooze. Trucks pulling flat-bottomed boats on trailers roared down the road and levee beginning sometime around 4 A.M. I found out later that these were the cray-fishers on their way to search the 12-foot-deep waters for this Cajun delicacy. Judging by the traffic, there is a substantial population of folks making a living catching "mudbugs," or as I grew up calling them, "crawdads."

General location: The trails loop through this park 30 miles southeast of Lafayette.

Elevation change: There are only nominal elevation changes.

Season: Although I rode nearly all this trail, the water came up near my knees where I turned around, and the trail could no longer be discerned. Had I been able to pick out the trail turns in the water, the bottom would have been hard enough for me to keep pedaling along.

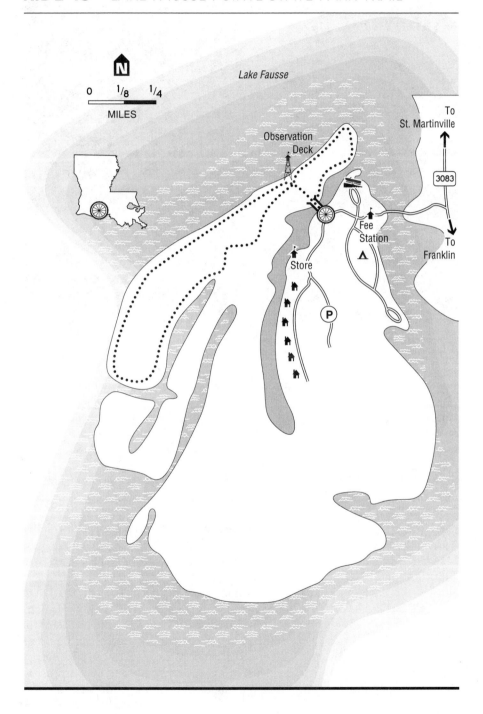

Lake Fausse

Observation Deck

To St. Martinville

3083

To Franklin

Fee Station

Store

P

0   1/8   1/4
MILES

Get enough pepper sauce in your mouth and you can pronounce "Atchafalaya" perfectly.

Services: You need to go back to Lafayette in order to get a wider selection of goods, but St. Martinville 30 minutes away) will have most supplies.

Hazards: Although I did not think of it at the time I was in knee-deep, gators both big and small patrol these waters. Likewise, I'm sure I would not have ridden as far on this underwater trail if I had thought about water moccasins. Poison ivy grows close to the trail in places.

Rescue index: Getting help with a mechanical breakdown would not be much of an inconvenience. Professional medical assistance is another thing: this area is not quickly reached.

Land status: This is a state park managed by the Louisiana Office of State Parks.

Maps: Maps are available at the entrance, where you'll be expected to pay admission. Just ask for the Lake Fausse Pointe State Park map.

Finding the trail: Numerous and conspicuous signs point the way to Lake Fausse Pointe State Park. The highway numbers from St. Martinville are LA 96 until taking the right onto LA 679. A right turn after crossing the bridge onto County Road 3083 takes you to the park entrance on the right. You'll notice the levee on your left as you make the turn. Follow the signs to the park store. The trailhead is across the bridge. Park inside Fausse Pointe and take at least a short ride along the levee either north or south of the park's entrance.

Sources of additional information:

Lake Fausse Pointe State Park
5400 Levee Road
St. Martinville, LA 70582
(318) 229-4764

Notes on the trail: In 1992 Hurricane Andrew hit this section dead-on. As a result, the "C" Loop (making up 3 miles of the total 6 miles of trails in the park) was blocked by debris and deadfalls, leaving only the .75-mile "A" Loop and the 1.75-mile "B" Loop intact. These trails are not blazed but are well worn and easy to follow if they are not flooded. Along the way, I was treated to my first fleeting sight of a wild mink as it scooted into the water 15 yards ahead of me.

RIDE 14 *THE LEVEES, ATCHAFALAYA SWAMP BASIN*

It may be an unfair stereotype, but levees and Louisiana go together like craw-fish and pepper sauce. And, like the pepper sauce, you can get too much levee if you're not careful. During my trips to Louisiana, I tried to be careful. But I also tried to arrange an extended ride on the levees. I had no luck doing so. But I did manage to contact someone who has ridden the entire 100 miles or so of the levee system looping around the Atchafalaya Swamp Basin on a gravel roadbed.

While the more adventurous biker may elect to ride the entire loop in the space of a few days, it is possible to make a great number of various lengths of out-and-back trips, begun at one of the many intersections where the levees meet with interstate, state, and local highways. If a section of the levee has been posted as private property, it is necessary to obtain permission from the landowner in order to ride across the property that lies *underneath* the levee. The levees themselves are controlled by the Atchafalaya Levee Board, which has servitude rights, meaning that the private landowner cannot do anything to the levees without first obtaining permission. But we, as bikers, cannot currently do anything on the levees if they are posted.

A word on the levees: completed with federal oversight after the over-whelming flooding that took place in the 1920s, they were first begun with Louisiana convict labor. The construction effort became serious after the destructive flooding of 1927. Two parallel mounds of muck were bulldozed into place with a space 50 feet wide left open in between them. These channels were then filled with more muck which eventually oozed its water out to form a sort of hardened surface. After the levee got to be about 15–20 feet high, gravel was spread on top to help hold things together.

RIDE 14 *THE LEVEES, ATCHAFALAYA SWAMP BASIN*

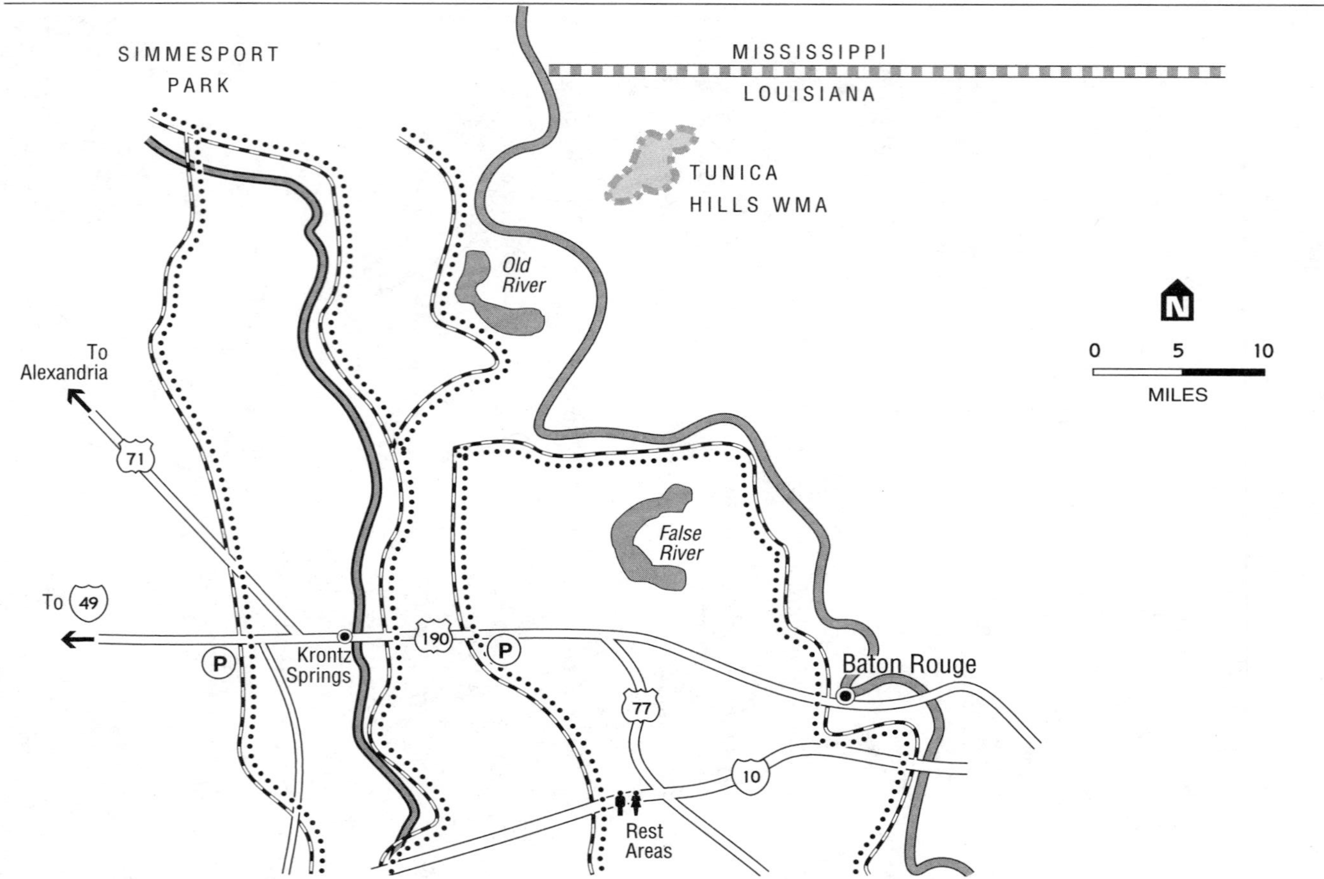

MISSISSIPPI
LOUISIANA

TUNICA
HILLS WMA

SIMMESPORT
PARK

Old
River

False
River

Baton Rouge

Krontz
Springs

Rest
Areas

To
Alexandria

To 49

71

190

77

10

N

0   5   10
MILES

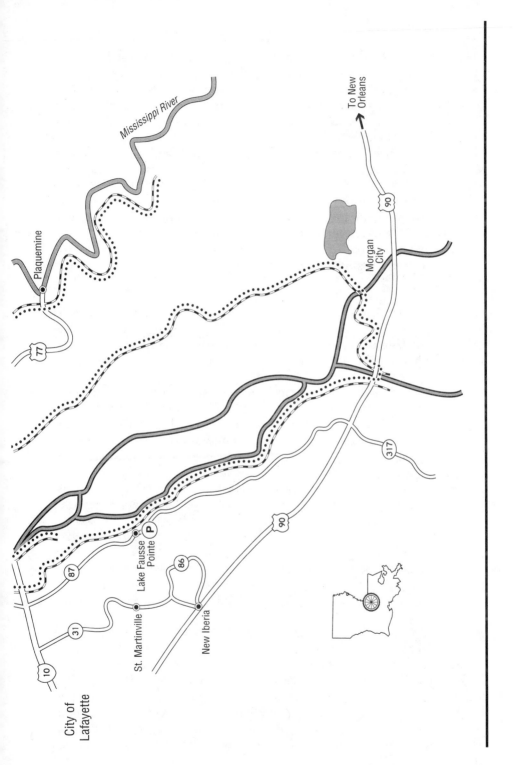

Control structures—gates to open and close the flow of floodwaters into and out of the basin—were installed in three places: on the east, the north, and the south. It is a critical junction for anyone wishing to ride the levees. If these structures are open for water flow, biking progress is pretty much halted until they are closed, which is after the flooding stops. I discovered that flooding in Louisiana does not operate on a regular timetable.

Despite these drawbacks, the Atchafalaya Swamp Basin Levee has, according to Joan Williams of Lafayette's Pack and Paddle, the "potential for [becoming] a fantastic linear park." A study being conducted by Louisiana State University in Baton Rouge (and monitored by the National Park Service's Rivers, Trails, and Conservation Assistance Program) is looking at the legality of the levee's remaining in its current use limbo. If you are interested in lending support for the conversion of levees to public property, you should contact the National Park Service regional office in your area or in Baton Rouge.

General location: The levee system goes through Simmesport in the north and Morgan City in the south and reaches a width of approximately 35 miles across the Atchafalaya Swamp as it completes its oval-shaped course.

Elevation change: The only elevation change occurs as you get up on and down off the levee.

Season: Floods either in Louisiana itself, or as far north as the Missouri River, east of the Rockies, can eventually affect the operation of the levee gates.

Services: Don't expect much curbside service along the levees. The occasional small town or village can supply basic food and drink needs, and a pickup heading back in from a day of fishing or mudbugging might be able to give you a ride if you break down, but don't count on it.

Hazards: Besides the floodgates, which need to be closed in order to pass over them to the other side, traffic on the levee—although not heavy (due to its being technically illegal, at least where posted)—is fast and basically unresponsive to any safety requirements of bikers. Disgruntled cattle owners—the cattle business is big in this part of Louisiana—could ask you to move off the high ground of the levee and turn around. And the cows themselves, used to being fed from slow-moving vehicles, congregate in front and around approaching bikers, encircling them and creating their own version of nasty conditions.

Rescue index: Go on a levee ride prepared to be totally self-sufficient unless you are planning a short day trip.

Land status: There seems to be some confusion about the status on top of levees. Although the system was built and is maintained by the federal government, this fact has not prevented some adjoining landowners from posting the levee as private property where "trespassing" is not allowed. According to the Atchafalaya Levee Board, landowners *can* post their property lying underneath the levee. So keep this in mind: it may be unposted one day and posted the next, and there's not anything you can do (legally) except turn back or get permission to ride on. And even if it's not posted, the landowner can request that you turn around. Failure to do so could result in a citation and/or arrest by the Atchafalaya Basin Levee District police.

Maps: Request the Atchafalaya Basin Map from the Louisiana Department of Wildlife and Fisheries, District VII, in Baton Rouge.

Finding the trail: Although any city along the way can serve as a point of entry, for those who wish to avoid many of the hazards associated with levee riding, consider beginning at either Lake Fausse Pointe or Henderson where Interstate 10 intersects with the levee. The stretch between these 2 western points offers approximately 30 miles of levee one-way (60 miles total) where no floodgates have to be negotiated.

Sources of additional information:

Greg Gilman
(318) 234-1575

Pack and Paddle
601 East Pinhook Drive
Lafayette, LA 70501
(800) 458-4560 or (318) 232-5854

Atchafalaya Basin Levee District
525 Court Street
Port Allen, LA 70767-2631
(504) 387-2249

National Park Service
Rivers, Trails, and Conservation Assistance Program
Baton Rouge, LA
(504) 388-1446
Atlanta, GA
(404) 331-5838

Louisiana Department of Wildlife and Fisheries
District VII
P.O. Box 98000
Baton Rouge, LA 70898
(504) 765-2918

Notes on the trail: Despite the obstacles, riding on these man-made dams puts you on the highest ground around where you can take in sights of a wondrous ecosystem. For those who are looking for a flat-ground challenge, looping the levee should be considered.

Baton Rouge Area Rides

Someone must have whispered in some young graduate's ear, "The future of Baton Rouge is in petrochemicals." The advice has been well taken because signs of petroleum processing define the horizon for many miles around Louisiana's capital. In fact, the first indication I was nearing the site of the nation's second largest oil refinery occurred when I spotted a dark plume of smoke.

Louisiana's state university is located on the banks of the Mississippi River, which forms the eastern border to this city whose name is French for "Red Stick." It comes from the French translation of the Choctaw word for "red pole," which probably was the dividing line between two tribes.

The loess bluffs, an unusual feature found from the Ohio River's confluence with the Mississippi down to Baton Rouge, provide the terra firma for mountain bikers and their machines. Although there is much low ground nearby, enough high and dry dirt comes together to form foundations for several good trails. Occasionally, however, even these trails become too wet to ride; many bikers resort to the flat routes around the university's lake where, as more than one biker has admitted, you can exercise your eyes as well as your thighs as you pedal by skimpily clad sunbathers.

The levee from Baton Rouge south to New Orleans provides about the only other all-season track for off-road biking in the area. Most mountain bikers who want a good workout head north to Mississippi and the trails in the national forest near Bude. I was able to inform some, though, that the Tunica Hills Wildlife Area (about an hour's car ride north) is an interesting and suitable alternative when time is shorter.

On the way to Tunica Hills, I suggest a stop by the eccentric displays found inside the Republic of West Florida Museum in Jackson, Louisiana. Besides early Native American artifacts, Civil War relics, and the prop off Lindbergh's plane, hundreds of tiny lead soldiers of various nationalities are mounted inside glass cases. The soldiers have been completely hand-forged by a Louisiana State University administrator. Antique cars, a working 1920-vintage pipe organ, and a natural history display complement the other artifacts. Across the hallway inside the same building is (what else?) a library.

For more information:

The Bicycle Shop
3315 Highland Road
Baton Rouge, LA 70802
(504) 344-5624

The Bicycle Source
5517 Jones Creek Road
Baton Rouge, LA
(504) 752-2453

Capitol Schwinn Cyclery
8424 Florida Boulevard
Baton Rouge, LA
(504) 927-1997
or 5778 Essex Lane
(504) 766-4004

Schwinn Bicycles
4628 Plank Road
Baton Rouge, LA
(504) 355-7761

The Backpacker
7656 Jefferson Highway
Baton Rouge, LA 70809
(504) 925-2667

BRAMA (Baton Rouge Area Mountainbiking Association)
P.O. Box 64652
Baton Rouge, LA 70896
(504) 752-2232 (contact: Cline Henagen)

Posse'
Independent Riders Association
P.O. Box 77934
Baton Rouge, LA 70879-7934

Baton Rouge Area Convention and Visitors Bureau
P.O. Box 4149
Baton Rouge, LA 70821
(800) 527-6843 or (504) 383-1825

RIDE 15 *HOOPER ROAD PARK*

One of the nicest surprises of trails in the Deep South comes from finding a great route tucked into a metropolitan area. This is the case with Hooper Road Park. Primarily a collection of ball fields adjoining a subdivision, the park has

RIDE 15 *HOOPER ROAD PARK*

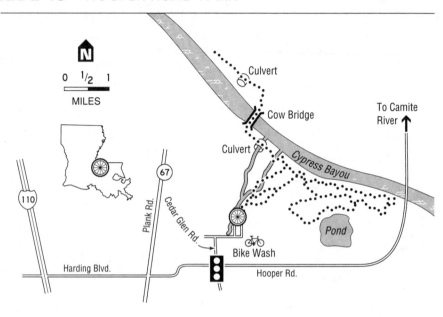

five to ten miles of technical single-track circling hither and yon, following creeks and burrowing into forests.

I wound up meeting two riders, Dave and Vince, who regularly ride this trail, and they allowed me to tag along. This trail was built and is maintained by volunteers from the Baton Rouge Area Mountainbiking Association (BRAMA) and Posse', the Independent Riders Association. Although no motorized vehicles are allowed on this narrow pathway, it suffers from a combination of heavy use and wet track, which wants to revert to its origin as a "pure mud-hole." As a result, many potholes and ruts lie in wait for the chance to send out gravity waves.

Once the trail dries out some, the claypan becomes hard and unyielding; however, beware the potholes. Despite their fairly innocent look (not very wide or long), these leftovers from heavy flooding become deep enough to nearly swallow a bike frame. At least that's what I was told.

General location: Hooper Road lies on the outskirts of Baton Rouge near the airport.

Elevation change: An area called "Frank's Place" by my guides has the most sustained change. Otherwise, you can expect relatively short, but steep, grade

Frank's Place—Hooper Road Park—proceed with caution!

variations. Some of them occur in rapid succession. The most dramatic change can be seen (or ridden by the intrepid and expertly balanced biker) where a small creek comes into the larger stream at a culvert on the southern side of Cypress Bayou. Concrete walls at extreme angles make a sudden end in a spillway. Black skid marks bear undeniable proof that this is ridden by some. The technique employed calls for laying the chest on top of the saddle and hanging derriere over the back wheel in what must be an amazing derring-do.

Season: The wetter this trail becomes, the more difficult it is to remain upright. Despite this, Hooper Road Park trail receives regular use throughout the year.

Services: Baton Rouge can provide what you're in need of. The park has facilities where you can wash your bike and replenish your water supply.

Hazards: Rigid forks and this trail do not a good mate make. The numerous roots, ruts, sudden dips, and climbs call for a more forgiving suspension. The heavy use seen on this trail also makes it likely that you'll meet some other bikers coming your way. Make sure you can avoid the oncoming traffic without mishap.

Rescue index: You are in close proximity to assistance.

Land status: The land is part of the city park system managed by Baton Rouge.

Maps: I was supplied the map as drawn and produced by Posse'. You can write or call BRAMA or Posse' and ask for the Hooper Road Park map.

Finding the trail: Exit Interstate 110 onto Harding Boulevard and head east toward the airport. Go straight through the light at Plank Road (LA 67) and turn left at the traffic light onto Cedar Glen Road. When it dead-ends, turn right and enter the park. Do a left buttonhook and park in the spaces along the third base line of the ball field. You will see the sign pointing where the trail begins into the woods.

Sources of additional information:

> Hooper Road Park
> 6261 Guynell Drive
> Baton Rouge, LA 70817
> (504) 357-7903
>
> BRAMA (Baton Rouge Area Mountainbiking Association)
> P.O. Box 64652
> Baton Rouge, LA 70896
> (504) 752-2232 (contact: Cline Henagen)
>
> Posse'
> Independent Riders Association
> P.O. Box 77934
> Baton Rouge, LA 70879-7934

Notes on the trail: You will find plenty of places on this techno-trail for you to employ expert moves. The terrain varies from dense forest, wide and wet bottoms, open fields, and high bluffs. Currently, 5 miles or so of trail cut through this Mississippi River floodplain. About a hundred yards of it ascends the ridge called "Frank's Place" that resembles formations found in the badlands of South Dakota. Area riders take a precipitous, narrow track back down to the main trail. This detour should only be attempted by those who have unerring balance and control. A mishap here could be, frankly, your last.

RIDE 16 *TUNICA HILLS WILDLIFE MANAGEMENT AREA*

A long time ago, hurricane-force winds ripped down from the northwest carrying with them glacial silt. This dirt, loess (pronounced like Superman's girlfriend), lost velocity, dropped from the sky, and piled up in drifts dozens of feet high along the eastern banks of the Mississippi River. After compacting, the loess weathered, plants and trees sprouted, creekbeds formed, and a unique landscape was ready for discovery.

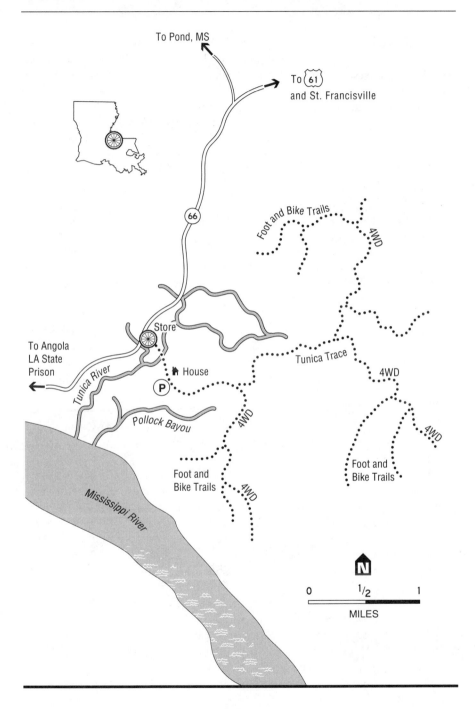

A gravel road leading to the trails in Tunica Hills Wildlife Management Area carves straight through the middle of this unique land formation. Three separate trails, each an out-and-back approximately two miles long (four miles total) branch off the main gravel road. Do not be deceived into thinking that these rolling hills are not rugged; they are. In fact, the Louisiana Department of Corrections opted to locate its state penitentiary just down the road at Angola, another type of wildlife management area.

The large oaks and gums, which form the canopy over the road leading into Tunica Hills, tower over what is part of the old Natchez Trace. There's no asphalt here, though. In places, banks 40 feet high create an almost tunnel-like environment where the huffing of your heavy breathing echoes and blends eerily with the calls of exotic sounding birds, such as the pinging of an alarmed yellow-billed cuckoo.

The flora and fauna found in Tunica Hills were once considered so unusual that The Nature Conservancy managed a section in the interior. It is now all watched over by the Louisiana Department of Wildlife and Fisheries. Many people I talked to were aware of this trail network, but few knew it was open for mountain biking. I count the ride here as one of my most fascinating in Louisiana.

General location: Tunica Hills lies just east of the Mississippi River where the ankle and top of Louisiana's foot join north of Baton Rouge.

Elevation change: Although the climbs are neither long nor especially steep, most people will find them sufficient to trigger the endorphins brought on by exertion.

Season: As a wildlife management area, hunting is allowed through the fall and late winter. This is also the time when ATVs can be heard roaring on these trails. However, from February 1 to September 15, the trails are for nonmotorized travel only.

Services: A convenience store is located just up the road from where you turn onto the Old Trace, but the most entertaining stop in the area is the old general store in Pond, Mississippi. To find it, take the right off LA 66 (heading north) at the tavern and follow it until you see the sign for Clark Creek Wildlife Area on the left. You'll cross a cattle guard and see the store on the hill. Your more specialized needs will be met in Louisiana's capital, Baton Rouge.

Hazards: I'll repeat the words of the wildlife officer I met there: "We got ticks real bad. With all the deer here, it gives them plenty to feed on. Of course, we've got snakes, but if you stay on the main trails, you shouldn't have any problem." The warning about hunters and ATVs bears repeating also.

Rescue index: You're pretty much out in the boonies. Be particular about the risks you take. While I was there, the bridge was washed out, which would've made any rescue even more complicated.

Land status: This is land managed by the Louisiana Department of Wildlife and Fisheries.

Loess banks create an echo-chamber at Tunica Hills.

Maps: A Wildlife Management Area Guide can be acquired from the Louisiana Department of Wildlife and Fisheries containing all of the maps for all the WMAs. The convenience store on the left just up from the Old Trace usually carries copies of the Tunica Hills map.

Finding the trail: Take LA 61 north out of Baton Rouge. Outside of St. Francisville, watch for the left onto LA 66 to Angola. Take LA 66 until the convenience store on the left about 17 miles down the road. At the bottom of the hill, before crossing the bridge, the Old Trace turns left. This is the entrance to Tunica Hills. After passing some residences and crossing 2 bridges, a big pasture is on the right. I was told to park here in the wide spot near the gate to the pasture. Don't block the gate. After riding up and down 3 hills, you'll see a trailhead on the right; another trailhead is farther down on the right; the final ATV trail is close by on the left. If you want to, you can park at the convenience store and begin your ride there. If you wind up at the imposing gate and flashing light at the Louisiana State Penitentiary, you've gone too far.

Sources of additional information:

Louisiana Department of Wildlife and Fisheries
P.O. Box 426
Ferriday, LA 71334
(318) 757-4571

Notes on the trail: It is a good idea to call and check the status of some of the trails and roads. Occasionally, they are closed to all but foot travel. However, if you don't call, pay special attention to the signs posted at the beginning of each trail and road. You will be treated to a special ride through a strange landscape. Approximately 6 miles of trail (one-way, 12 miles total) exist in the 3 separate trails which go out and back. This does not take into consideration the nearly 20 miles of improved and unimproved roads open for exploration. In addition, other trails open up during different times of the year.

New Orleans Area Rides

Although I have visited some of the planet's most exciting and unfettered cities—Hong Kong, Tokyo, Paris—I had only been a cinematic and literary tourist to the Big Easy, Louisiana's Crescent City, prior to researching this book. As I made my way nearly 25 miles across the Pontchartrain Causeway and into the heart of New Orleans, my pulse rolled like the six-foot swells on the huge lake below me. A friend of mine says he is attracted to the city's sordid excitement much like a moth goes toward a flame. Somehow I found the idea a little unnerving. But I couldn't come to the Deep South and not cross over into the land of Pete Fountain, Louis Armstrong, and streetcars with names like "Desire."

So I screwed my courage to the sticking place and headed toward Bourbon Street and cobblestone. I found St. Charles Avenue and its sugar-baron mansions and universities. At the end of Carrollton Avenue where it comes into St. Charles, I parked, disembiked, and got on top of the levee. I was a little nervous and by myself, so I cut my bike trip short after I thought I saw a young Marlon Brando strutting toward me with a cigarette dangling from his mouth.

I likewise cut my car trip short after I unknowingly found myself headed the wrong way down a one-way street. I didn't realize it at first because the street lights were pointed in my direction. But after several close calls with swerving vehicles and an especially scathing curse, I made my way to more rural surroundings. Two weeks later, I saw three feet of water where I had been riding and biking.

I had meant to make my way downtown after sundown and after the vehicular traffic into the French Quarter was restricted, but I settled for a beignet and cafe au lait at Cafe Beignet at the crack of noon. For someone like me who has cultural norms not quite on the wild side, it was intense enough. Coffee, sugar, and culture. Hey, I'll be back (maybe) to ring out the millennium at Pete Fountain's Night Club.

For more information:

> Bayou Bicycle, Inc.
> 3534 Toulouse Street
> New Orleans, LA 70119-4907
> (504) 488-1946

> Bike Zone
> 1300 West Thomas Street
> Hammond, LA 70401-3046
> (504)543-0000

Northshore Schwinn
1169 Robert Boulevard
Slidell, LA 70458-2059
(504) 646-0620

Don's Bicycles
200 Joseph Street
Slidell, LA 70458-8412
(504) 641-2341

The Bikesmith of New Orleans
4716 Freret Street
New Orleans, LA 70115-6321
(800) 264-7335 or (504) 674-1343 or
(504) 897-2453

Cleary Bike Center
3001 Clearview Parkway
Metairie, LA 70006-5301
(504) 885-8191

GNO Cyclery
1426 South Carrollton Ave
New Orleans, LA 70118-2810
(504) 861-0023

RIDE 17 *FONTAINEBLEAU STATE PARK*

This state park lies on the north shore of Lake Pontchartrain, the large body of water north of New Orleans. Massive live oaks and their twisted boughs, hundreds of years old and draped with long strands of Spanish moss, stand as the next most prominent landmark. White oaks and red oaks tower over the palmetto understory and provide habitat for a diverse number of songbirds.

As you would expect, there is much low-lying ground which holds water for long periods, as the terse lady at the entrance told me. But I was determined to ride the short mile-and-a-quarter loop even if I had to swim part of it. Fortunately, I was able to ride it all without too much splashing. Most of the water lay concentrated in the sloughs that provided brief, but messy, crossings. However, since many mountain bikers—and I am one—had moms who encouraged playing in the mud, sloshing through the mire and muck is just an added attraction to this incredibly beautiful trail.

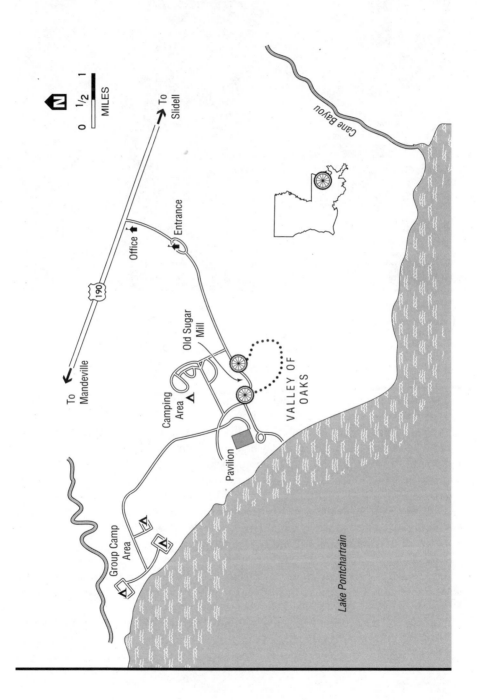

Valley of Oaks on the banks of Pontchartrain: "Remember the groves were God's first temples."

General location: Almost directly north of New Orleans on the north shore of Lake Pontchartrain, this park also lies on the route of the soon-to-be-completed Tammany Trace.

Elevation change: There is negligible change, and it all seems to be down. The land does that sometimes in Louisiana.

Season: Apart from becoming flooded from too much Mississippi being diverted in the lake, this trail can be ridden year-round.

Services: It may make you a different person, but you can get whatever you need in New Orleans. For less exotic needs, Mandeville is a dependable source.

Hazards: Although the trail has a rather firm bottom, you do run the risk of sinking up to your axle in mud. This is a little problem unless you happen to be going 20 mph a split-second before hitting the hole.

Rescue index: You can be easily reached in a short time.

Land status: This is another park managed by the Louisiana state government.

Maps: The hiking trail is shown on the map of the park you can pick up at the entrance.

Finding the trail: Exit Interstate 12 onto Highway 59 north of Mandeville (#65). Go south to Mandeville and take a left heading east on LA 190 (Florida Street). Approximately 3 miles farther on the right you'll see the park sign and entrance where you will be asked to pay a fee. The trailhead is straight past the camping area and on the left just past the ruins of an old sugar mill.

Sources of additional information:

Fontainebleau State Park
P.O. Box 152
Mandeville, LA 70470-0152
(504) 624-4443

Notes on the trail: Although this trail is short, the scenery along it makes length unimportant. After beginning the trail near the sugar mill and traveling in a clockwise direction, you pass through growth so lush it seems a yell from Tarzan would not seem out of place. The other trailhead is found at Oak Valley where the arrangement of live oaks with their mossy limbs creates a huge hallway of trees on the bank of Pontchartrain. Whether making a side-stop off of Tammany Trace or staying a few days to partake of the wonders of Lake Pontchartrain, a relaxing ride on the everglade trail of Fontainebleau will be a pleasant diversion.

RIDE 18 *TAMMANY TRACE*

I have frequently heard of attempts by groups and organizations to convert old railway beds to multi-use trails. Unfortunately, the Deep South has had little success in doing so. And it's too bad, especially considering the absolute fervor with which people have adopted one such trail in the toe of Louisiana, Tammany Trace, an out-and-back, level treadway.

I showed up in the middle of a Monday morning expecting to find little, if any, traffic on this 8.5-mile (one-way), asphalt, ten-foot wide trail. It's 17 miles total if you choose to do the entire out-and-back beginning from either Abita Springs Park in the north or Mandeville at the southern end. Or you can halve that distance by parking at Koop Drive, near the green caboose office, and ride either north or south, making an approximate 8.5-mile out-and-back.

As I unloaded my gear and got going, I saw several older couples walking, two small groups biking, and even a guy on rollerblades streaking down the trace, coming awfully close to exceeding the 20 mph speed limit. I did not see anyone on horseback, but this is also an approved mode of traveling the trail.

The first stage of trail opened up on September 17, 1994, thereby completing the changeover from the Illinois Central Railroad corridor to pedestrian and equestrian thoroughfare. Tammany Trace has been approved for a total length of 31 miles, linking Covington in the northwest to Slidell in the south-

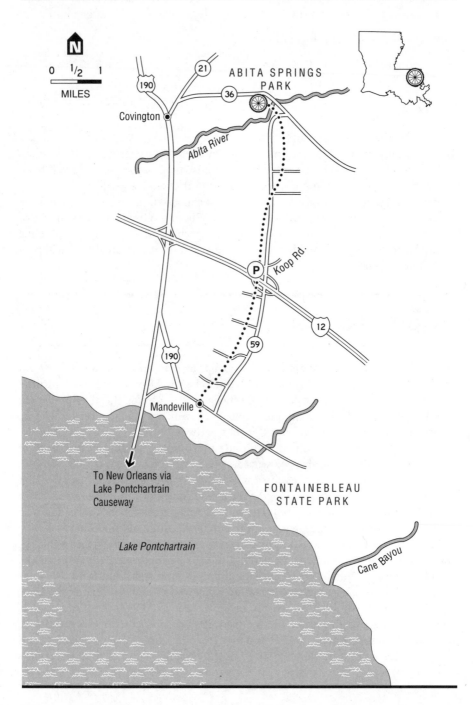

Father and daughter take a spin on Tammany Trace in Abita Springs.

east. The next section of trace—from Mandeville to Lacombe—is scheduled to open sometime in the summer of 1996.

General location: The current 8.5 miles lies between Abita Springs and Mandeville.

Elevation change: The locomotives that chugged along here had little more than their cargo to pull along this flat terrain. One factor, however, can require an increase in necessary power: wind. On the day I rode this trail, the wind was blowing briskly out of the north, thereby making the ride up to Abita Springs difficult to make in my large ring. On the ride back, I constantly had to slow down to the 20 mph speed limit.

Season: You may have to choose drier times to ride the horse trail, but if you stay on the asphalt, you can ride even in a driving rainstorm.

Services: Mandeville has many goods and services as does the beautiful town of Abita Springs. If you need something outlandish, New Orleans is just a few shouts away.

Hazards: There is a strict policy of yielding to other users: rollerbladers to cyclists; cyclists to joggers; joggers to walkers; and walkers to horses. Also, you need to obey all traffic signs. Tammany Trace crosses some busy highways in places; cyclists yield to motorized traffic!

Rescue index: I would think that if someone using the trail for pleasure didn't happen by soon, one of the rangers assigned to patrol the trace in a golf cart would be along shortly.

Land status: St. Tammany Parish is the governing body for the trace.

Maps: Maps are available at the Koop Drive parking area.

Finding the trail: Exit Interstate 12 onto LA 59 and head north. Look for the Koop Drive sign on the left. Turn and follow the gravel road until you come to the green caboose. Park in the lot across from it.

Sources of additional information:

> The Tammany Trace Foundation
> 21411 Koop Drive
> Mandeville, LA 70448
> (800) 438-7223

Notes on the trail: I rode from Koop Drive to Abita Springs and back. There are 4 intersections along the way before coming to the "Tourist Park" in Abita Springs. As I was getting ready to turn around there, I met a guy with a knowing look about him unloading his mountain bike from the back of his pickup. He turned out to be a native Louisianan, and we talked for several minutes on the ride back to Koop Drive. He explained first that there was a single-track you can ride by crossing the bridge over the Abita River inside the park in between the gazebo and picnic tables, provided it isn't above its banks, which it was that day. After I told him that I was surprised to find that no matter what kind of trail it may be—rocky, flat, wet, dry, gravel, asphalt—there is always someone out there who loves it. When I asked him what his favorite is, he quickly told me, "I can't get enough of any of it." Now there's a biker. Roll on.

MISSISSIPPI

When I first considered trying to find mountain bike trails in Mississippi, I was prepared to discover only swamps, bayous, and sucking mud. I had learned this unfortunate stereotype as a boy. But I already loved enough about the state—home of great writers and musicians—to make me want to penetrate the mystery in my mind called Mississippi.

As I began the search, plenty of people looked at me as if I had been out in the sun too long when I told them I was looking for mountain bike trails. But by the time I found Tishomingo and followed the Natchez Trace to Jackson, where I talked to Tom at The Bike Rack, I could already enthusiastically agree with his statement: "Mississippi is an absolute biking heaven."

Woodall Mountain, Mississippi's highest land at 806 feet above the Gulf of Mexico, is privately owned by a paper company and is off-limits to mountain bikers. Despite this relatively low elevation, the highland ridges in northern Mississippi contain several sites where nearly vertical slopes await your challenge. Overall, 16 million acres of woodlands, many of which lie within the numerous national and state forests, offer a wide variety of terrain.

The steeper sections on the northeast fall off to the southwest where sandy plains and piney woods are home to not only logging equipment (which processes two billion board feet of lumber each year) but also to the red-cockaded woodpecker and the gopher tortoise. The Endangered Species Act has finally provided the legal mandate for protecting some of the old growth forests where these and other animals try to hold on.

One of the first non-native visitors to the region, De Soto, discovered a land rich in just about everything except what he was searching for: gold. When the white planters arrived, pushing aside the Choctaw, Creek, and Natchez Indians who had lived in Mississippi for thousands of years, they felled the massive oaks and pines and replaced them with cotton, rice, and indigo. But these land owners were ignorant of cultivation methods designed to protect the fine glacial silt which grew these crops and the soil became depleted in many areas. Diversification of crops has helped reverse the damage done. In a stroke of Deep South genius, Mississippi farmers looked at their rain-flooded lands—and the catfish walking their way from slough to pond—and said, "Aha!" The result has made Mississippi the world's largest producer of farm-raised catfish.

Another industry not normally associated with Mississippi has been the development of the gaming business. Along the Gulf Coast, casinos—on land and gulf—line the principal coastal highway where tourists roll into town looking for roulette wheels and one-armed bandits. It is a gamble that, so far, has paid off for its investors, helping the tourism dollars double in less than four years to nearly $4 billion.

For those of you who, like I did, think you've got the most glorious mountain bike trails and experiences in your own backyard, sit back and flip through the pages describing what may well be the best-kept secret in two-wheeled fun. What lies ahead are trails cut to meet every need. If you're the aspiring NORBA racer who's looking for a change in training scenery, experts and pros alike call Mississippi home. If you venture out into the woods on your rubber-spoked legs with more of a naturalist's spirit, you won't find land or wildlife any more beautiful and varied. No doubt you'll be downright inspired.

Biloxi Area Rides

Mississippi developed gambling in August 1992 as a dependable source of revenue and has encouraged the construction of many casinos along its more than 70 miles of coast. Should you find such attractions to your liking, there will be no end to your fun—provided you remain financially solvent. If you hit the jackpot, you can spend some of the winnings on many of the area's other attractions, such as deep sea fishing, shops, restaurants, or even getting yourself another mountain bike at Hagan's Biloxi Bike Center, located right across the street from the only lighthouse in America to bisect a highway.

The area shows little evidence of Hurricane Camille, which devastated Mississippi's coast in 1969. Hurricane Gilbert refreshed the memory of what awesome power such storms produce when it swept through in September 1988. Keep in mind when planning a trip to the gulf that hurricane-producing conditions are more likely to occur in August and September.

However, this section of coast usually gives nothing but reasons to relax and thousands of people come here each year to do just that. If you're looking for a place that's more remote, a trip offshore to the National Forest Service's Ship Island (where Fort Massachusetts still stands despite a direct hit from Camille) creates a remote island atmosphere while still providing many conveniences found in other national parks. But overnight camping is not one of them.

The trails found in the De Soto National Forest just north of Biloxi offer a motley of rides. The beginner can roll along on the fairly easy (yet sandy) tracks at Bethel ATV trail where, during the quieter days, the endangered red-cockaded woodpecker can be seen. At the very least, you will be able to view the sites set aside for the nesting of these birds.

Bigfoot Horse Trail demands more of the mountain biker, both in mileage and technique needed to make some of the stream crossings. As difficulty goes, Longleaf Horse Trail fits somewhere in the middle between De Soto and Bigfoot. Unfortunately, the National Forest Service's plans to construct a mountain biking trail in the De Soto National Forest have been canceled due to Congressional withdrawal of funding. Instead of scrapping the whole shooting match, they should have headed down to Biloxi and shot some craps.

For more information:

Hagan's Biloxi Bike Center
178 Porter Avenue
Biloxi, MS 39530
(601) 374-3508

The Wheel House
Edgewater Village
2650 Beach Boulevard
Biloxi, MS 39531
(601) 388-0096

Biloxi Ranger District
USDA Forest Service
Route 1, Box 62 (on US 49 South)
McHenry, MS 39561
(601) 928-5291

RIDE 19 *SHEPARD STATE PARK*

Tucked away on Mississippi's Gulf Coast, where the Pascagoula River first puts its mouth to salt, tiny Shepard State Park offers the mountain biker a taste of something sweet. Regardless of its relatively short and flat route, the wide, grassy, single-track loop of approximately five miles, used by hikers and bikers alike, offers an experience found nowhere else in the Deep South.

With the sound of roulette balls clacking in waterfront casinos only a few miles away in Ocean Springs, Biloxi, and Gulfport, few people would expect such a natural setting so close by. But natural it is. A salt marsh, where rails, egrets, and ibises search for meals in its brackish backwaters, is also home to raccoons that search the shore for shellfish. A wide variety of plant life, including large colonies of hooded pitcher plants, grow along the seldom-used, turf and pine-needle trails.

General location: This is the only true Gulf Coast trail found in the Deep South; it is located in Gautier, Mississippi, just west of Pascagoula.
Elevation change: Except for areas along the creek, little elevation occurs.
Season: I rode this trail for the first time just after a thunderstorm had dumped a couple inches of rain. Although it was a little tricky getting over to dry land from where the creek flooded the bridge, I managed to keep my boots dry. Some sections of the trail held water several inches deep, but the firm trail surface underneath allowed easy travel.
Services: All services are provided in the heavily developed coastal communities.
Hazards: This is a hiking trail, as well as a bike route: watch for pedestrians. Some low-lying areas have been equipped with various types of crossings, some rather difficult to ride. Cinch up your helmet strap and do a balance check before attempting any you're unsure of. I took the safe route on some and pushed. Should you fail to cross upright, more damage would probably

RIDE 19 *SHEPARD STATE PARK*

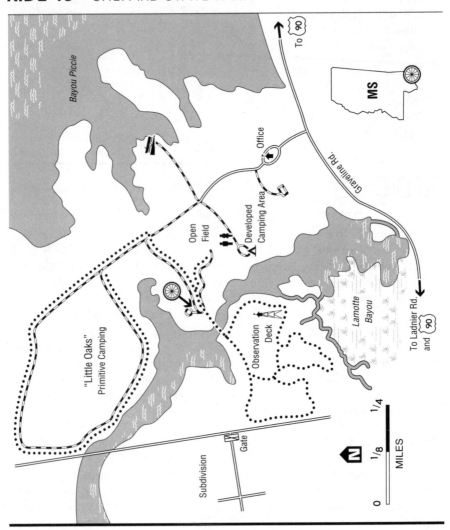

be done to the wetlands than to your body or bike. But why hurt anything? If you travel on the horse trails, be prepared to yield the trail to equestrians.

Rescue index: A subdivision borders one side of the trail, which would make any rescue easily done, even though a fence separates the homes from the park.

Land status: This is land managed by the Mississippi Department of Wildlife, Fisheries and Parks.

Maps: A map of Shepard State Park showing the trails can be picked up at the office during normal business hours, or you can request one by mail.

Let your front wheel be your guide at Shepard State Park.

Finding the trail: From Highway 90 (the coastal highway) follow the signs to Shepard State Park on Graveline Road. After paying your day-use fee at the entrance station, continue straight past the soccer field on the left and take the next left. You can park at the end of the road. The trail begins dead ahead and crosses the creek via the bridge.

Sources of additional information:

Shepard State Park
1034 Graveline Road
Gautier, MS 39553
(601) 497-2244

Notes on the trail: There are two sections of single-track: one on the opposite side of the bridge and the other on the near side of the bridge. The far side offers more easily navigated pathways; they are level, grassier, and wider than their counterparts on the near side, which wind through narrow stands of yaupon shrubs and thickets and through bogs with challenging boardwalks. In addition, some exposed roots and steep banks call for increased concentration. You can continue your ride on the gravel road to the boat launch where some other short sections go off into the woods and connect to other roads in the park. Horse trails—free to ride with a bike as well—also cut through meadows to link park roads. A gated road near where you turn left to find the single-track can be explored as well.

RIDE 20 *BETHEL ATV TRAIL*

The Bethel trail typifies much of what is going on in the Deep South as far as trail maintenance and construction are concerned. This is a rather recent addition and exact locations of pathways have not been firmed up, although the general location cuts through a sandy section of loblolly and slash pines, the staple of Mississippi forests. The north loop goes 38 miles; the southern circuit (sharing the same trailhead) meanders 31 miles before completing its loop. An expert NORBA competitor training for the big race will avoid this type of trail due to its lack of technical demand; however, if you're interested in getting plenty of chances to observe wildlife—mainly deer and turkeys—without a great deal of variation of scenery, then Bethel beckons.

Tall pines with little undergrowth provide a view of what the earliest settlers of this region saw. The forest service has taken great care to ensure that the integrity of the landscape has not been compromised for the sake of a trail. And there's good reason for that. The map makes note of areas described as "RCW Colony Site." These mark where the Forest Service has located nesting sites of the red-cockaded woodpecker, an endangered species that requires old growth pines afflicted with heartwood disease in order to nest. Therefore, you might want to enjoy this course just to say you have frolicked in the woods with an extremely rare bird. Also, if you're quiet—and lucky—you might come away having sighted the red-cockaded woodpecker (look for the tell-tale sign of pine pitch oozing down the tree trunk) or the gopher tortoise, another endangered species whose habitat is being preserved in this section of the De Soto National Forest.

General location: This trail is located approximately 12 miles east of Highway 49 in the Red Creek Wildlife Management Area in the De Soto National Forest.

Elevation change: The most significant elevation changes occur up the tree trunks of the towering pines growing here.

Season: Due to its sandier structure, this trail holds up better in wet weather—and rides smoother—than many of the trails north of here. The pines, however, don't provide much shade during the hotter months.

Services: Head south toward Biloxi and Gulfport to replenish your supplies.

Hazards: The loose sand will play havoc with traction; get a firm grip and anticipate sudden direction changes as a result of any sandy outcrops. Also, ATVs will be thicker than gnats if you choose weekends to visit Bethel. And, like gnats, you'll either have to put up with them or go somewhere else.

Rescue index: This is a remote and seldom-visited part of the national forest (except for weekends). There aren't many obstacles to overcome to effect a

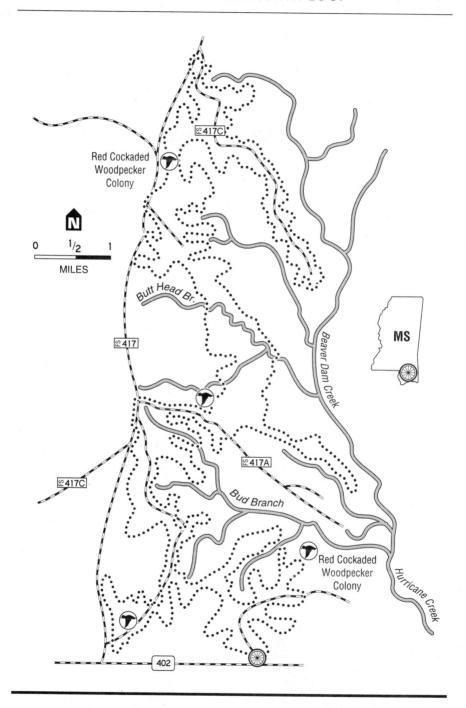

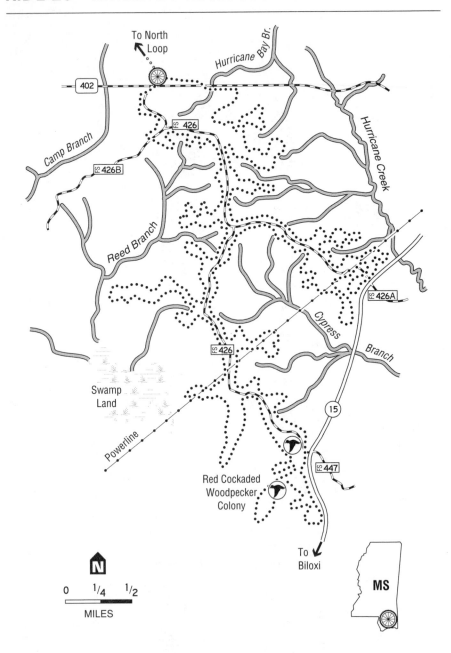

rescue once the need is determined, but you could lie there until black buzzards picked you clean before anyone would notice you missing.

Land status: This is national forest land.

Maps: The De Soto National Forest map is a good one to buy because of all the many fine places to visit in this huge (501,000-acre) natural setting. You can also pick up or order a map of the Bethel ATV Trail from the Biloxi Ranger District's office in McHenry on Highway 49.

Finding the trail: Take Highway 49 south to McHenry where you can stop at the ranger's office. Go on to Saucier where you need to be on the lookout for Highway 67 on the left. About 5 miles on 67, you'll come to an intersection where you'll go straight for about 5 more miles past the sign to the POW Camp. The Bethel ATV sign will be on the left about 1 mile farther on Forest Service Road 417. Turn down it and go until you see the parking area on the left. Park and enter either the north or south loop by following the signs and info at the bulletin board. The trail is currently blazed with white paper arrows.

Sources of additional information:

Biloxi Ranger District Office
National Forest Service
Route 1, Box 62 (on Highway 49)
McHenry, MS 39561
(601) 928-5291

Notes on the trail: As a result of trying to replace habitat for the red-cockaded woodpecker and the gopher tortoise, the forest has a wide-open look to it on the loop across the road from the trailhead. Consequently, the twists and turns among this airy course are seldom hidden from view in places, and many miles must be ridden before finally losing sight of where you began.

RIDE 21 *RATTLESNAKE BAY ATV TRAIL*

Of all the bike trails I rode in Mississippi, this one may be the sandiest. However, its four-foot-wide pathway still holds some wet spots despite attempts to keep it out of the low-lying areas. This is quite a feat considering the 31-mile loop is squeezed into a space not much bigger than 3 square miles, thereby offering at least a partial explanation for its name. The moderate grades present a good location for the new biker to get in a moderate workout, without being overly taxing. Still, its hills are steep enough for a nine-year-old to proclaim them mountains.

Along the roads on the perimeter of this trail, military exercises occasionally are carried out by the forces stationed at nearby Camp Shelby.

RIDE 21   *RATTLESNAKE BAY ATV TRAIL*

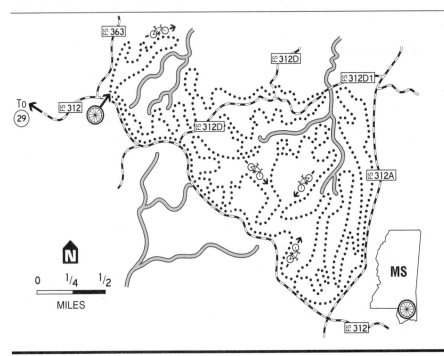

These maneuvers normally occur between the months of May through September—months you may wish to find shadier and cooler places to ride—but you can enjoy this trail even though the military may be on the move. Just be alert.

The terrain is comprised of a relatively young pine forest broken up by grassy meadows where deer and turkeys sprint at the sound of a gear change, especially around dawn and dusk. It was on this trail where I stopped to catch my breath and drink some water. While trying to retrieve my bottle after it slipped out of my hands, a covey of about twenty quail shot up out of the high grass near the trail in an explosion of beating wings and wheeling bodies. It was a good thing I wasn't in mid-swallow when it happened because I probably would've choked.

As I was leaving the parking area after I finished riding, I met a national forest ranger who had a K-9 unit with him. I was approached by the ranger and "interviewed." I met his steady gaze and answered his dubious questions about other bikers on the trail. Not long after that encounter, I ran across the regulations governing use of our national forests. Remember that some equipment and accessories legal in other settings are not good to carry with you into the national forest.

General location: This long trail is located in the De Soto National Forest just south of New Augusta, Mississippi, near an U.S. Army installation, Camp Shelby.

Elevation change: The only times you will need the small crank ring are to acquire purchase in the sandier sections; however, changes in elevation do take place, but nothing drastic.

Season: Due to the lack of shade, I prefer riding this during the cooler months, which also corresponds to the times when military exercises are not being held. The sand makes it a more accessible trail in wet weather, but it does have some mudholes to either shoot through or walk around.

Services: All services can be obtained in Hattiesburg. There are no water sources close by.

Hazards: Obviously, since this is an ATV trail, motorcycles and wheelers will be on the trail at times. There is only one legal direction of travel—clockwise—so you can relax to a certain degree about meeting oncoming traffic. The mudholes can be grabby, so be careful about how fast you roll through.

Rescue index: You're never more than a straight-line mile from one of the forest service roads. Just carry a map so you know which one; otherwise, you can get turned around and not know which way is out.

Land status: This is land within the boundaries of the De Soto National Forest.

Maps: Request the Rattlesnake Bay ATV Trail map from the forest service offices in Laurel, Wiggins, or Biloxi. The same map is also posted inside the bulletin board at the trailhead.

Finding the trail: Take Highway 98 east out of Hattiesburg until the intersection with Highway 29; turn off to the right (south). A little over 2 miles on Highway 29 leads to the left turn onto Forest Service Road 312, which goes less than 2 miles before the trailhead sign appears on the left. The trail is marked with 5-inch orange diamonds.

Sources of additional information:

Camp Shelby (United States Army)
Highway 49
Hattiesburg, MS 39407
(601) 584-2709

Chickasawhay Ranger District
National Forest Service
Box 426 (418 South Magnolia Street)
Laurel, MS 39441
(601) 428-0594

Hattiesburg Bicycle Center
2103 Hardy Street
Hattiesburg, MS 39401-5963
(601) 582-9777 or (800) 748-2068

Moore's Bicycle Center
707 North Hutchinson Avenue
Hattiesburg, MS 39401-4138
(601) 544-1978

Champion Cycle and Fitness
104 South 37th Avenue
Hattiesburg, MS 39402-1634
(601) 264-8233 or (800) 273-4158

Notes on the trail: You probably won't want to ride the entire 31 miles in one day unless you get an early start. The trail always remains fairly close to a forest service road that can be taken back to the trailhead parking fairly quickly, thereby making a variable loop length possible.

RIDE 22 *BIGFOOT HORSE TRAIL*

The whole time I rode this trail, I couldn't help but think I had one pedal in the past and one in the future as I straddled down the narrow line of the present. Part of the mood was created as I entered the parking lot and saw a row of six cement munition bunkers leftover from the area's days as a WW II POW camp for German soldiers, who built the lake behind which the trailhead is found.

This course, which winds its way in a combination of loops totaling over 15 miles, covers terrain that would be the perfect setting for a movie showing bloodhounds chasing an escaped convict through the swamp. Large roots stretch across the narrow pathway, which slices through a canopy of live oaks, sweet gums, bays, and maples growing among dense undergrowth of yaupon and sparkleberry.

Although I didn't meet up with any horses on this trail, I did come across some hikers who looked as wide-eyed about seeing me as a horse would've. Despite being far less than an ideal mountain biking track—long and deep potholes guarded sections requiring a portage through the woods—I count this trail as one of my personal favorites.

One of the strangest transformations that occurred on this challenging course involved the sound of my back axle bearings, which had been growing progressively louder and making me wonder if I would suddenly grind to a halt in the middle of nowhere. After the repeated, required runs through

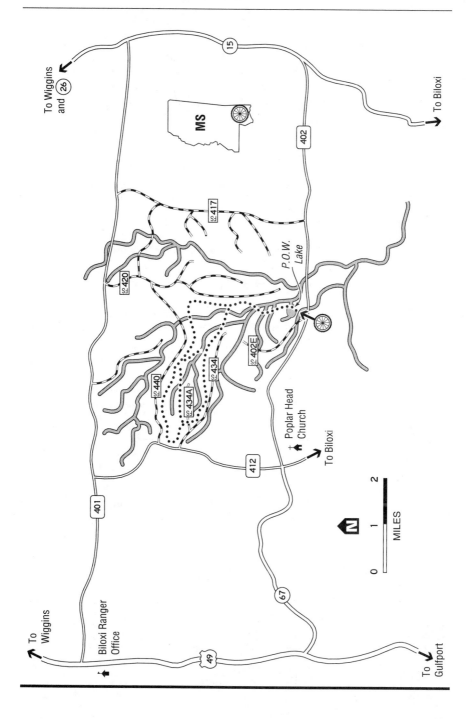

feet-wetting potholes, the sound stopped. The fine, oily texture of the silt in this region apparently works as a lubricant, at least temporarily.

I also collected my favorite souvenir of my days in the Deep South here on this trail. As I sped along a silent Forest Service road, I spied a square brown object lying directly in the middle of the road almost as though it had been placed there on purpose. Before I could slow down, I rode past what turned out to be a homemade pillow, decorated in a strange manner. The brown nylon covering has attached to it varying shapes and patterns of leather, felt, and Naugahyde. On top of these strips are hot-glued 33 buttons, most of them different sizes, shapes, and colors. The seams of the pillow are hidden by a length of workboot shoestring. The same string has been cut into odd sections and attached in a crazy arrangement. The piece is finished off with a six-penny nail, a heavy-duty zipper, a corporal's chevron, an ear-bob, and—finally—a cluster of buttons centered inside a small metal picture frame.

General location: This trail is way out in the boonies in the De Soto National Forest.

Elevation change: Hardly any change occurs except along creek banks and potholes.

Season: This is a summertime (dry) route for the most part, although I rode it during the winter's wet season. As with all national forests, hunters frequent these woods during various spells. Although some bikers head to different locations then, I have always felt comfortable on the national forest trails while wearing a fluorescent orange vest and ringing my bell frequently. Some bikers feel, however, that this only makes a better target for disgruntled, disappointed "trackers of the white-tail."

Services: All services can be found in Biloxi. Be sure to bring plenty of liquids unless you have means of treating the water from the creeks.

Hazards: The creeks could be too high to cross safely during periods of much rain. Deep potholes and roots require creative crossings at times. You may have to wade through some spots or get off the trail and go through the undergrowth. Watch for the slithering critters at rest on logs—just look where you will place your foot!—a cottonmouth bite is no souvenir to take back.

Rescue index: The remoteness is not misleading. While you may run across some fellow bikers or hikers, it is not an easy place to get out of quickly.

Land status: This is national forest land.

Maps: The De Soto National Forest map—and the one in this book—show the Bigfoot Horse Trail.

Finding the trail: From Highway 49 leaving Wiggins, go south until the sign on the left points to the beginning of Highway 67. Take this road until the stop sign and go straight. Forest Service Road 402E has a sign for the POW camp on the left. The road passes the munition bunkers on the left. Park there. The combination trailhead for the Tuxachanie Trail (foot-travel only) and the

Bigfoot Horse Trail begins at the narrow opening of the fence. Go across the dam and take the left fork leading behind the lake; the right fork is the Tuxachanie and is off-limits to bikes.

Sources of additional information:

> Biloxi Ranger District
> National Forest Service
> Highway 49
> McHenry, MS 39561
> (601) 928-5291

Notes on the trail: This trail lacks the frequent markings of some of the other trails. The first couple of miles will be challenging in the wettest sense of the word and also serve as the last leg of your trip back to the lake (unless you opt for travel on the Forest Service and asphalt roads). Plan plenty of time to explore this interesting section of Mississippi. The white blazes, which occur fairly regularly at first, peter out after a while. The trail has been heavily used, so you should not have any trouble finding the loop back to the trailhead. Taking the first fork to the left sets a clockwise route. Pay attention to this intersection. If lefts are taken at each of the remaining 4 intersections (forks), 1 more stream crossing will occur before coming back to this intersection. Then, of course, a wet 1.5 miles (4 creek crossings and 1 bridge) lead back to the trailhead. But you're a mountain biker and you love it.

RIDE 23 *LONGLEAF HORSE TRAILS*

Some horse trails are better off left to the horses because of the many potholes, deadfalls, and other horsey obstacles that take the two-wheeled fun right out of the experience. Longleaf does not fit in that category. The two loops—a short one of 6 miles and a long one of 23 miles—capture the sweet essence of biking bravura.

The routes lead through a heavily managed section of the De Soto National Forest where prescribed, controlled burns keep the underbrush negligible. The day before I rode the short loop, the forest service had set the woods on fire. The white ash was still on the ground, and stumps smoked and smoldered. Deer, still unnerved by it all, I suppose, nearly jumped over my head as I rode down the six-foot wide trail.

Graveled stream crossings make the travel through the bottoms easy. The climbs back up to the piney ridges are never very long, and if you look carefully, you might see the endangered gopher tortoise crawling toward a den. Songbirds like northern flickers, tufted titmice, and chickadees constantly appear in escort as they glean the bark and branches for insects.

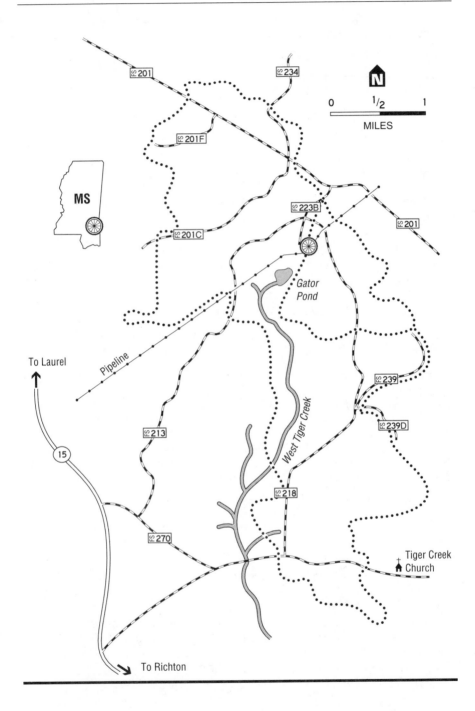

FS 201

FS 234

N

0   1/2   1
MILES

MS

FS 201F

FS 223B

FS 201

FS 201C

Gator
Pond

To Laurel

Pipeline

FS 239

West Tiger Creek

FS 239D

FS 213

15

FS 218

FS 270

Tiger Creek
Church

To Richton

And, as you would expect on a horse trail, there are horses. These magnificent animals do not usually react rationally to a bicycle in motion. If you ever happen upon one headed your way, stop and get well off the trail until it has passed. If you come up behind one, ring your bell or toot your horn from a distance. If you don't have a bell or horn, you can call out in a friendly voice as soon as you see the horse. Ask permission to pass by (on foot if possible) and thank the riders.

I met two horseback riders in the parking lot as they were beginning their ride. I spoke, made friendly with them, and asked which way they were headed. After I learned they were going on the same trail I was riding, I told them I would see them later going the opposite direction. I was not trying to be overly nosy, just cautious. I've spent enough time around horses to know that some of them are entirely too skittish to be trusted with surprises. I wanted to be able to pass the horses head-on, not from behind, so I could sidle safely off to the side as they walked by. I believe my consideration was appreciated.

General location: These two loops are located inside the De Soto National Forest.

Elevation change: Although there are some sections requiring short bursts of energy to make the top, there are not many, and the gently rolling terrain holds a bike like a curved palm.

Season: The stream crossings along the way shouldn't pose any problems unless rain has fallen in flash-flood fashion, which happens more often than not during winter and spring. Since people hunt in the forest, a quick call to the forest service office to determine which, if any, season is open would be a good idea.

Services: Most services can be acquired in Laurel; however, water should be carried in and any supplies you need for your bike will most likely have to be purchased in Hattiesburg; Laurel has no bike shops.

Hazards: Have you ever had a close encounter with a deer while on your bike? You should be alert for the possibility here. One jumped over the path in front of me so close I could smell its breath as it passed by. Also, horses deserve your undivided attention when overtaking them or when they're passing you.

Rescue index: There is a Forest Service work center not too far from the trailhead, but you are fairly far from any substantial first aid facility. The closest is in Laurel, 13 miles away once you get to the blacktop (Highway 15), which takes 15 minutes to get back to. So be particular.

Land status: This is part of the De Soto National Forest, Chickasawhay District.

Maps: The well-marked trails make a map unnecessary; however, you can pick up or order a map of the Longleaf Horse Trails from the Chickasawhay Ranger District Office in Laurel. Since there are so many wonderful trails and backroads in the De Soto National Forest, it is worth the investment; over

A biking encounter of the equine kind: yield the trail.

300,000 acres are described in 3 districts, many of which have graveled road-ways and gated access to motorized vehicles.

Finding the trail: Take Highway 15 south out of Laurel. Watch for the sign to the Gavin Auto Tour on the left about 11 miles out. The next road to the left (Forest Service 202), should be marked and will need to be taken. Go about 3 miles before turning left onto FS 218 for no more than 6 miles. Take the left at the sign and park near Gator Pond (occupied!). The short loop is marked with white diamonds, and the long trail is marked by orange diamonds. You can travel in either direction.

Sources of additional information:

Jones County Chamber of Commerce
Laurel, MS 39441
(601) 428-2043

Chickasawhay Ranger District
Box 426 (418 South Magnolia Street)
Laurel, MS 39441
(601) 428-0594

Notes on the trail: Leaving the trailhead traveling clockwise, both the long and short loop share common treadway until shortly after crossing FS 218 when the short loop turns right. Soon after, a pipeline intersects the trail. Two streams are crossed before the short loop rejoins the long one where they turn and head west toward FS 218. After crossing this road and dropping slightly down to West Tiger Creek, they turn north to the trailhead.

The long loop, taken in a counterclockwise direction, shares the tread with the short loop until a left turn near FS 213B, which it crosses. It meets up with FS 201, FS 201C, and FS 234. After reaching the other (north) side of FS 201, the trail arcs over to FS 234, crosses it and FS 201 again headed south. It parallels FS 201F briefly before crossing FS 201C once more. After merging with the powerline and following it for nearly a mile, FS 213 is crossed. From this point until riding over FS 202, the trail stays near West Tiger Creek and its feeders. The next section of trail loops back across Tiger Creek Church Road and FS 202 for a final time and delves deep into the forest until reaching FS 239D. It follows this road and heads northeast onto FS 239 for over a mile before finally rejoining the short loop east of FS 213.

Natchez Area Ride

Natchez, Mississippi, marks the southern end to the Natchez Trace Parkway, the remarkable epic roadway spanning over 400 miles. Actually, the end of the Parkway does not enter the bounds of Natchez proper, stopping a tad over eight miles from the city limits. Natchez has a rich past linked to its importance as a river port. Many graceful homes still stand and can be toured all year long. As beautiful as some of these homes are, Natchez also has a rather sordid history engrained in the "under-the-hill" neighborhood situated closer to the river. Yes, you can visit there, too, but it has tamed its reputation considerably since the days of unbridled riverboat gamblers.

The Natchez Indians lived years ago in this area, building ceremonial mounds of earth piled many feet high. One example of this type of structure can be found at Emerald Mound, which dates back to the fourteenth century. It encompasses nearly eight acres, making it the second largest mound of its type anywhere. Take time to walk the trail to the top and ponder for a moment all the other ancient footsteps that took this same path celebrating a simpler lifestyle.

Up the Trace is an interesting example of the winds of change. Loess Bluff was created during the Ice Age when topsoil blown from hundreds of miles away was deposited here. Of course, you'll be riding on some of the same topsoil—and the ridges it formed—just to the east in the Homochitto National Forest. However, the great force always in motion and always bringing change is the "Father of Waters," the Mississippi River.

For more information:

> Frank Moak
> Natchez Bicycle Center
> 334 Main Street
> Natchez, MS 39126
> (601) 446-7794

RIDE 24 *CLEAR SPRINGS TRAIL*

Located in southwestern Mississippi near the small town of Bude, this national forest trail offers the mountain biker everything: hills and ridges, creeks and bottoms, flora and fauna so strikingly beautiful that the sight of it all draws bikers here from all over the Deep South. The single-track loop of over ten miles saw only hikers at first, but the biker-friendly National Forest Service in Mississippi evaluated the situation and determined Clear

RIDE 24 *CLEAR SPRINGS TRAIL*

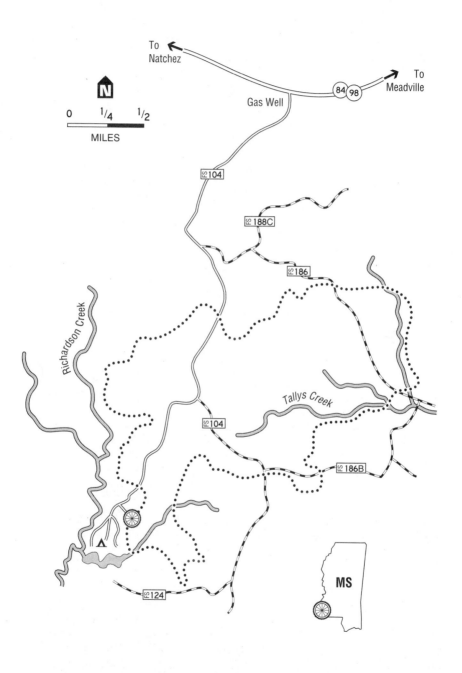

Springs big enough for both hikers and bikers although the steep climbs may make hikers out of the best bikers.

There is a bulletin board where users can register and read tips for a more enjoyable ride; for example, the day I rode in early December also happened to be open for several types of small game hunting, and wearing an orange vest was recommended even though hunters were not supposed to be bagging bunnies near the trail. Also, logging was being done that day—not an uncommon sight in our national forests—and note was given to watch out for trucks and skidders hauling and loading timber.

One of the many nice things about this trail is how the length can be customized by getting on one of the Forest Service roads bisecting the trail at six different spots. By taking an alternate route and following the sound of a chainsaw I came up on a full-blown logging operation in progress. I don't know who was more amused—me, or the loggers looking at me in my orange vest taking pictures of them.

General location: This trail is located entirely within the Homochitto National Forest boundary.

Elevation change: As with so many of the trails in the Deep South, forget about having to crank up any extended climbs at Clear Springs; however, it does have short, steep sections that will test legs, lungs, and courage.

Season: Discover the many moods this trail has to offer by riding it year-round. Gonzo bikers have begun riding harder than the trail can handle; therefore, wet weather can produce muddy, slick spots hazardous to your cycle and self.

Services: All services can be found in nearby Natchez. Clear Springs is a great place to do some camping. The facilities are top-notch.

Hazards: Hunters can be spotted slinking among the tree trunks or—more likely—parked up in a tree-stand. Ring your bell or toot your horn often. Some technical sections require discretion. Also, some unnecessary wear and tear has been inflicted by overzealous riders skidding and sliding to compensate for their ill-advised quest for speed. Life is long; try to moderate your riding gait when conditions dictate.

Rescue index: If you bump up and need assistance, you can be reached fairly easily by using one of the gravel forest service roads.

Land status: This is part of a National Forest.

Maps: There are maps of Clear Springs Trail at the trailhead clearly showing the turns and roads. The National Forest Service Office in Meadville is the primary source for the map

Finding the trail: Take Highway 84/98 out of Natchez for approximately 30 miles. Look for the familiar National Forest brown-and-white sign pointing to the right. A gas well may be pumping at the turn. Stay on the paved road until the sign directs a left turn into the trailhead parking lot. The trail begins just to the right of the bulletin board. Don't forget to sign in.

Morning breaks at Clear Springs near Bude, Mississippi.

Sources of additional information:

Homochitto National Forest Ranger's Office, Bude District
Route 1
Meadville, MS 39653
(601) 384-5876

Notes on the trail: After a short leg at the trail's beginning from the parking lot, you can elect to take a left or right, going either a clockwise or counter route. I took the clockwise direction and found out later that the mileage posts marking the trail start out at zero if you go counterclockwise. If that matters to you, make the adjustment. Otherwise, I don't think it makes any difference in difficulty or decorum which direction you travel, although at least one person told me going clockwise "is backwards."

The layout of this trail can be best characterized by rolling terrain that drops off sharply to the many small creeks that flow into the Homochitto River, which drains this area just east of the Mississippi River. If you're looking for an easy beginner's trail, this isn't the one. There are plans underway to add on at least 3 more 3-mile loops on the southwest section of the existing trail. Added to the existing 10.5 miles, the count would reach nearly 20 miles. Those who have ridden this loop call it one of the best.

Jackson Area Rides

Because I come from a small mountain town, I am sensitive to the presence of heavy traffic. After having driven on the Natchez Trace Parkway to cross the state, the end of this tranquil transit onto Interstate 55 in north Jackson comes crashing in as suddenly as cymbals from a marching band. Lucky for me I'm a mountain biker and can handle anxiety attacks.

The sleepiness that surrounds most of the other cities in Mississippi does not penetrate this large metropolitan area. It is, after all, the capital and should be expected to serve as the gathering place for the movers and shakers. You won't be disappointed. Jackson is a city of infectious, positive energy.

Before you get too far into the city, stop at the Mississippi Crafts Center located just off the Natchez Trace. As well as being a good source of general information, it contains one of the most compact collections of Mississippi folk art anywhere. Despite my hectic schedule, I spent nearly an hour going through the displays of cane baskets, pottery, weaving, quilting, and jewelry. A word of advice: save your money ahead of time for purchase of one of the baskets; they are magnificent works of art. On the other end of the city, you can stop at a similar place, the Chimneyville Crafts Gallery, where you can learn about the profound cultural legacy of Mississippi's Native Americans.

Besides being able to attend the Dizzy Dean Museum April through August—except for Mondays—you can entertain yourself with a wide variety of activities as diverse as the International Ballet Festival, held every four years in June, to the International Red Beans and Rice Festival held in October every year. Junes in Jackson also provide the chance to catch a hot air balloon race. But what you'll probably enjoy the most are the two fine trail systems found within the Jackson area: Forest Hill Park and "Little Colorado."

For more information:

Metro Jackson Chamber of Commerce
201 South President Street
Jackson, MS 39201-4308
(601) 948-7575

The Bike Rack
Colonial Mart on Old Canton Road
Jackson, MS 39211
(601) 956-6891

The Bike Rack
5403 Robinson Road
Jackson, MS 39204-4138
(601) 372-6722

104

Indian Cycle
P.O. Box 1287
125 Dyess Road
Ridgeland, MS 39158-1287
(601) 956-8383 or 922-0014

The Bicycle Hotline
Le Fleur's Bicycle Club
P.O. Box 515
Jackson, MS 39205
(601) 372-8949

Bicycle Advocacy Group
P.O. Box 515
Jackson, MS 39025
(601) 982-8353

RIDE 25 *FOREST HILL PARK*

This city park is where local bike shops direct new mountain bike owners to ride first. Its many single-tracks looping hither and yon give the impression—and opportunity—to string together a much longer ride than its six miles would suggest. The fairly easy-to-navigate terrain also provides a good place to practice basic skills required for the more challenging trails of Jackson's other nearby trail, Little Colorado.

Although this is the site of races and events put on by the local bike organizations, it remains fairly unknown and uncharted. The list of city parks in the Jackson brochure even neglects to include this park's trail in its descriptions. Local bike riders, however, have spent a great deal of time and effort in making this a safe and enjoyable place to ride your mountain bike.

Signs and pieces of surveyor's tape mark the most commonly used trails, but disorientation is likely if you don't have a homing pigeon's sense of direction . . . or the map. Of course, you may just luck up and run across some of the younger neighborhood boys on bikes who will offer to take you "down some trails you haven't seen before." If you have time, take them up on it.

General location: This is located within the property boundaries of Forest Hill City Park located off McCluer Road.

Elevation change: This area provides only gently rolling terrain without any significant changes in elevation; however, there are those sudden changes in direction along banks and creeks that will keep you on your toes—one way or the other.

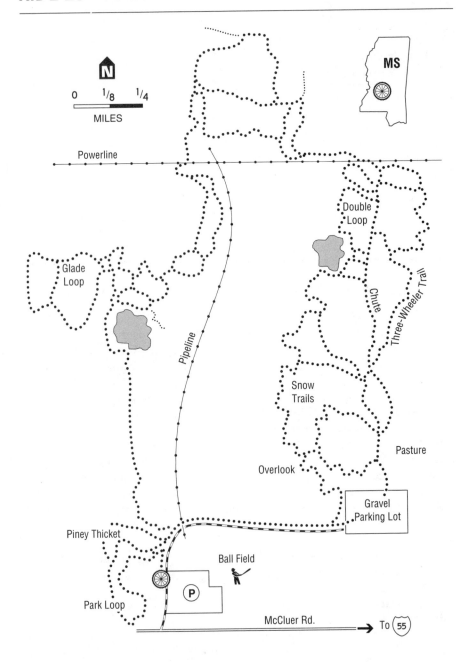

These Jackson riders "know where the real trails are" in
Forest Hill Park.

Season: This trail can be muddy and difficult to travel after the rains. Allow
ample time for it to dry out before riding it; at least one source suggests that
riders wait a week after a good soaking winter rain. But if you have to ride it
when it's wet, like the racers did during a deluge, you can. It's good preparation for riding trails in Louisiana.

Services: Water for your bottles can be easily obtained at the park. The rest
of your services can be acquired at convenient outlets in Jackson.

Hazards: Other than the mud, you'll probably only have to watch out for
briars during the summer and the low-hanging branches and occasional
deadfall. Bikers coming head-on at high speeds can be a problem, too.

Rescue index: These trails are located on the edge of the Forest Hill sub-
divisions, and as a result, you will not be very far from help.

Land status: This is Jackson city property, which seems to assure it will
remain protected and available for mountain biking. Some sections of Forest

Hill trails skirt the boundaries of private property and are subject, therefore, to the whims of these individuals. The saving grace of this park comes from the potential for expansion: one estimate maintains that at least double the current trail length can be developed inside its borders.

Maps: Jackson's bike shops have copies of this trail map on hand. Just ask for the map of Forest Hill Park on McCluer Road.

Finding the trail: Take Interstate 55/20 south out of Jackson and take the left fork of I-55 heading to New Orleans. Look for the exit to Savanna Street and take it. Turn to the right and follow it through the residential districts surrounding this park. Go straight through the traffic light; you'll be on McCluer Road. Stay on this road until you see the park on your right at 1300 McCluer Road. Park in the lot beside the ball field. One trailhead is directly across from the parking area; another is down the first-base line by the gravel parking lot.

Sources of additional information: Call the Jackson city parks number at (601) 960-1840 if you need to get more info on this or any of the other 42 city parks.

Forest Hill Park
1300 McCluer Road
Jackson, MS 39209-3943
(601) 960-1840

Notes on the trail: Races put on here cover a loop of almost 5.5 miles beginning with the trailhead on the left as you enter the park, near the right-hand turn across from the center-field fence. Bear to the left until reaching the pipeline. The pipeline leads to the powerline, which you cross and take the second right. When the trail dead-ends, take another right alongside the pasture until coming out at the gravel parking lot. Take the next right back onto single-track and bear left again until reaching the powerline (again). The single-track is on your right as you snake your way to the powerline inside the main loop. Familiarize yourself with the main outer loop before exploring any of the inner loops. It can be quite confusing the first time around.

RIDE 26 *LITTLE COLORADO TRAILS*

This collection of single-track and old jeep trails located on Rankin County Board of Education property has over 15 miles of trail that should pose no difficulty for the experienced mountain biker. Plenty of places, though, give a challenge. Tight turns in the middles of climbs or descents keep concentration from wavering off the front forks. Although a large outer loop defines

RIDE 26 *LITTLE COLORADO TRAILS*

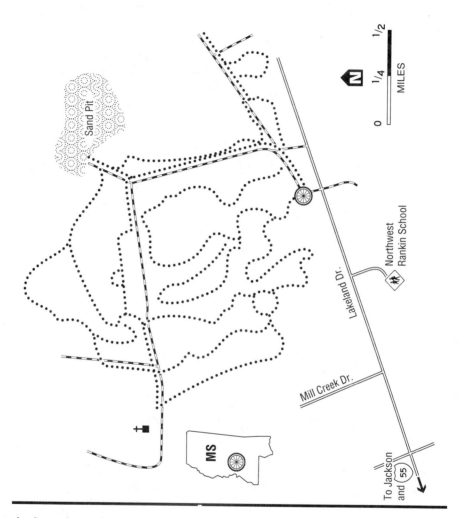

the boundary of the square-mile territory, smaller loops make several inside connections.

The excellent condition of this trail system belies the fact it is also used by motorcycles occasionally. In fact, the trails were originally cut in by the area's motorcyclists. Its primary visitors, however, are the Jackson fat-tire trippers, who use it quite a bit. I showed up on a January Thursday just past noon and found two vehicles already parked and bikers embarked.

I met up with one of the bikers there that day, James Petrovich, who showed me the spot that gives this trail its name. A large area of excavation nearby has laid the ground bare. The rain has cut through the leftover mounds and banks to give the sandstone a look similar—although smaller—to the canyons found in its more famous counterpart.

The only bad part about this trail may be its future. The property is deeded over to the local school system as part of a square-mile gift from the Mississippi state government. It is currently being leased to landowners who allow its use for biking. As superintendents change and policy swings, this prime mountain biking venue could become something entirely different. Until then, enjoy.

General location: This trail is just off Lakeland Drive east of Jackson.

Elevation change: The short but steep climbs are the only elevation changes encountered. Some of them will call for everything you can apply to your pedals in order to make the ascents.

Season: Except for in a downpour, you will be able to ride this trail when you won't be able to ride most others in the Deep South. The dense shade provided by the mixed hardwoods should make even the hottest days bearable.

Services: All services are provided in Jackson; however, bring all your water along with you.

Hazards: Some passes between trees along the single-track may require more caution than what you may expect. I had to wiggle, then wamble my way through more than one tight sapling gate. Until you become familiar with this trail, go slow and enjoy the setting as much as possible.

Rescue index: This is a fairly remote and widely scattered trail system. The sound of the highway in between you and help may cause all but the loudest of alarms to go unnoticed. However, once you've been located it won't take long to get you to aid.

Land status: This is Rankin County Board of Education property. It is perfectly legal to ride on this trail now, but the future is uncertain. A timely letter to the Rankin Board of Education in support of keeping this trail open for mountain bikes may prove beneficial.

Maps: The map used as a guide for this book was picked up free at Indian Cycle. Ask for the Little Colorado Map at any of the other area bike stores.

Finding the trail: Take Interstate 55 south out of Jackson until the Lakeland Drive exit. Leave the interstate, turn east, and go several miles until passing the shopping centers and gas stations. Cross the Hinds County line into Rankin County and notice the entrance to Northwest Rankin High School on the right. Look for the dirt road on the right at the top of the hill and turn left across the highway. Park in the small area provided. The trail begins directly behind the parking area.

Sources of additional information:

Rankin County Board of Education
408 South College Street
Brandon, MS 39042-3310
(601) 825-9714

Notes on the trail: This trail is unmarked by any blazes or signs. The only indication of being on the trail will be the well-worn paths. Your boundaries are the dirt roads on every side but the west, with a section of the trail crossing the dirt road on the north. You can easily put together a ride of 20 miles or more without getting on too much of the same territory twice. Plan to arrive early and stay as late as your legs and companions will allow.

RIDE 27 *DELTA NATIONAL FOREST*

There won't be any need to consider a topo map for this region of Mississippi. The land starts off ankle high and just gets lower no matter where you go in this tupelo bottomland swamp. The Delta National Forest is remarkable for being the only national forest that preserves the character of what used to be so commonplace along the banks of the Mississippi River. It is here where the waters meet and back up at the Mississippi River, flooding the Forest Service roads occasionally.

Most of the curves will be found in the Big Sunflower and Little Sunflower rivers and not on any of the roads or ATV trails. You can, therefore, take the 21-mile loop comprised of gravel Forest Service roads and let your eyes search the murky waters for the eyes of gators, otter, beavers, and ducks when they look back. As I rode down the road in this strangely spooky place, I couldn't help but wonder about how the former inhabitants, the Choctaw, dealt with the floods and muck.

Most ATV trails described in this book are largely accessible by mountain bikes. The ATV trails in the Delta can only be ridden by three- or four-wheelers for much of the year due to the extremely soggy conditions, but if you want to have some fun and see how much mud you can go bog on your bike, this is the place. However, after talking to the sole remaining bike shop owner in Vicksburg, ten or so miles to the south, he informed me that due to the massive erosion problem here, all off-road biking has been suspended for periods of time. The quality of soil, which is actually silt, does not repair easily, if at all.

Despite the tender nature of the ground here, many of the locals own ATVs, which they use to get back into the forests where they hunt for deer and boar. This is good to remember as you explore the deeper sections of this

RIDE 27 *DELTA NATIONAL FOREST*

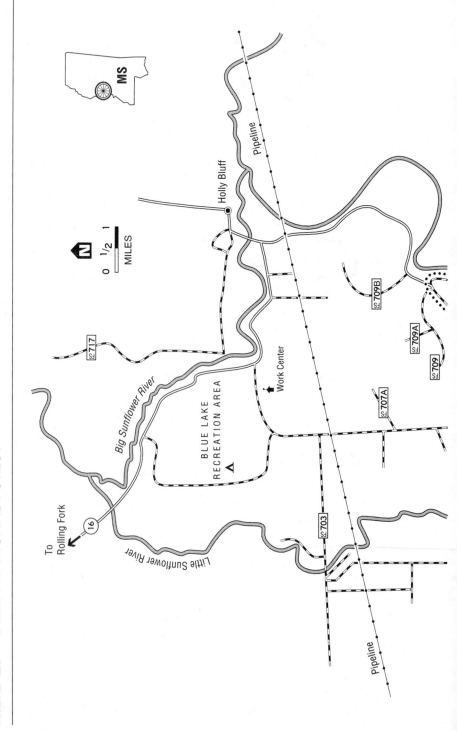

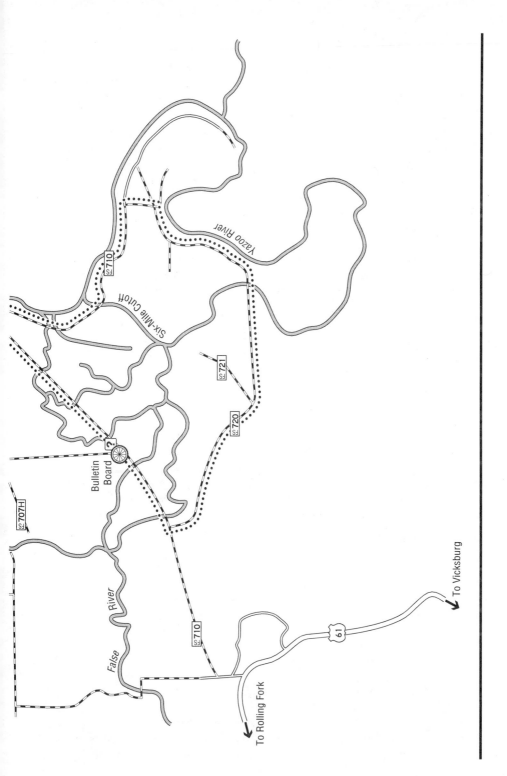

forest. I saw a huge boar bigger than my bike strapped to the front of an ATV parked at a trailhead. It would be a mighty funny feeling to meet up with one of these cantankerous, tusked monsters with only a couple of water bottles and a helmet for protection.

General location: Just east of the Mississippi River, north of Vicksburg and south of Yazoo City.

Elevation change: None . . . well, okay, almost none.

Season: Wait until the dry season and you may be able to get into the backcountry; otherwise, you will probably have to be satisfied with staying on the developed Forest Service roads.

Services: You can get what you need in Vicksburg. Tote whatever water you need to drink with you because it is a rather long ride to get replenished.

Hazards: The greatest hazard is posed by the landscape. The silt track you'll find in this area does not suffer the tread of bikes lightly. If you ride during the wetter season, an immediate furrow three inches deep and wide will be laid open with the first tire crossing if you get off the developed roadways.

Rescue index: You're not very far from civilization, but civilization is not very developed in the immediate area.

Land status: This is the Delta National Forest, a rather small area of interesting land.

Maps: Ask for the Delta and Homochitto National Forest map when you call, write, or go by the National Forest Service office in Rolling Fork.

Finding the trail: Leave Vicksburg on Highway 61 and about 18 miles north, as the road takes a bend to the left, look for the National Forest Service sign indicating a turn to the right and take it (Forest Service Road 710). Shortly after making the turn, look for the second road to the right, which is still FS 710 and constitutes much of the trail. Park anywhere off to the side after making the turn.

Sources of additional information:

Delta District Ranger
National Forest Service
402 Highway 61
Rolling Fork, MS 39159
(601) 873-6256

The Vicksburg Bike Shop
1622 Clay Street
Vicksburg, MS 39180-3018
(601) 638-7046

Notes on the trail: As indicated by the name of the national forest, this is delta country, and the signs along the road advise against traveling down them during periods of high water. But when it's dry enough to put a tire down, a ride down one of the forest service roads—more levee than road—can take you back in time to when the Native Americans cultivated the richness afforded by all this water. The quiet and remote waterways on both sides of the roads give this land a slightly ominous feel.

The suggested loop of 21 miles begins where FS 710 splits with FS 707. (FS 710 actually seems to turn right.) As FS 710 turns to pavement a little over 4 miles toward Big Sunflower River, take a right and follow the river. After crossing Six Mile Cutoff, take a right at the junction of another paved road. Pass 2 unimproved roads on the left and 1 on the right as the road again meets the Yazoo River. This is FS 720, which crosses the river and passes 1 unimproved road on the right before dead-ending into FS 710. Take a right back to where you parked. Congratulations, you've done the Delta!

Meridian Area Rides

I remember meeting my father as he returned from occasional business trips to Meridian, Mississippi, and feeling somehow he had made a pilgrimage to some far and distant land. I don't know if it was the fact he was in Meridian or Mississippi that impressed me the most; all I know was that I felt it was a place I would always want to visit.

It was with this thought that I left the interstate on a winter Sunday morning looking for Bonita Lake. I didn't know where to start looking. Since it is a city park, I headed downtown. The only signs I saw were the ones for the Jimmie Rodgers Museum at Highland Park. I didn't think that was where I would find the trails, but traffic was light, and my Lewis-and-Clark spirit encouraged the adventure of direction-less exploration.

I crossed the Sowashee Creek and followed the beacons of the tall buildings on 8th Street. For a city of over 45,000, it was as sleepy looking as any place could be. But I saw it rousing. Plenty of Jimmie Rodgers Museum and Highland Park signs kept me headed confidently deeper in to the city until I made the final turn into the park.

Jimmie Rodgers, of course, is the singing brakeman whose country yodels gave rise to country music as we know it today. As I passed by the closed museum, I was struck by the rich musical legacy Mississippi musicians have given us: blues from Greenwood, rock from Tupelo, and country from Meridian. And not too far south from where these people sang and played, another prominent American musical contribution—jazz—got its start in Louisiana. It must be something in the water.

Besides the musical museum, you can also see and ride a Dentzel carousel manufactured in the 1890s—the only one of its type in the United States. And to round out the Mississippi musical trip, a tour can be made of the visitors center at Peavey Electronics—the largest manufacturer of amplifiers in the world.

For more information:

Meridian/Lauderdale County Partnership
(601) 693-1306

Meridian Parks and Recreation
(601) 485-1850 or 485-1801

Heart & Sole Cycle and Fitness
3104 23rd Avenue
Meridian, MS 39302
(601) 693-2453

RIDE 28 BONITA LAKES TRAIL

Upwards of 20 miles of wide and narrow single-track are connected by gravel-surfaced roads that crisscross up and down the slopes near a set of three lakes just off Interstate 59 in Meridian, Mississippi. These routes are shared by hikers, bikers, and horses alike, but despite heavy use, they are some of the best maintained trails anywhere. If time doesn't allow for your riding every trail, pick out one or more of the many loops to fit the mood or time constraint.

Built by motorcyclists years ago, the trails around Bonita Reservoir are now owned and maintained by the city of Meridian. The cutoffs to the right and behind the most northerly of the lakes provide a moderately strenuous track used by local organizers for races. However, this area has got the go-ahead for construction of a new shopping mall. The verdict is uncertain regarding whether or not these trails will be altered. Keep your fingers crossed.

The left fork that leads along the eastern bank of the largest lake will take you to the top of what can only be fairly described as precipices. A rider I met there, Keith, called these trails the icing on the cake of techno-riding. The steeper and more dramatic the direction changes, the better Keith likes them. He is young and has good shocks. However, most of the loops can be negotiated with an eye reserved for surveying the quiet splendor of this mature, mixed hardwood forest. Towering beeches and oaks attract a wide range of birds into their limbs. You'll likely find several places along the way to stop and admire all the living things, great and small, that congregate here.

General location: These beautiful pathways can be found just a short distance from I-59/20 barely outside of Meridian proper.

Elevation change: As is the case with so many of the classic rides in the Deep South, the overall, sustained change is not significant, but the immediate change can pin your ears back "flat agin yo' haid."

Season: These trails are well made and have held up well under all conditions. The shade of the large trees provide as much relief from the Mississippi heat as possible.

Services: All services can be found in Meridian.

Hazards: Some exposed roots on the steeper sides deserve discretion. Horses and hikers are also commonly seen.

Rescue index: You will notice the barn housing the horses used by the Mississippi Mounted Police on your left by the rest rooms and pay phone as you enter the park from the Highway 19 entrance. I imagine a fairly quick rescue would come galloping along should it be necessary.

Land status: This is Meridian city land.

Maps: No map is currently available other than the one drawn up for this book by Keith. Thank you, Keith.

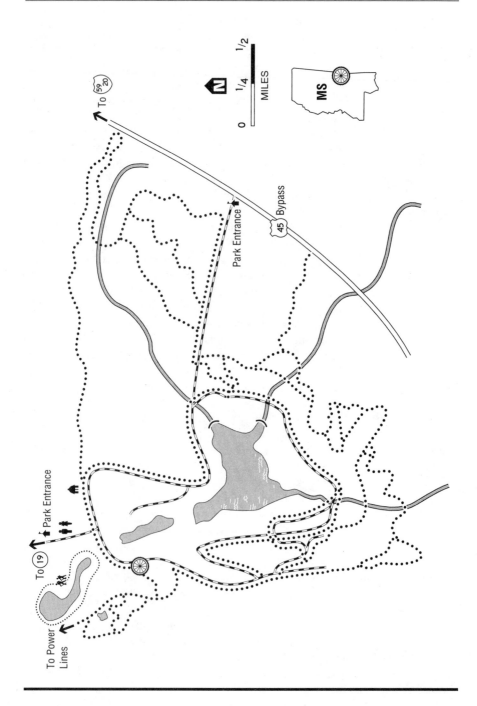

Bonita Lakes in Mississippi—living up to its name.

Finding the trail: Take exit 154 off I-59/20 and turn east on Highway 19. Less than a mile later you will see the entrance to Bonita Reservoir on your right. Turn and follow the road until it crosses the dam in between the first and second lake and goes down into a parking lot. The trailhead is right in front of you on the other side of the split-rail fence.

Sources of additional information:

Meridian Parks and Recreation
(601) 485-1850 or 485-1801

Notes on the trail: As pointed out earlier, the more easily negotiated sections are off to the right after you make the first climb and take the fork. These are also the ones most likely to get closed should the shopping mall nightmares become reality. A map is not really needed to keep yourself within the frequently traveled trails on this side. However, bear left at each junction until arriving at the powerline right-of-way. At the bottom of the hill where twin giant beeches stand, take a right and ride past a small pond on the right. The single-track trail rejoins the double-track above the trailhead.

If you feel equipped for more technical riding, take the first left fork that starts off by hugging the contour. You will soon be challenged in a most mountain biking way as the single-track parallels the lakeshore. Trails continue on the other side of US 45 Bypass if you want some more.

RIDE 29 CLARKCO STATE PARK

One of the reasons why I took a full year to explore the Deep South was so I would have enough time to fall into some lucky finds like this three-mile loop around Lake Ivy inside Clarkco State Park. After a long day on the road and trails, I pulled into this beautiful park just south of Meridian on US 45. The ranger who checked me in to the campsite seemed excited and proud that I would be riding the nature trail.

After getting up early and chattering through a breakfast in subfreezing temperatures, I headed down to look for the trail just after it got light enough to see the trailhead near the primitive camping area. A wide, pine-strewn roadbed invited me inside the forest. While I was standing there, two sharp-shinned hawks glided into the trees in front of me. The bite of the cold on my fingers and face was suddenly gone and replaced by the roar of pulse in my ears.

General location: The park is located off US 45, just south of Meridian.

Elevation change: There is probably less than 100 feet of change; most of it comes in a 50-yard climb that will have you doing the huff-and-puff. This is an ideal training site for the young, aspiring mountain biking legs of any little ones you may have. They won't be able to pull all the hills, but they will get a good taste of what mountain biking is all about.

Season: This trail gets very little use and is very well maintained. As a result, you should be able to ride this even in a downpour.

Services: Most services can be found in Quitman, and what you can't find there will be available in Meridian.

Hazards: You will be sharing the treadway with hikers, for whom this trail was primarily built. Please respect their rights to passage and this trail will be kept available for our mutual enjoyment. If you want to fly like the wind, choose another trail. The bridges are for foot travel only unless you are a trials expert. One short stretch of deep sand can cause much front tire slippage if you are caught unawares.

Rescue index: The trail is easily accessible from many directions.

Land status: This is park land owned by the state of Mississippi.

Maps: The park office has a map of Clarkco State Park, which clearly shows the nature/bike trail and is available at no charge.

Finding the trail: Head south out of Meridian on Highway 45 until taking the left-hand turn into the park. Pay your user's fee, take the first left, and park in the office parking lot. Head toward the primitive camp area and pick up the trail on the left just past the bath house.

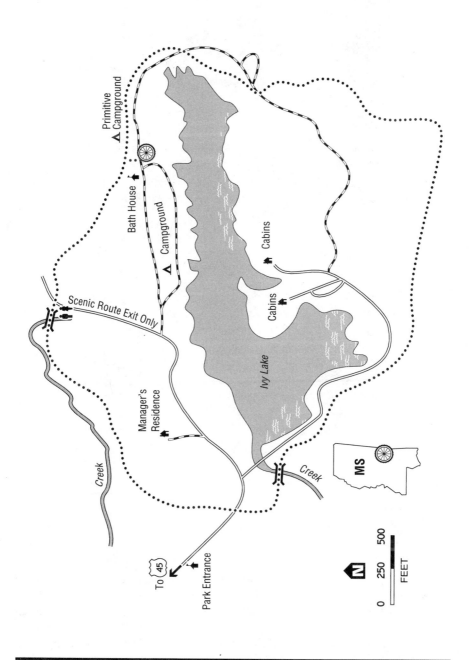

Primitive ▲ Campground

Bath House

Campground ▲

Cabins

Cabins

Ivy Lake

Scenic Route Exit Only

Manager's Residence

Creek

Creek

MS

To 45

Park Entrance

N

0 250 500
FEET

A meditation station at Clarkco State Park.

Sources of additional information:

Clarkco State Park
Route 1, Box 186
Quitman, MS 39355
(601) 776-6651

Notes on the trail: The first mile of this 3-mile loop runs near the other, more developed, camping areas, but the only sign they're near are the access trails coming down from the ridge on the left. A rest area has been developed on an island formed by a fast-moving creek. The white sands at the base of tall turkey oaks and gums make this a place you will want to stop, look, and listen. Benches have been placed there to encourage you.

The next section is long and steep enough to make you slip into your weenie gear before it levels off on a contour overlooking a serene creek valley. The downhill that follows produces some significant speed, but try to restrain yourself and remember this is a trail you should slow down on and enjoy.

After crossing the park entrance road, you're led toward the backwaters formed from a beaver's dam. Go slow and you may be able to see this master engineer perched up on a log in the middle of the pond. I was a little too slow and unsuspecting, so I only caught the sound of its plump body dropping into the water and the subsequent waves. You're getting close to the 65 acres of Ivy Lake where you may see kingfishers, coots, and old coot fishermen. If you began your trip at the primitive camping sites, you will circle back to them shortly after crossing the last bridge. If an extended ride is called for, make as many loops as you need.

RIDE 30 *NOXUBEE WILDLIFE REFUGE*

According to at least one published source, *noxubee* is the Choctaw word for "stinking water." Perhaps the association comes from this area's location on the great waterfowl migration path. Here you can ride miles of gravel service roads. One loop of 6.5 miles represents the best of what Noxubee has to offer the off-road cyclist. Its relatively flat grade crosses creeks (via bridges) and connects gated roads where thousands of mallards, wood ducks, gadwalls, widgeons, and teals make their winter homes—only to be replaced by egrets, herons, and songbirds arriving in the spring. The result is cacophony in the air and great amounts of "caca" on the ground.

From October to March, much of the ground is inundated by waters from Bluff Lake (1,200 acres) and Loakfoma Lake (600 acres), providing what is called "green timber reserves," referred to as a "GTR" on the maps. These flooded sections are drained in the early spring after the ducks and their kin head north to nest. Consequently, many of the roads available for mountain biking within the refuge cannot be ridden during the winter months.

Wildlife refuges are managed as part of the U.S. Fish and Wildlife Service, one of many divisions of the U.S. Department of Interior. Another responsibility of the Department of the Interior that mountain bikers are probably familiar with is the United States Geological Survey, makers of the 7.5 minute topographical quadrangles. There's little need for consulting such a map while on the relatively flat refuge, unless you are interested in finding the sources of the Noxubee River and the Chinchahoma Creek flowing into it.

General location: The 47,000 acres are located south of Starkville, Mississippi, where Oktibbeha, Winston, and Noxubee counties come together.

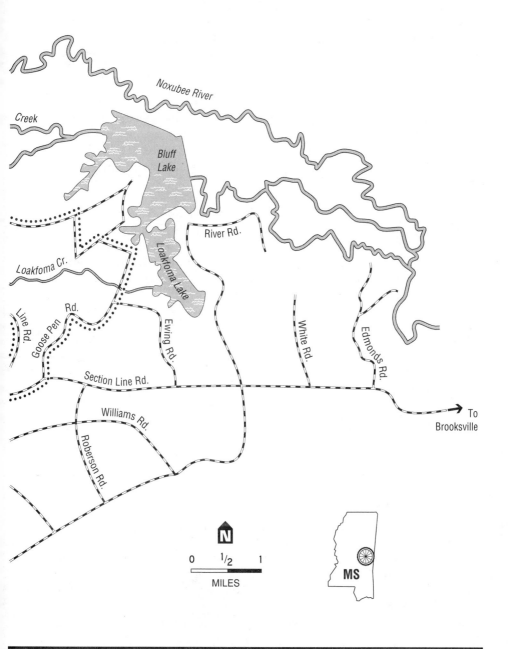

Noxubee River

Creek

Bluff
Lake

River Rd.

Loakfoma Cr.

Loakfoma Lake

Line Rd.

Goose Pen Rd.

Ewing Rd.

White Rd.

Edmonds Rd.

Section Line Rd.

Williams Rd.

Roberson Rd.

To
Brooksville

N

0   1/2   1
MILES

MS

Elevation change: One of the curious characteristics shared by several trails in the Deep South is that, somehow, the trails never seem to create much of an uphill grade. Yet, occasionally, you go flying effortlessly downhill at helmet-whistling speeds.

Season: Many of the closed roads open to mountain bikers are flooded October to March and are, therefore, not suitable for travel, although—unless it is posted as closed—you wouldn't be prevented from trying it by foot. However, a gander with its dander up can apply a daunting dent to your flesh with its formidable beak.

Services: All services can be acquired in nearby Starkville where the students of Mississippi State University have created a diverse and dynamic market.

Hazards: Ganders notwithstanding, relatively few obstacles should impede your safe and scenic travel along the roads inside Noxubee Wildlife Refuge. Vehicles can be found on some of the roads, although most of the roads are gated and remain closed for service access only.

Rescue index: Rescue from most areas of the Noxubee can be executed swiftly and easily because most, if not all, of the routes you can take follow gravel roads.

Land status: This is one of the over 475 National Wildlife Refuge areas located in America and is under the U.S. Department of the Interior's control.

Maps: If you get to the office before it closes, you can ask for and receive one of the two available maps of the entire Noxubee Wildlife Refuge.

Finding the trail: Take Highway 25 south out of Starkville. After crossing the Chinchahoma Creek and Noxubee River, look for a dirt road on the left and a sign pointing to the refuge. The dirt road will dead-end into Louisville Road, on which you will turn left. The Refuge Headquarters is to the left at the next intersection. Be advised that there are hiking trails open only for foot travel. Biking is restricted to refuge roads unless specific permission is obtained to do otherwise.

Sources of additional information:

> Noxubee Wildlife Refuge
> Route 1, Box 142
> Brooksville, MS 39739
> (601) 323-5548

Notes on the trail: For making the 6.5-mile loop, leave the parking lot and head back west on Louisville Road, passing by the Noxubee Cemetery on the left. Take the next left (Dummy Line Road) until the intersection with Section Line Road where you turn left again. Another left onto Goose Pen Road leads past where Ewing Road comes in from the right, just before crossing the Loakfoma Creek. Turn right or left at the next intersection; either one dead-ends into Louisville Road where a right turn goes back to the office and the lakes.

You can be as creative as you want in mapping out various routes inside the refuge. Levees, gated roads, and ungated roads lead all through this unusual landscape where over 254 species of birds have been sighted, including the seldom-seen red-cockaded woodpecker and wood stork. The easily navigated roads allow you to take in the scenery where farms flourished, then disappeared due to massive erosion. The wasteland was taken over by the government and planted in pines. As you will discover, this refuge has created a retreat where mountain bikers won't find many mountains, but will find plenty reason—and over 200 miles of roads—to return for another ride.

Columbus Area Rides

The Tombigbee River, whose name comes from the Choctaw words for "coffin maker," is the chief topographic feature of this east-central region. Before being linked to the Tennessee River via the Tenn-Tom Waterway, this river was the principal means of transporting King Cotton to downstream markets.

The largest city that grew in the area is Columbus, originally called "Possum Town" due to the marsupial resemblance of one of its early settlers, Spirus Roach. I guess it could've been worse. By 1821 incorporation was complete and any danger of such a stigma was avoided.

Within 70 miles of Columbus lies the Natchez Trace Parkway, two distinct areas of a national forest, the largest tribe of Choctaws, two universities, and the only place in the world named for the Polish military leader, Tadeusz Kosciusko, who waged campaigns for the soon-to-be United States in the Revolutionary War. "Kozzy," as it is called by the younger citizens and neighboring communities, is also the home of Oprah Winfrey.

Perhaps one day Oprah may have on her show mountain bikers who got stuck in the region's notoriously sticky clay. A local bike store owner and I were talking about the adobe nature of the moistened mud. He told me he laughed every time he read an ad by a bike tire company claiming it had developed the ultimate mud tire. He was sure they hadn't tested it in this part of Mississippi.

A friend and I, unforewarned and anxious to ride, coasted downhill on a Forest Service road that had alternate patches of exposed clay and slash pine needles. We rolled through the first section of mud which stuck to our tires like glue and then picked up those long needles. It looked cute at first until both tires quickly gained twenty pounds of adobe and completely locked down. The hike up the half-mile hill back to the truck with my bike on my back was enough to convince me that there is some mud you should never fight.

For more information:

The Bicycle Shop
La Galerie Shopping Mall
Starkville, MS 39759
(601) 323-2555

Holeshot Bicycles
Highway 82 East
Columbus, MS 39701
(601) 327-9461

RIDE 31 *OPOSSUM TRAIL*

For those who have read the introduction to Columbus Area Rides, you will understand the connection to opossums in this land of armadillos. What you may not recognize is the opossum quality of this trail; it's a real sleeper. Few people pointed this trail out to me as I did initial research into the area, but I'm sure you'll agree that this trail ranks as one deserving a good reputation.

After construction began on this 150-acre lake in 1961, Lowndes County Lake opened in 1964 and became part of the Mississippi Park Commission in 1972. By 1980, when the 3.5 miles of single-track nature trail—part of the total 5-mile loop—was built by the Youth Conservation Corps, it joined the sports complex, pavilion, marina, and campground to provide the entire family with an outdoor experience surpassed by few Mississippi State Parks.

Along with the difficult single-track, the serene beauty of the lake will stand out in my memory. I had pitched my tent on the banks in the primitive camping area. When I got up (before sunrise as was customary on the trail), I saw the first glimmer of sunlight replacing the moon's glow. I took my breakfast down closer to the water and watched and listened as I sipped my coffee. Mallards began moving into the water. Peewees chirped and wrens warbled. Two pairs of great blue herons glided inches above the glassy surface in near-perfect synchrony. They landed on the far shore where I had ridden my bike the day before and gave a loud and raspy honk. It's a wonderful thing, riding bikes in the Mississippi woods. Sometimes you don't even need tires.

General location: Lake Lowndes State Park, where this trail is located, lies south of Columbus.

Elevation change: Some sections may make you think you need to put your chest on the saddle on the way down. The climbs can be made via bike only if you have steam-powered thighs.

Season: Avoid this trail during the wet times, although its loamier track allows wet riding more often than most soils near here.

Services: Columbus has been around for a long time and has the services to prove it. The park is well equipped to provide many of the basics and incidentals you need.

Hazards: Hikers as well as bikers can be just around the bend, so be prepared to meet them either head-on or stopped in the middle of the trail soaking up the sights.

Rescue index: Although sections give the impression of being remote, most of the trail lies close enough to some aspect of civilization to effect a quick and timely rescue.

RIDE 31 *OPOSSUM TRAIL*

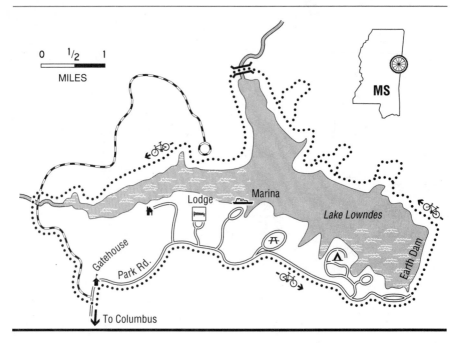

Land status: This is another fine state park taken care of by the people of Mississippi.

Maps: You can pick up a map for Opossum Trail inside the lodge located across the street from the sports fields.

Finding the trail: Leave downtown Columbus headed south on Highway 69. Signs will lead to the entrance of Lake Lowndes State Park, 8 miles southeast of town. The trail begins past the campgrounds where the road dead-ends. There is a sign with "Possum Trail" on it at the south end of the dam.

Sources of additional information:

Lake Lowndes State Park
3319 Lake Lowndes Road
Columbus, MS 39702
(601) 328-2110

Notes on the trail: I came to this park late in the day, looking for a fairly easy ride. I thought, "It's only 5 miles, piece of cake." Well, as sometimes happens on unfamiliar trails, I went through a time and place warp. The harder I pedaled, the slower I seemed to cover mileage, and the faster the sun seemed to sink. Compounding this Kafkaesque turn of events was the fact that the

The trail begins on the dam for Lake Lowndes.

trail has several unanticipated forks. Although I did not corroborate it with any official source, the right-hand forks (which I took) seemed to lead up and down the lakeside ridges. The left forks appear to come back in from the left and stay closer to the lakeshore. The single-track ends at the gate, and the remaining 1.5 miles back to the trailhead is asphalt. As a consideration, you may want to turn around at the gate and ride it as an out-and-back, taking the right forks again, which in the reverse direction, will be the unridden forks from the first pass.

RIDE 32 *CHOCTAW LAKE TRAILS*

Although no trails have been developed solely for bikes in this national forest, the allure of riding here comes from the numerous chances to investigate inviting roads and trails of all types. Some go only a short distance before stopping at wildlife clearings. Some hook back into other roads and can give lengthy rides. Practically every ridge and hollow has a road or the remnant of one used long ago when this area was originally timbered. And each has its own surprise waiting. One particular 17-mile loop-on-a-string of moderate difficulty, however, should whet your appetite for more of what this national forest presents to mountain bikers.

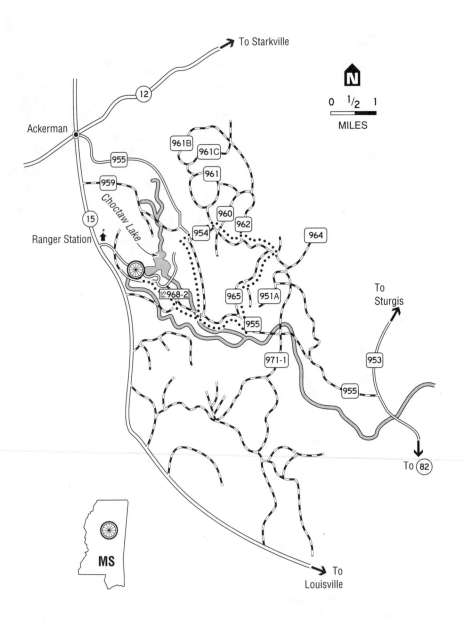

It's hard to imagine a prettier place than the recreational area southwest of Ackerman, Mississippi, called Choctaw Lake. Green-backed, little, and great blue herons stalk the grassy edges of this central Mississippi impoundment. Huge carp wallow in the shallows, carving out spawning grounds. Kingfishers cackle and chase each other from bank to bank. Eastern kingbirds patrol the meadows overlooking otters swimming after a snack as pied-billed grebes submerge until only their necks and heads show. The fascinating pictures of winged and unwinged animals hold so much attention, you will be hard-pressed to go out and explore the roads on bike.

I had just traveled down this promising road—looking for a long loop—when it abruptly ended on the edge of a large clearing. Before I had time for my face to fall, I saw three turkeys scooting off into the high grass to the right and a coon ambling off to the left. I grabbed my water bottle and started to head back when I saw hundreds of ladybugs flying straight at me and my orange sweatshirt. The fact that I was probably the foulest smelling flower they had ever approached didn't stop them from landing on me until I was wearing a black-speckled coat. I counted over a hundred on the front of my shirt before I decided to leave. I didn't think there was any danger in having too many ladybugs land on me, but I saw more streaming toward me. It was just a bit unnerving to have so many of anything coming after me.

General location: These trails and roads are typical of the ones in east-central Mississippi.

Elevation change: Some of the hills can be atypically long and steep for what you would expect, but the Deep South landscape here prevents long, sustained climbs.

Season: I wouldn't ride any of these trails or gated roads after a rainy time; they can be treacherously gooey and capable of stopping you in your tracks. Avoid getting off onto the gated backroads and trails during any season if you see a vehicle parked nearby. This probably signals a hunter of some sort. There are too many opportunities to find an unused area to disrupt anyone else's trip into the forest.

Services: Most services can be found in nearby Ackerman. The recreational area—closed from November 15 to March 15—is the finest one I've ever visited. Biking services can be found in Starkville and Columbus.

Hazards: Avoid the mud!

Rescue index: Although you can get off into remote places, you're not too far from help in most cases. If a solo trip is planned, a good move would be to leave word with the rangers at the entrance to Choctaw Lake.

Land status: This is National Forest land.

Maps: The map for the Tombigbee National Forest should be enough for finding most trailheads; however, you may want the topo maps to aid in further investigation of possible routes. Six separate quad maps are needed to completely cover the area, although the most important ones are the

7.5 minute series Ackerman, Sturgis, Louisville North, and Highpoint quads; the other two are Betheden and Bradley.

Finding the trail: Because there are no particular trails developed for off-road use, you have to pick your way through the Forest Service roads and explore the numerous gated sections. An excellent place to begin is at the parking lot on the west side of the lake (where the beach is); ride back toward the entrance. At the first intersection, turn left and zoom down the asphalt section by the lake.

Sources of additional information:

> Tombigbee Ranger District
> Route 1, Box 98A (right outside of the Choctaw Lake entrance)
> Ackerman, MS 39735
> (601) 285-3264

Notes on the trail: After riding down the pavement by the lake, note the work center on the left. Bear right on Forest Service Road 968-2. After crossing a creek, look for County Road 955 coming in on the left and take the left. At the next intersection turn right onto CR 954. After passing 3 gravel roads on the left, take the next right, FS 965. It dead-ends back into CR 955 where you turn left. After approximately a mile, you should return to the intersection you were at approximately 11 miles ago. Take the previously ridden section of 968-2 back to the parking lot. You can easily spend all day taking roads down into secluded valleys and along ridges where you can easily be the first one to set tire there since the logging operations which made these roads necessary.

Don't be put off by the lack of developed trail systems in this National Forest. Let your spirit of exploration take over and find the hidden ponds and streams few people have the pleasure to relax by. On a 3-mile stretch on FS 971-1, I counted 10 gated roads or open trails leading off to either side. Any of these roads or trails may lead into an oxbow of a languid creek or up along a ridgetop where you can reclaim the sense of what this land must've looked like when the Choctaw were this region's first inhabitants.

Oxford Area Rides

Those who carry around the image of Mississippi being a backward little state with nothing going on have obviously never been to Oxford. This northern city is home to the University of Mississippi and has a history going back to 1848; its students keep the hustle and bustle center focus. The inner-city neighborhood reflects the diversity of stately architecture of antebellum buildings and spontaneous behavior of the residents, all with distinguished Southern decorum, you hear?

The Oxford city square's atmosphere blends young and old, near and far, into a place you will find hard to leave. If you love to eat, you need go no farther than a few blocks to gorge on everything from Lebanese to Cajun to catfish and hushpuppies. For the lowdown on what's happening, go to the Visitors Center on the east side of the square where you will walk in and be greeted by a nice lady in a rocking chair who will while away the time with you as long as you have the desire.

North Mississippi's literary traditions run deep. Nobel Prize winner William Faulkner lived nearby in a beautiful home and wrote his stories based on much of what he saw around him in Oxford. And you might run across John Grisham strolling down the same streets making some of the same observations.

Next to its literature, Mississippi's musical heritage lays claim to the nativity promoting what many feel is the first truly American form of expression: the blues. The university has its archives on display where you can go and explore extensive recordings, reference books, and other memorabilia tracing its development. For those who poo-poo the blues as a significant event in music, remember that barely 50 miles east in Tupelo, the King took the blues one more step—as the song says, "The blues had a baby and named it rock 'n' roll."

Another culture is rapidly growing in the Oxford area as well. Mountain biking expert class racers, Don Massey and Adam Dorsey, can be found hanging around Oxford Bicycle Company when they aren't either training or racing in one of the National Off-Road Bicycle Association's events. The Oxford-NORBA connection goes even further; champion rider John Tomac married one of the many beautiful young ladies from Oxford.

Put this town on your schedule for a biking holiday and experience some of the best of what Mississippi has to offer.

For more information:

Oxford-Lafayette County Chamber of Commerce
Oxford, MS 38655
(601) 234-4651

Oxford Bicycle Company
407 Jackson Avenue
Oxford, MS 38655
(601) 236-6507

Base Camp, Inc.
2008 University Avenue
Oxford, MS 38655
(601) 234-5982

RIDE 33 ROWAN OAK TRAIL

Either before or after visiting William Faulkner's home on Old Taylor Road, take your thoughts about Yoknapatawpha County along and ride this nearly two-mile out-and-back (3.5 miles total) of dirt single-track with two small loops—one at the Buie Museum and the other on the Rowan Oak side of the creek. Despite the relatively short length of this trail, be prepared to put in play some of your best moves in order to stay upright.

On one side of the route, antebellum homes—like Rowan Oak—ring the lip of the creek valley the trail winds through, although you will feel their presence rather than see them. You might be able to detect the faint, musty odor from closets where hoopskirts hung a hundred or so years ago.

The openness of the forest created by the wide variety of mature hardwoods allows long views to open, especially in the winter. On a fall Saturday, you might choose to stop a few minutes and catch some of the football game at the Ole Miss Stadium, which is on the far side of the trail. You'll hear the band playing and the crowd cheering no matter where you are on the trail.

General location: Take Highway 6 toward Oxford from Pontotoc and exit to downtown. Turn left onto Old Taylor Road a mile before you get to the square. Go straight at the stop sign and look for the entrance to Rowan Oak on your right. Go past the entrance or park outside the gate and head down the gravel drive. The single-track begins where the gravel stops.
Elevation change: There is basically one ascent and fall on either side of the bridge. Though steep, it should not present much difficulty to an experienced rider.
Season: Avoid this trail during wet weather.
Services: All services are readily available in Oxford, which may surprise you with its fashionable shops and restaurants.
Hazards: One short, sandy section of trail becomes very narrow and canted downhill. I rode it one way and walked it the other; walking is safer unless

RIDE 33   *ROWAN OAK TRAIL*

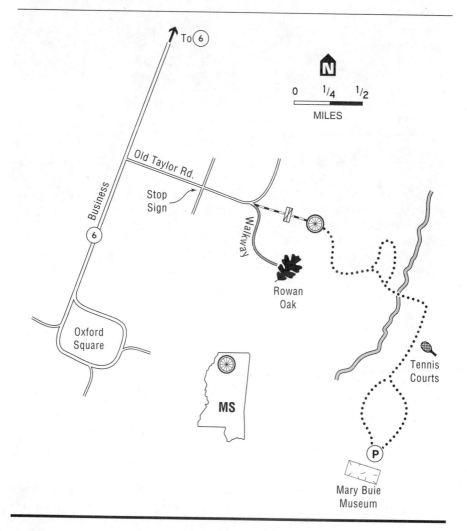

the University of Mississippi, which maintains this trail, has done some repair on it.

Rescue index: A good rebel yell or whistle blast should bring several folks running on the double, unless it's during a Saturday football game.

Land status: The University of Mississippi owns the land.

Maps: No map is currently available, other than what is found in this book.

Finding the trail: Look to the right after the gravel section of the parking area for Rowan Oak ends.

The trailhead lies to the left of Faulkner's home, Rowan Oak.

Sources of additional information:

The Curator at Rowan Oak
Old Taylor Road
Oxford, MS 38655
(601) 234-3284

The University of Mississippi
200 Lyceum
Oxford, MS 38677
(601) 232-7378

Notes on the trail: The first descent to a wash below Rowan Oak needs to be negotiated slowly in between roots anchoring the large oaks, maples, and sweet gums growing in this urban forest. Bridges across the draw are maintained by the University of Mississippi (as are Faulkner's grounds), but some slides have occurred that make at least one pass a tricky maneuver.

The climb up the other side ends in the parking lot of the Mary Buie Museum, established in 1939. Buie, an Oxford artist who moved to Chicago and made her living painting copies of masterpieces for the wealthy, moved back to Oxford late in her life. The museum was established with funds from her will. Along with examples of her work, the museum contains a folk art exhibit, children's hands-on displays, and other art.

After riding along the backside of the parking lot, look for the worn bike trail heading back down the hill. After crossing the bridge again, the trail forks to the right in a loop that reconnects to the main trail not far from the beginning.

RIDE 34 *FRUIT LOOP*

This series of trails winding through a mostly pine forest serves as the arena for the serious mountain biking challenges in Oxford. Built largely by students from the University of Mississippi on land owned by the university, this 5.5-mile series of loops is not designed with the beginner in mind.

Its dirt single-track cuts through trees so close, you may have to wiggle your handlebars and hold your tongue just right in order to get through without touching. Slopes exist so steep that riding down them may not be possible without the gift of wings, and going back up is just a fantasy for most mortal mountain bikers. There are even some low, wet spots to test your mudslinging gears.

But the difficult nature of Fruit Loop should not be reason to avoid this beautiful trail in north Mississippi. An honest use of caution and discretion will prevent all but the unluckiest mishaps. You can comfort yourself when you need to hop off and hike by knowing that expert NORBA racers often use this trail as a training course. If you're not walking some on this trail, we'll most likely be reading about you soon in NORBA News as winning some of the big bucks.

General location: This trail is located just off Highway 6 headed toward Pontotoc from Oxford.
Elevation change: The overall change is not significant, although there are short sections closer to being perpendicular to flat ground than parallel.
Season: Most sections of this trail hold up well under wet conditions. However, as is generally the rule, avoid riding if much rain has fallen recently.
Services: All services are found in Oxford, my favorite urban Mississippi destination.
Hazards: Besides the extremely steep portions, deadfalls from the February 1994 ice storm may still obstruct in places. Recent construction along the powerline right-of-way may make riding bumpier or muddier than preferred.
Rescue index: You're close to help, but the terrain could make it tough to get to you in places. A strongly blown whistle might bring aid if you're not the only one riding the trail.
Land status: This property is owned by the University of Mississippi.

RIDE 34 *FRUIT LOOP*

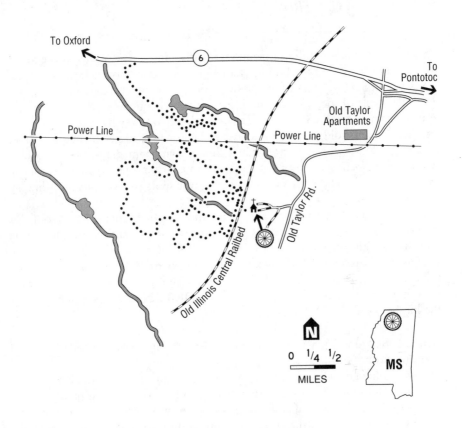

Maps: A very good map exists (besides the one found in this book) and can be picked up at Oxford Bicycle Company. Ask for the map of Fruit Loop.

Finding the trail: Two trailheads exist: one off of Highway 6, and the other off of Old Taylor Road. Use the one off Old Taylor Road. Take Highway 6 toward Pontotoc and exit after passing the Coliseum on your left and going under the abandoned railroad overpass. Turn right onto Old Taylor Road, go approximately 1 mile, and turn right. Take the second road on your left and park in the small church parking lot. Follow the road on the left of the church

A steep descent on Fruit Loop—helmets recommended.

leading down to the former railroad bed of the Old Illinois Central Railroad, which now serves as the trailhead. Take a right at the bottom of the hill and look for the single-track turning off to the left.

Sources of additional information:

The University of Mississippi
200 Lyceum
University, MS 38677
(601) 232-7378

Notes on the trail: By beginning behind the small church off Old Taylor Road, roll down to the rail-less bed of the Old Illinois Central Railroad and turn right. Look for the single-track going uphill on the left 50 yards or so. The right fork leads toward the powerline right-of-way, more or less directly, with either of the next forks going across the powerline. The left fork has a small loop on the northeastern side of a creek (no bridge) before winding clockwise back across the creek feeding a small lake. Continue on to the powerline and take a right. Almost immediately, look for the single-track reentering the woods on the left. Bearing left at the next 2 intersections leads to Highway 6. The 2 intersections on your right headed toward Highway 6 form 2 ends of a loop going near another small lake. On the back side of that loop, a trail leads back to the railbed, after first recrossing the powerline right-of-way.

RIDE 35 *TRACE STATE PARK*

Despite what you may have thought, Mississippi's state parks are prime territory for mountain biking. Most offer nature trails that are open for bike travel and provide a wide range of difficulty. The king of state park trails, however, is represented by the over 40 miles' worth of loops within loops located in Trace State Park in northeast Mississippi. These trails present an extremely challenging arrangement of wide mountain bike single-track that is frequently used (legally) by motorcycles.

Down the road ten miles in Tupelo, you can visit Elvis Presley's birthplace, memorial chapel, and park; five miles north of the park the Elvis Presley Lake and Campground has entertained plans for building bike paths. Museums acquainting visitors with Tupelo's Chickasaw and Civil War past, along with modern Mississippi art, and headquarters for the Natchez Trace Parkway are also found in Tupelo.

You can also visit the John Allen National Fish Hatchery where millions of fish are hatched yearly. The hatchery received, no doubt, an excited call on February 17, 1984, when Billy Cother caught over 63 pounds of bass from the park's Trace Lake. You can see the ten fish he caught hanging from a plaque in the park office. The others he caught that day had to be returned where they probably still swim with the catfish, redear, bluegill, and crappie kept stocked in this 600-acre lake.

This lake is also home to great blue herons, scores of ducks, beavers, otters, and countless songbirds. The mixed hardwoods and large pine forests around the water provide the perfect habitat for all sorts of critters, including *bicyclus montanea*.

General location: Seven miles east of Pontotoc and 10 miles west of Tupelo on Highway 6.
Elevation change: Short, but substantial, drops and rises require uncanny balance and Olympian leg power.
Season: The best riding can be done from July through November when Mississippi traditionally goes through a drier season.

Your ears get pinned back on descents such as this at
Trace State Park.

Services: All services are found in Tupelo.

Hazards: The ice storm of February 1994 closed off many sections of trails,
but they are being reopened gradually. Check with the park ranger at the
entrance to get the latest information on any subsequent openings or closings;
ice storms are regular levelers of pine forests—and trail blockers—in this
region. Roots exposed on hillsides and wet bottoms can give the inexperienced
biker fits.

Rescue index: Although these trails are in a state park, some are remote
enough to require several hours to bring about a rescue.

Land status: Trace State Park is owned and operated by the Mississippi State
Park System.

Maps: Stop and go inside the park office and ask for the map of Trace State
Park showing the mountain bike trails located on it.

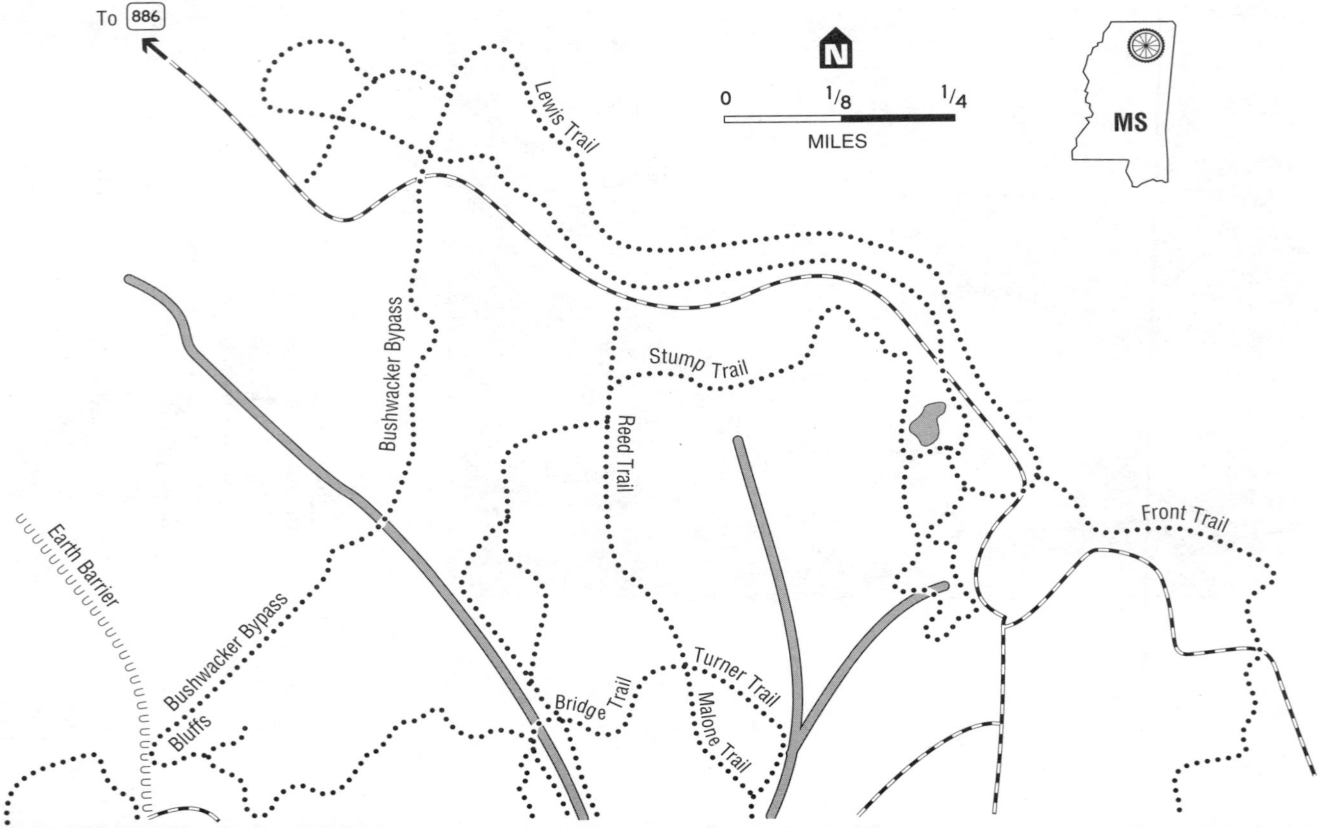

MS

N

0   1/8   1/4
MILES

To 886

Front Trail

Stump Trail

Lewis Trail

Reed Trail

Turner Trail

Malone Trail

Bridge Trail

Bushwacker Bypass

Bushwacker Bypass

Bluffs

Earth Barrier

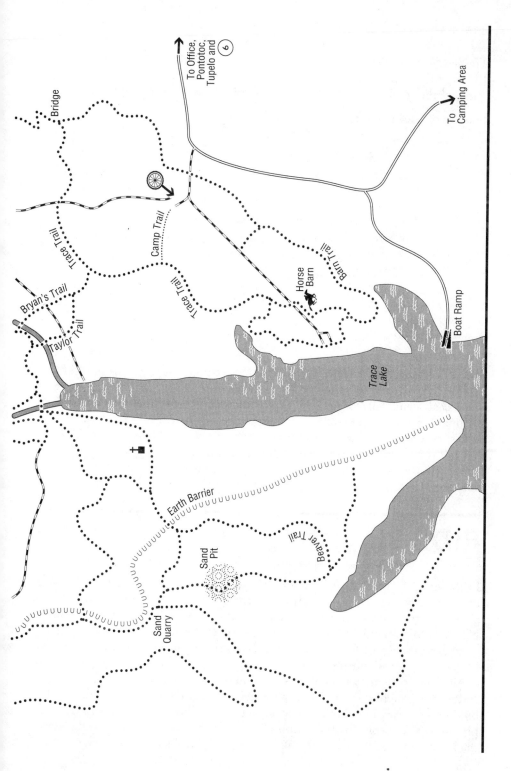

Bridge

Trace Trail

Bryan's Trail

Taylor Trail

Camp Trail

Trace Trail

Horse Barn

Barn Trail

To Office, Pontotoc, Tupelo and

⑥

To Camping Area

Boat Ramp

Trace Lake

Earth Barrier

Beaver Trail

Sand Pit

Sand Quarry

145

Finding the trail: After stopping at the office and paying your user's fee, head toward the campground. The road to the trailhead is marked in the left-hand curve of the road. Take it and park at the top of the hill near the pavilion.

Sources of additional information:

Trace State Park
Route 1, Box 254
Belden, MS 38826
(601) 489-2958

Bicycle Shop and Racquets, Inc.
1143 Main Street
Tupelo, MS 38801
(601) 842-7341

Bicycle Pacelines
1905 Holly Hill Drive
Tupelo, MS 38801
(601) 844-8660

Notes on the trail: Bikers of all kinds (motorized and non-) come from all over to ride the wide-ranging trails at Trace. Because of their being adapted to the more challenging hill climbs desired by motorcyclists, some trails may be totally unsuitable for your skill level. But with such a wide assortment to choose from, who's to complain? If you'd rather not venture onto Bushwhacker Trail, you can opt for Bushwhacker Bypass or Bridge Trail, or take Swamp Trail where there is no bridge. Pick your path and immerse yourself—literally at times—in double-tracks along high dry ridges and through low bogs.

RIDE 36 *NATCHEZ TRACE*

In the early 1930s a man by the name of Jeff Busby worked diligently for travelers of all sorts for generations to come. The result of his effort is the greatest single piece of roadwork ever preserved. Stretching from just outside Natchez, Mississippi, in the southwest, nearly to Nashville, Tennessee, in the northeast, the Trace follows over 400 miles of the ancient trading route of Native Americans and early settlers.

Although primarily intended to accommodate noncommercial motorized traffic, the Natchez Trace is also an official bike route used by hundreds of bikers each year. Lori Finley's excellent book on biking the Natchez Trace provides all the spin for those times when you have a hankering to replace the knobs for 1.25 or 1.5 slicks. While the thought of sharing so many miles

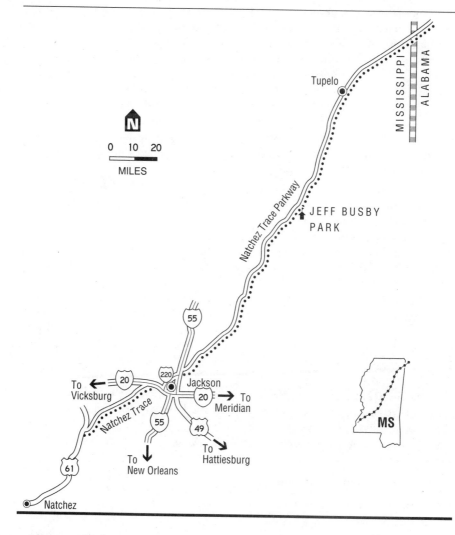

with motorized companions may put some people off, travel on the Trace is an enriching biking experience.

Sections of the Old Trace have been marked along the way, which can be ridden short distances by mountain bike. Although not recommended by this biker, a horse trail called Witch Dance (off the Natchez Trace and south of Tupelo and Davis Lake Recreation Area) can be ridden by the biker undaunted by large potholes and otherwise hoofed-up pathways. You'll wind up finding out why it's called "witch dance."

General location: The Natchez Trace begins 8 miles northwest of Natchez, Mississippi, and heads northeast, bisecting the state of Mississippi until it clips off the northwest corner of Alabama before heading into Tennessee.

Elevation change: The city of Natchez lies 100 feet above sea level, and Woodall Mountain just off the Trace near Tishomingo is the highest point in Mississippi at 806 feet. Generally, the farther you go northeast, the higher the elevation. No dramatic elevation changes occur along the Natchez Trace.

Season: The spring and fall offer the best scenery and color. The annual Bike Across Mississippi (BAM) is scheduled for the second weekend in October and is organized by Le Fleur's Bluff Bicycle Club in Jackson.

Services: All services are available at regular intervals, usually short distances off the Trace; however, some services may be obtained only after traveling upwards of 8 miles off the route.

Hazards: Of course, you must contend with motorized vehicles going the posted speed of 50 mph down the 22-foot wide highway. Finding your way around Jackson can be testy at best.

Rescue index: Help is usually not far away. However, if you become someone's hood ornament, the phone number FOR EMERGENCIES ONLY on the Trace, (800) 300-7275, won't do you any good at all.

Land status: The Natchez Trace is a unit of the National Park System

Maps: The Natchez Trace Parkway Bicycle Route map is an essential guide for anyone planning a trip on the Trace. This can be ordered by sending a $2 check payable to Eastern National Park Association at the Natchez Trace Parkway address below. Include a note requesting the map along with your address. The Bicycle Bypass put out by Le Fleur's Bluff Bicycle Club is indispensable for getting around Jackson on a bicycle.

Finding the trail: Travel Highway 61 north out of Natchez and follow the signs for Mississippi's southern terminus. Take Highway 72 either east out of Corinth, Mississippi, or west out of Tuscumbia, Alabama, until you see the signs pointing out the northeasternmost Mississippi intersection of the Natchez Trace .

Sources of additional information:

Natchez Trace Parkway
RR 1, NT-143
Tupelo, MS 38801
(800) 305-7417

Le Fleur's Bluff Bicycle Club
P.O. Box 515
Jackson, MS 39205
(601) 372-8949

Notes on the trail: Three hundred miles of The Natchez Trace run through Mississippi, less the 23.3 miles around Jackson where alternate routes must

Part of the Old Trace you can explore on the
Natchez Trace.

be used in order to reconnect. Although this is primarily a route designed for
thin tires, rather than knobbies, sections of the Old Trace can be explored—
sometimes for several miles—which require an off-road bike.

RIDE 37 *GREAT RIVER ROAD STATE PARK*

There is only one great river road, the Mississippi River itself, and you probably won't ever ride a trail closer to its mighty currents than at this state park.
Its distant location, 20 miles west of Cleveland, Mississippi, home of Delta
State University, prompted the ranger at the park to tell me, "We have a lot
of people pass us by."

RIDE 37 *GREAT RIVER ROAD STATE PARK*

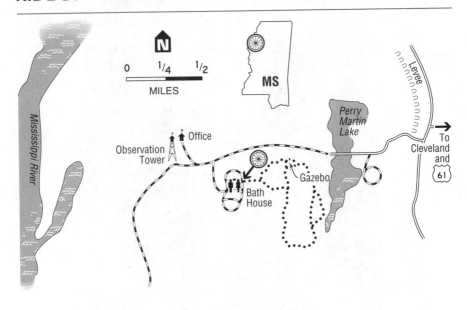

Although it is remotely situated on the river side of the levee, the Great River Road State Park is worth the trip for the mountain biker who is looking for a true taste of the old cotton fields back home. The trip north from Natchez on Highway 61 shows why this land has been, and still is, heavily farmed—tractors can plow in fifteenth gear it's so flat. Mountain bikers experiencing the short, 1.5-mile single-track leading from the camping area to Perry Martin Lake can likewise run in a high gear, providing the flood waters have not left behind a fresh deposit a gooey silt.

Just across the river in Arkansas, the famous White River, destination of the true trout fisher, empties its flow into the Mississippi just upriver of the confluence with the Arkansas River. Check the weather reports before deciding to make this park your stop; rainy spells will show you why the bath house is set up on 15-foot-high stilts. As a result, spring is not the best time to plan a bike ride here. Even if the Mississippi is in its banks, the mud left behind is slow to dry and quick to stick to your tires. But despite these adverse conditions for biking, do try to be one of those who "don't pass by."

General location: This infrequently visited state park lies west of Rosedale at the end of Highway 8, 20 miles west of Cleveland, Mississippi, home of Delta State University.

Rolling between the levee and the river, Great River Road State Park.

Elevation change: Very doggone little.

Season: This is the tough part. If you arrive when the water's up, forget it. You can only ride the trails when long periods of the Mississippi in its banks have occurred, which coincide roughly with election years.

Services: Cleveland and its university atmosphere seem oddly out of place, but can provide you with a source of many supplies. Rosedale is a small town where just the basics can be had.

Hazards: Getting swept away or stuck in mud present the primary hazards, both of which are easily avoided. But you should call ahead of time if you aren't keeping track of what the Mississippi is doing; the park does close due to floods.

Rescue index: This is a remote park.

Land status: This is a Mississippi State Park.

Maps: Maps of the state park, showing the nature trail (as it is called in park parlance), are available at the park's office.

Finding the trail: After entering the park, turn into the campground and travel counterclockwise around the campsite loop. Just about directly opposite of where you entered the campground is a brown railing masquerading as a type of bridge. This is the trailhead leading to the gazebo less than a mile away.

Sources of additional information: The toll-free number for Mississippi's State Parks is (800) 467-2757.

Great River Road State Park
P.O. Box 292
Rosedale, MS 38769
(601) 759-6752

Notes on the trail: Despite the difficulties associated with finding a dry enough time to ride in this park, it is a rewarding experience. The trails cut through lush river bottom land with cottonwoods turning late spring into a flurry of snowy seed pods floating through the air. The huge maples and oaks hang out boughs where a myriad of melodious songbirds chortle, cluck, and coo the whole day through. Plus, there's just something about riding a bike so close to the mighty Mississippi.

ALABAMA

When over 50,000 square miles were lopped off the original Georgia territory to set the borders of the Yellowhammer State in 1817, the smell of gunpowder still hung in the air from battles with the Creek Indians. To the west, Mississippi had already become a state as negotiations with the Spanish were completed for Perdido Bay in Mobile. When Alabama finally came into the union in 1819, it was already established as an agricultural power in the production of cotton and would remain one until the lowly weevil—combined with the crippling effects of the Civil War—forced pursuit of other industries.

Mountain bikers who take the time to explore the entire length of the state will discover a great change in the topography from north to south. Up north in Birmingham, where agriculture comes harder due to the uneven, steep terrain, mining discovered rich deposits of limestone, coal, and iron ore. In 1880 the first blast furnace was built in Birmingham, which went on to become a major producer of steel and iron. If this development had happened 20 years earlier, the Civil War could have wrought much bigger changes than it did in this land whose motto is, "We dare defend our rights."

The Tennessee River Valley Authority gave rise to numerous dams along the Tennessee River in the northern part of the state, and made production of hydroelectric power a principal industry. Perhaps it was this availability of cheap energy and technology—along with nearby Birmingham's steel—which encouraged national officials in 1949 to locate a primary aerospace research and development center in Huntsville.

The Bankhead National Forest in Alabama's northwest corner commands over 180,000 acres of rough and ready terrain for exploration on a mountain bike. As with all national forests, it is managed with an eye to timber: over two billion board feet per year. The resulting access roads that cut across many of its ridges and slopes await the adventurous biker who is attuned to the older, overgrown roads of the earlier logging of 50 years ago. That is, if the more modern, gravel byways are not to your liking.

Unfortunately, the rockier, bygone days are what crop up in many people's minds when Alabama is mentioned. Civil War and civil rights are an inseparable fact of Alabama's history, but recent times have served to ease many of the tensions created by demagogues at university doors and the occasional redneck playing the devil with firehoses. Most Alabamans, instead, have focused their sights on the dreams set in motion by a brave woman, Rosa Parks, whose footsore fatigue became a wellspring of energy for an entire country's attempt at social equality.

Motorists crossing the state line on interstates may glance at the "Alabama the Beautiful" welcome signs and consider it pure hype. But after taking a year to seek out the backroads and small towns to find places to straddle my saddle, I discovered that this phrase was understatement. Alabama has beauty cascading not only from rock cliffs, but also meandering through coastal plains and cane thickets.

This is an ancient land first settled by people who cleared the thickets over 17,000 years ago and built mounds in celebration. More recently, it is a place which gave rise to incredible genius and talent. Who can look at the life of Helen Keller, born in Tuscumbia, Alabama, and not be inspired to perform great feats? The young Henry Aaron, playing stickball on the streets of Mobile, overcame the prejudice of a country to become an inspiration to millions. My childhood days were likewise driven by the image of Willie Mays breaking at the sound of a baseball no one else could've caught . . . and catching it.

Helen Keller, Hank Aaron, Willie Mays, Hank Williams, Tallulah Bankhead, Booker T. Washington, George Washington Carver, Harper Lee, Nat King Cole, Bo Jackson, Hugo Black, and Jesse Owens are just a few who sunk their roots deep into the fertile soil of their Alabaman Imagination and drove themselves to achieve what others said they could not—and would not—achieve. That's Alabama for you. Land of possibilities limited only by the ability to dream. Ride it; you'll like it.

Huntsville Area Rides

John Hunt, Huntsville's first settler and the community coroner, probably would not be let down by the way his settlement has turned out. Besides having one of Alabama's oldest state parks, the site of a spectacular mountain bike trail, Huntsville has had a commanding influence in our country's space program since 1949 when Redstone Rocket Center was established. Today, at One Tranquility Base, the U.S. Space & Rocket Center not only contains a complete space museum—advertised by an ominous-looking SR-71 Blackbird parked out front—but also Marshall Space Flight Center is stationed on the premises as a command post for shuttle and other space missions.

A tour of the high-tech facility takes a good portion of the day and comes strongly recommended. Take the bus tour of missiles and check out the special exhibits. One exhibit, the moon landing's twenty-fifth anniversary, was being celebrated while I was there. The cultural trappings of the late 1960s that surrounded the moon mission, complete with a drum set from The Beatles, were on display in the upstairs hall. I suggest packing a picnic just so you can eat lunch beside one of the Titan boosters. After lunch, file into the theater, lean back in a comfy chair, and watch one of the neat space movies on the largest indoor dome screen in the southeast, OMNIMAX.

To the west, the Tennessee Valley Authority dammed the Tennessee River to make the Wheeler impoundment, backing up the river for 74 miles. Southeast of Huntsville, Guntersville Dam creates 30 more miles of lake from the Tennessee River. The only area where the Tennessee flows unimpeded in Alabama lies just south of Huntsville as it makes the turn from southeast to head northwest into Tennessee at Pickwick.

Before this river leaves Alabama, it sluices past Tuscumbia, then falls through Muscle Shoals, dropping 134 feet in 37 miles. This region is rich in history other than the hydroelectric sort; it's home to Ivy Green (Helen Keller's birthplace), Alabama Music Hall of Fame (Hank Williams, W.C. Handy, Tammy Wynette, Emmylou Harris, The Commodores), and the Key Underwood Coon Dog Memorial Graveyard.

Those who consider mentioning that a coon dog memorial is immaterial to Southern culture need to read *Where the Red Fern Grows*. Few possessions are more precious to a true Southern man than his dog, beginning with the redbones and blueticks that bay the night away as they lead lamplit hunting parties through the woods. This is good to remember if you ride at night and hear a sound like the hounds of Baskerville are upon you. They're probably only coon dogs.

Another place you're likely to run into all things wild is the Bankhead National Forest, southwest of Huntsville. Remote and scenic, the Bankhead holds a wealth of wilderness for the biker who wants to make an extended stay. Just on the western fringe of the forest, the country's longest natural bridge east of the Rockies—60 feet high and 148 feet long—spans some of the most beautiful countryside in the Yellowhammer State.

To Huntsville's southeast lies the mountain town of Gadsden, named for the politician James Gadsden who negotiated the deal with Mexico to purchase the southern section of Arizona and New Mexico (for a cool $50 million) in what is known as—what else?—the Gadsden Purchase. In this east Alabama town a long knuckle of the Cumberland Plateau has been traversed for centuries by Native Americans and settlers alike. Now called Lookout Mountain Trail, it is a popular destination for bikers, hikers, climbers, and spelunkers.

Huntsville served as Alabama's first capital from 1819–1820, during the time when Alabama became the twenty-second state. The brief tenure as capital may have resulted from Huntsville's confusing traffic engineering. Anything as frustrating as Huntsville traffic must have been a long time in the making. But once you're off onto the backroads and bike trails of north Alabama, reasons surface for making Huntsville a biking capital. The cool forests, dark river corridors, and airy ridges have all the ingredients for the ideal mountain bike ride. You need hunt no further.

For more information:

> World Class Bicycles
> 7950 Highway 72 West Madison
> Huntsville, AL 35802
> (205) 430-0033

> Bicycles, Etc., Inc.
> 8100 Memorial Parkway
> Huntsville, AL 35802-3037
> (205) 881-6947

> The Pedaler
> 9009 Memorial Parkway
> Huntsville, AL 35802-3019
> (205) 880-1350

> The Outdoor Omnibus
> 2806 Memorial Parkway
> Huntsville, AL 35801-5654
> (205) 533-4131

> Werner's Hardware
> 1115 4th Street
> Cullman, AL 35055-3329
> (205) 734-5673

Madison County Convention and Visitors Bureau
700 Monroe Street, Department A
Huntsville, AL 35801
(800) 772-2348

RIDE 38 *MONTE SANO STATE PARK*

Few places will surpass the natural beauty of Monte Sano, a park on the southern side of Huntsville, Alabama. The 7.5 miles of rocky single-track, where mountain bikes can make the loop on Mountain Mist Trail at approximately 1,600 feet above sea level, comes close to Appalachian Trail scenery. The only objects higher than you are the rockets tracked at the nearby Space and Rocket Center . . . or maybe the wild goats who live here. The difficulty of parts of the trail will make you wish you had a mountain goat's sure, cloven-hoofed purchase and climbing strength.

This park has been around since the mid-1930s when the Civilian Conservation Corps fought the Depression and created art. Native stones and logs were hewn into shape to construct the buildings at the park. The cabins and taverns even contain beautiful handmade pieces of furniture, something the CCC is not noted for.

What I remember most about this trail, though, is the scenery. Large and graceful oaks and maples, undisturbed for over 60 years, spread bodacious boughs over road and trail alike. Although your typical furry critters have made Monte Sano home, the quiet seclusion of these woods works as a magnet for birds. Summer tanagers, blue jays, brown thrashers, and wood thrushes warble, cluck, and chirp endless daytime melodies.

But my favorite sighting at Monte Sano occurred one morning when two male cardinals squared off and flew into each other, breast to breast. They parried like this for several minutes until I moved and startled them. If each had been equally stubborn about his territory, the joust could have taken days. At my home one summer, a cardinal flew into a large window, pulling up at the last second and pasting a wax-print of scapulars on the window in a violent thrust of wings. Its automatic battle began at first light and continued until last—every day—for three months. Since then, I've regarded cardinals and their tenacity, however misdirected, with much greater respect.

Also worthy of our mountain biking respect are the volunteers of the Spring City Cycle Club. One such volunteer, Keith, has been the prime trail designer in this rocky land. After Keith's first trail was put in and named "Keith's Trail," he put in another ("K2"), then another ("K3"), and most recently adapted the trail used by the wild goats living among the precipices to add an additional 3.5 miles to an already extensive network of over 20 miles.

The sky above and ground below embrace the biker at Monte Sano.

General location: Find this trail south of Huntsville city limits, high atop one of the last fingers of the Lookout Mountain range.

Elevation change: There is significant elevation change at Monte Sano.

Season: Except for extremes in temperature and moisture, you should have no trouble riding this trail year-round.

Services: Huntsville is a big place and can accommodate most of your needs; however, you'll have to contend with the confusing layout of some of the major roads if you need to run back to town from Monte Sano. Plan on at least a half-hour round-trip ride down the mountain in order to get to most stores. Late one Friday afternoon in Huntsville traffic looking for a Wal-Mart, I felt transferred to highway hell. When I came to, I was somewhere north of Redstone Arsenal.

Hazards: Large rocks, a-la-Appalachian Trail, can turn a front tire as easily as an ankle. Loose rock outcrops on steep slopes give no traction.

Rescue index: Rangers patrol the park constantly. Whistles, bells, or flares should bring 'em in.

Land status: State park.

Maps: The office outside the camping area check-in has the map for Monte Sano State Park inside and other mountain biking information posted on the bulletin board outside. Those desiring more detailed topographic info can consult the Huntsville quad in the 7.5 minute series. Monte Sano's trail system is, like many others in the Deep South, in a state of transition. Much of the

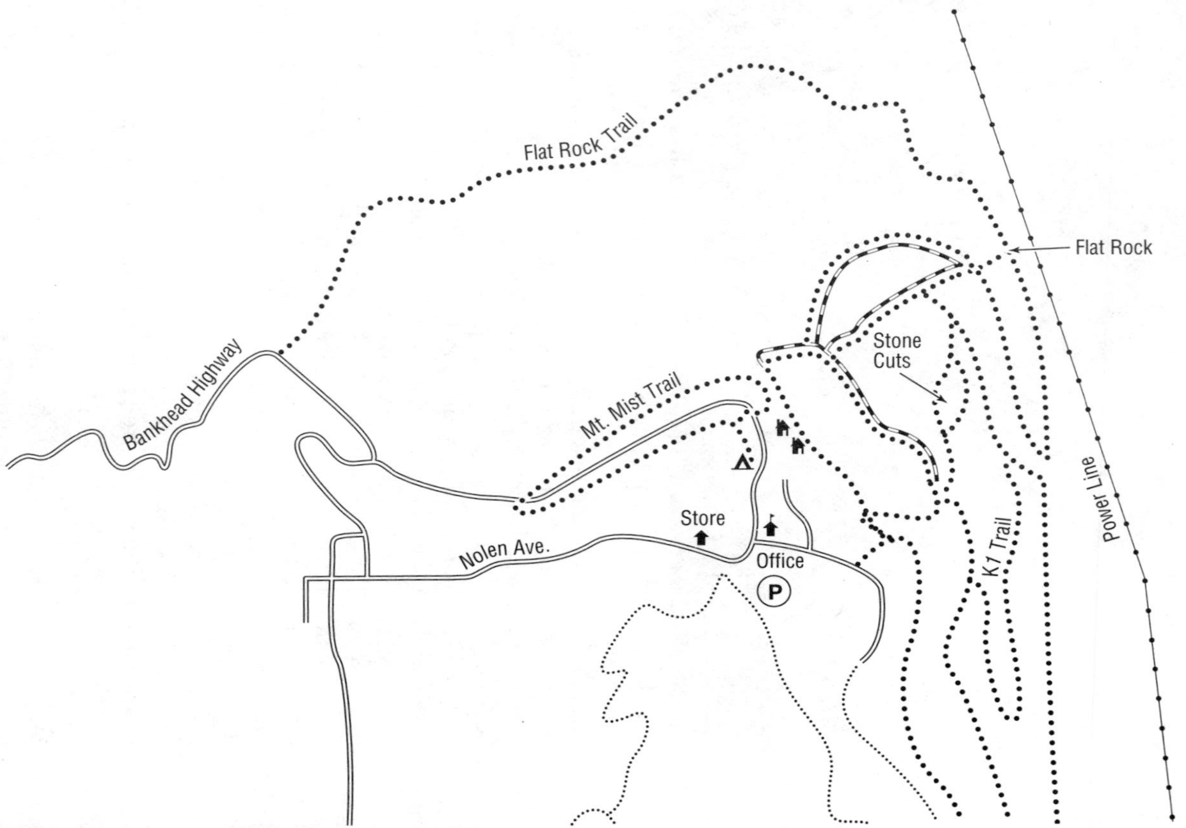

RIDE 38 *MONTE SANO STATE PARK*

Flat Rock

Power Line

K1 Trail

Stone
Cuts

Office

P

Store

Flat Rock Trail

Mt. Mist Trail

Nolen Ave.

Bankhead Highway

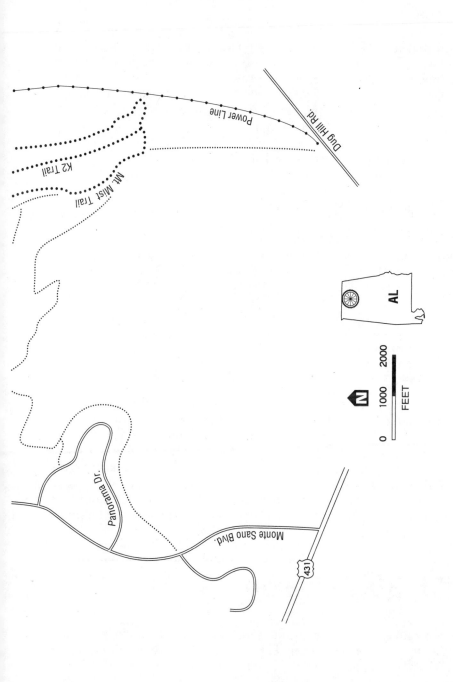

single-track that can be ridden does not appear on the park's "official" map. Another survey of Monte Sano's trail system is scheduled to be published in the near future. When it is completed, visitors will be able to use the new map to direct them to Flat Rock Trail, 2 flat rocks—1 the size of a football field, and the other about ⅓ of a gridiron. Until then, you can contact Spring City Cycle Club and obtain an updated map of Monte Sano.

Finding the trail: Take Highway 431 south out of Huntsville, following the signs to Monte Sano State Park. Turn left at the light at the top of the mountain and follow the signs to the entrance. Parking is on the right across the street from the country store. Ride your bike down to the lookoff. The single-track begins on the left before the gated road.

Sources of additional information:

Spring City Cycle Club
P.O. Box 2231
Huntsville, AL 35804
(205) 533-5050 (Greg Dempsey)

Monte Sano State Park
5105 Nolen Road
Huntsville, AL 35801
(205) 534-3757

Notes on the trail: The trail takes off on single-track at the Black Walnut Trailhead (blazed yellow) across from the parking lot at the "Look Offs." It descends on a narrow, worn, rock-strewn pathway until crossing the road at the bottom. Mountain Mist Trail (blazed orange) begins after the second fork on the right. Its 5.5 miles contain open understory among massive trees. Many forks split off and lead into strange and exotic rock formations, some on single-track and others on double-track service roads turning into single-track from use by mountain bikes. Some trails have been set aside for hiking only, basically the ones closer to the park's entrance.

RIDE 39 *BUCK'S POCKET*

The steep canyon formations in this gorgeous state park provide a rugged place to roll your knobbies. The trail that will be used most by bikers goes out to the primitive camping area on a wide, rough double-track of 2.5 miles out-and-back (five miles total) that can accommodate four-wheel-drive vehicles. The rest of the five trails—open to mountain bikes—are better suited for walking, although I was able to ride short sections of each.

RIDE 39 *BUCK'S POCKET*

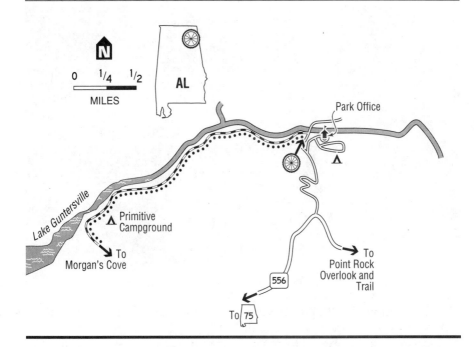

The park, traditionally a retreat for defeated politicians, got its name based on an old Native American legend. Apparently, a hunting party cornered a monstrous buck at the edge of one of the many precipices. Instead of taking an arrow in the heart, the buck leaped to his death. The picture of a flying buck will be easy to imagine as you ride along this rocky region, a northern extension of the formations found south of here at Cherokee Rock Village.

Springtime riders will see a mature hardwood forest of beech, butternut, and blackjack oak sprouting leaves over thick stands of foam flower and wild blue phlox. The boulder-strewn streambed (on the right, headed in) floods during and after periods of heavy rains. Eagles fly over their winter homes here, close to Lake Guntersville, a huge impoundment of the Tennessee River.

It will seem like a world away from the "peace and tranquility" of Buck's Pocket, but after a ride you may want to swing by the town that became an outlet, Boaz, Alabama. Hundreds of stores open their doors as cut-price sites for common and obscure items you may have been waiting to buy. A tiny book store had a good bike repair book I bought to take along with me on the trail. It proved to be an economical investment; by following the easy steps, I am now competent to repair most ills that befall my bike.

The backwaters of Lake Guntersville, Buck's Pocket.

General location: Buck's Pocket State Park is north of Gadsden and south of Lake Guntersville, located in 3 counties: Dekalb, Jackson, and Marshall.

Elevation change: Some of the trails change vertically over 400 feet; the one described in this book—Primitive Campground Trail—has only short sections of significant elevation change, that is, unless you make the rocky way to Morgan's Cove.

Season: I had to reschedule a trip to Buck's Pocket once because the park was under several feet of water. Call ahead to make sure the water's down.

Services: Try to get all supplies stocked before arriving at Buck's Pocket. A few small stores are found closer, but if you need much more than a loaf of white bread or some gas, you'll have to make the long trip back to Gadsden or the somewhat shorter drive to Guntersville.

Hazards: For those who ride with the balance of a mountain goat, you will be right at home on the softball-size stones frequently found where I wanted to place my tires.

Rescue index: Civilization is nearby; however, the roads take a circuitous route getting there. Park rangers would most likely hear a well-blown whistle anywhere in the park.

Land status: This park is part of the Alabama State Park System.

Maps: The office by the campground has the map of the park's trails. They are fine reproductions of the topo maps of the area. Each of the 5 trails is clearly marked on the map.

Finding the trail: Follow the frequent signs pointing the way to Buck's Pocket off Highways 75 and 431. Or you can travel on Highway 227 out of Gadsden or Guntersville. Once inside the park, go past the right turn to the office. Park on the left in the next curve. The trail goes off to the left.

Sources of additional information:

Buck's Pocket State Park
Route 1, Box 36
Grove Oak, AL 35975
(205) 659-2000

Boaz Chamber of Commerce
306 West Mann Avenue
P.O. Box 563
Boaz, AL 35957
(205) 593-8154

Notes on the trail: The old roadbed that serves as the trail is wide and easily ridden for its 2.5 miles one-way (5 miles total on the out-and-back) to the primitive camping area. From the campground on, many more rocks need to be avoided and ridden over on the way to Morgan's Cove, 3.5 miles away. Maintaining traction and balance becomes a problem even for the experienced biker. In places, the double-track resembles one of the creekbeds coming off the mountains. Rock ledges of a foot or higher are not uncommon, giving the kamikaze cranker plenty of opportunity for excitement.

RIDE 40 *CHIGGER RIDGE*

Deep South mountain bikers who get the itch for thigh-groaning climbs can take the Redbug Express out to Chigger Ridge. This network of ATV and motorcycle trails just off Interstate 65 south of Cullman, Alabama, contains launching pads where experiments can be run to find out how close to vertical you can ride your bike. Nearly 15 miles can be put together in the two basically single-track loops (six miles in the southern trail, almost nine miles in the northern loop at the end of an approach along the powerline), which are as demanding as anything you will ride in the Deep South.

If you show up on a weekend, be prepared to find it busy with vehicles zooming up, down, and around the various loops curling through thin woods. The best time for mountain biking this trail falls on Monday through Friday. Although it takes some high-octane hormones to do it, I know of at least one mountain biker who mixes it up with the gassers and loves it. He says he's going to place a shrine where bikers of both sorts can deposit significant relics, like broken spokes, chains, and Gonzo rings.

RIDE 40 *CHIGGER RIDGE*

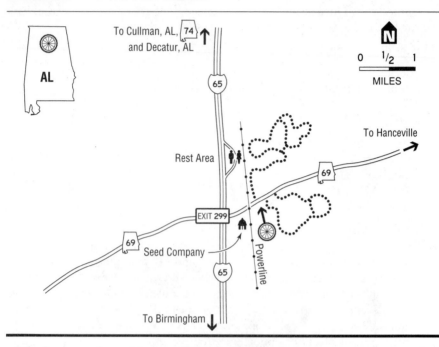

The bottom of your shorts will probably be what gets put on display after riding down Chigger Ridge's "Rocket Chair." Although you will be headed toward Mother Earth after you lift off, this steep section of heavily rutted trail could be used as a site to challenge the world's speed record for mountain bikes: currently 111 mph by French biker, Christian Taillefer. That's no escargot!

General location: This trail system lies east of I-65 and south of Cullman, Alabama, on both sides of the road to Hanceville, Alabama.

Elevation change: Don't show up expecting to crank up everything put in front of you on this trail. In fact, you may want to consider getting off your bike and doing a combo walk-slide up and down some of the more extreme slopes. Then again, this type of elevation change may be exactly what you grease your chain for.

Season: Motorized vehicles should be avoided when they're in season, usually on weekends. Rain does not treat the treeless sections of trail with much kindness.

Services: Cullman is a fairly large town and should be able to provide what's needed in most cases; however, Birmingham lies not too far to the south on speedy I-65.

Hazards: Big potholes can be more than a nuisance, as can the machines that are responsible for making the majority of them. Steep slopes and wide ruts call for equal amounts of courage and skill . . . and discretion. Know when it's OK to say, "I'm walking down this one today, Bubba!"

Rescue index: If you shot off a flare, you could have the entire Alabama National Guard to you in no time.

Land status: My sources and detective's sense both failed me on this one, folks. I could in no way see any signs preventing public access. I will continue to investigate, but if you find out before the next edition comes out, let me know.

Maps: No maps, to my knowledge, have been made available for this course other than the one made from my notes. The Hanceville 7.5 minute series quad depicts this area.

Finding the trail: Take I-65 south out of Cullman. Exit on #299, which is right after the interstate rest area. Turn left (east) after stopping and pass the seed company on the right. Look for the bare clay banks going up a power-line right-of-way on the left. Across the road on the right more trails perform pretzel logic in and out of the pine forest.

Sources of additional information:

Werner's Hardware
1115 4th Street SW
Cullman, AL 35055
(205) 734-5673

Notes on the trail: Begin your ride by taking the single-track on the right side of the road heading in (opposite the interstate). Ride past the high bank on the left and take the path going behind it. This loop continues through a young pine forest with a couple of intersections. The trail leading off to the right climbs along the side of the hill and hooks back into the main trail close to the highway. You can ride several loops on this side of the highway, amounting to about 5 miles all said and done.

On the other side of the highway (interstate side), you will immediately see the steep and wide double-track leading up a powerline right-of-way. Ride it if you can. Once you get on top of the ridge, the trail goes off toward the interstate rest area. After arriving at the rest area, you can turn around the way you came for the thrill of the ride as you fly, more than ride, down the powerline right-of-way. YEE-HAA! Look, Ma, no brakes!

RIDE 41 CLEAR CREEK

Don't get on the phone and call NORBA to tell them you have found the perfect site for next year's Finals. A challenging course this is not. In fact, when I talked to someone about riding this one-mile out-and-back trail, I was told it is so accommodating you can complete the two miles (total) in a wheelchair. I

RIDE 41 *CLEAR CREEK*

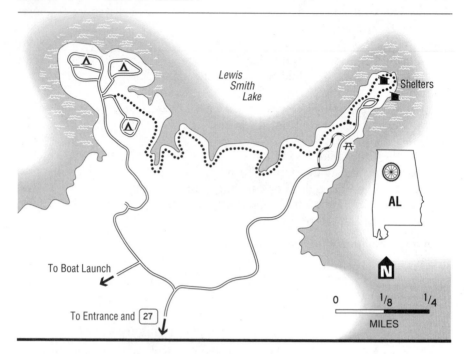

Lewis
Smith
Lake

Shelters

AL

To Boat Launch

To Entrance and 27

N

0   1/8   1/4

MILES

wouldn't necessarily suggest that (although I know people who can take a wheelchair in places I would fear to tread), but it is true the wide, short trail leading from the campground to the beach makes a scenic spot for a beginner to get a taste of what mountain biking is like.

A National Forest Recreational Area, Clear Creek offers enough in the way of family fun to keep everyone happy while the more hard-core bikers do nearby exploration on abandoned single-track leading off Forest Service roads. Swimming, fishing, hiking, boating, camping, and picnicking are just some of the other activities to enjoy after a hard ride.

But if you're like me, a quiet ride along the shores of Lake Lewis Smith at dusk does more than a Goody's for unwinding those stress knots in the neck. I stopped by a large beech and was looking out across the water when I heard the unmistakable sound of a barred owl calling, "Who-cooks-for-you, who-cooks-for you-all?" I was not lonely, but I wanted to see if I could call in Mr. Owl. I began my un-owl-like hooting, trying for all the world to mimic Mrs. Owl.

I was not convinced and stopped after a couple-three rounds. Just as I was about to swing my leg over and remount my bike, my heart nearly flew out of my throat as I saw a large, dark figure float silently on a bough twenty yards away. "Mr. Owl," I thought, "is lonely tonight and looking for Ms. Right."

Screech in a beech—do not disturb!

As he began his call again, I could feel the powerful hoots vibrate in my chest. Sometimes descending a single-track in a quest for a new personal record for speed, or balance, or endurance matters little. Sometimes all it takes is for something to give a hoot.

General location: This trail is found slightly northwest of Birmingham near Jasper, Alabama, off Highway 195.

Elevation change: No appreciable change occurs.

Season: This trail has an all-weather track.

Services: For the basics, Jasper can provide that forgotten can of beanie-weenies, but if you want knockwurst, head over to Birmingham. The recreational area has water, rest rooms, camping, and showers.

Hazards: The 2.5-mile Raven Trail is for foot travel only. The bike trail is open for bikers—and hikers—of all ages. Be alert for the unpredictable actions of a surprised walker; they sometimes impersonate an armadillo or opossum and try to get run over.

Rescue index: Few places in the Deep South will allow an easier rescue.
Land status: National Forest Recreational Area.
Maps: You can pick up a map of the entire Clear Creek facility at the entrance station or at the Ranger District Office at Double Springs.
Finding the trail: Leave Jasper, Alabama, headed north on Highway 195 to Manchester. Turn right onto Walker County Road 27. The entrance is 8.5 miles down this road. After entering and paying a fee, take the left at the fork toward the campground. Take the right into Fawn Loop where the trail begins on the left in between site 65D and 67D. The other trailhead can be reached by going to the beach and parking.

Sources of additional information: Reservations for camping at this area can be made by calling (800) 280-2267.

> Bankhead National Forest
> P.O. Box 278 (South Main Street)
> Double Springs, AL 35553
> (205) 489-5111

Notes on the trail: This short out-and-back hugs the southern shore of lake Lewis Smith.

RIDE 42 *BRUSHY LAKE*

This National Recreation Area in the William Bankhead National Forest by itself does not represent much of a challenge to a serious mountain biker wanting to bust a lung and stretch a thigh. However, the 33-acre lake and nine primitive camp spots do satisfy the need for a staging area to arrange some physically challenging rides nearby. The half-mile one-way (one mile total) paved path leading to the dam from the campground and two gravel roads (a one-eighth-mile loop and a quarter-mile out-and-back) within the area present a good setting for beginning bikers of any age to practice.

The roar of Brushy Creek spilling over the dam at the end of the path fades into the background as dusk falls. It seems every frog in Alabama contributes to the palpable, rhythmic ribbiting of summer nights along the shore. The very air heaves in croaks of thunder, making conversation forced. For those who enjoy a frog leg or two on the supper plate, this is the place to come.

An old gentleman arrived one evening with his son, a flat-bottomed boat, a powerful headlamp, and a deft wrist on the other end of a pole equipped with a three-pronged gig. I sat around the campfire for more than three hours watching the gigger's light circle the lake. Occasionally, sections of the lake fell silent and the light wiggled. Across the water I could hear something plop into the bottom of the boat.

RIDE 42   *BRUSHY LAKE*

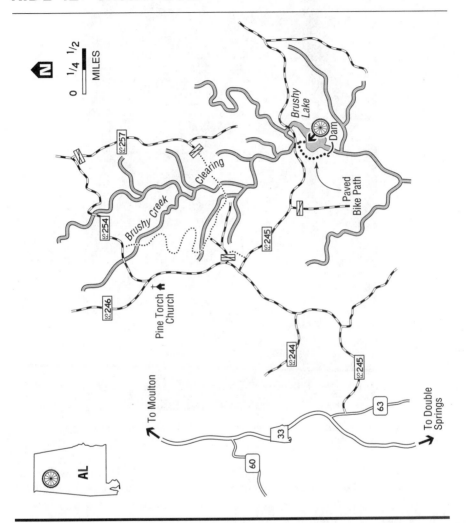

General location: This trail is located in the northern half of the 180,000 acres of the William Bankhead National Forest.

Elevation change: Nothing steep and nothing long is on this short trail.

Season: It is an all-season trail.

Services: Get your services taken care of before you head out to Brushy Lake. This is a remote area. Water can be drawn from the area's spigots. Showers, cold as well diggers' feet, are available in the bathhouse.

Hazards: Any biker with more than rank beginner's skills will have no trouble on this trail.

Rock cliffs vibrate to the sound of bullfrogs at night—
Brushy Lake.

Rescue index: You will have a long ride back to Double Springs where the closest medical facilities exist. If anyone else is using the area, your call for help will be easily heard as it echoes off the cliffs nearby.

Land status: This is National Forest land.

Maps: The only map available for this area is the Bankhead National Forest map, which you can get at the new National Forest headquarters in Double Springs.

Finding the trail: Leave Double Springs on Highway 33 heading north. Approximately 15 miles down the road, look for County Road 63 coming in from the right at a sharp angle and going to Grayson. A sign at the first gravel road (Forest Service Road 245) on the left (100 yards) points the way to Brushy Lake. About 5 miles on FS 245 look for the road sign that says Brushy Lake Road on the right. Turn down it and follow it to the entrance on the right.

Sources of additional information:

USDA Forest Service
2946 Chestnut Street
Montgomery, AL 36107-3010
(205) 832-4470

Bankhead National Forest
P.O. Box 278 (South Main Street)
Double Springs, AL 35553
(205) 489-5111

Notes on the trail: Although this trail is short, it is a good trail to discover, especially for the novices on knobby tires. The gravel roads within the recreational area wind around and through the campground so that a long loop (for short or inexperienced legs) can be put together nearby while the other family members catch 40 winks or catch one of the many fish stocked in the lake.

RIDE 43 *HOUSE TRAIL*

This trail gets its name from the Double Springs biker who (along with help from his friends) pieced together old sections of abandoned horse trail in the Brushy Lake area of the Bankhead National Forest. The single-track leads down to a small creek crossing before fording across the upper flow of Brushy Creek near the final ascent up to Forest Service Road 257; this amounts to a total of 2.5 miles one-way, five miles for the total out-and-back. Or if riding a gravel road fits the mood, a loop of a little over five miles can be completed.

You may want to take the trail back on the single-track, but by taking a left onto FS 257 and climbing the hill, an interesting visit can be made at Pine Torch Church. This church still stands from its initial construction "sometime in the 1840s." Take a moment to admire the skill used to fit and fashion the logs together; its modern counterpart is set back from the road. Inside, cattle yokes hold the incandescence of the twentieth century, but the overall atmosphere keeps pulling you back to "sometime in the 1840s."

On my first trip down the trail and onto FS 257, I came around the bend at the bottom of the hill and beheld a sight directly out of the last century: a man was working a harnessed horse pulling felled timber in between standing trees and down to his log truck. The man "talked" to his horse by whistling in different tones depending on whether he wanted the horse to stop, turn right, or turn left. Another horse, waiting his go at a log pull, stood tied to the parked log truck. During a lull, I told the man he had some beautiful horses. Showing typical mountain reserve, the man answered, "They'll do."

RIDE 43 *HOUSE TRAIL*

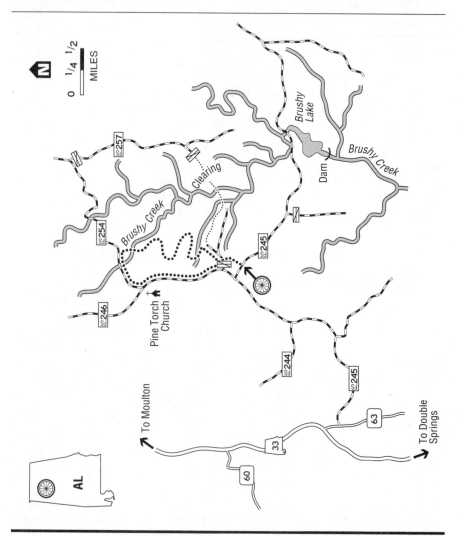

General location: The trail is a natural extension of any rides you created from Brushy Lake Recreational Area.

Elevation change: You will encounter some slopes long and steep enough to get you blowing like a horse pulling a tree. Gee! Haw!

Season: This trail gets little use and has held up well. I would say if you can make it to Brushy Lake, conditions should be right to ride this trail.

Services: Double Springs carries the basic supplies. The Brushy Lake Recreational Area has water, showers (cold water only!), and camping spots.

Hazards: The trail has some double-track which has washed out pretty badly in places. Pedal with some anticipation of these and you should maintain cycling equilibrium. Remember you are in some remote territory. Practically anything in the great woods can be spotted, from bear to bumblebee. I had an unexpected confrontation with a black hog-nosed snake just before reaching FS 257. I say it was a confrontation, but it reminded me more of two pacifists being surprised (and scared). The snake, having recently swallowed breakfast and sunning itself, slithered a few anxious feet away before coiling, flattening its head and hissing. The effect was unnerving for someone who had recently been face-to-face with a water moccasin, which is the whole idea. The snake, basically defenseless, puts on a show designed to fool the other into thinking what lies before it is an angry cottonmouth; this masquerade has probably caused many to become decapitated by scared humans. I confess I extended the snake's performance after I realized it was not poisonous. How did I know? A cottonmouth never shows you anything but its deadly, white throat and holds its ground, twitching its tail all the while. The hog-nose presents its back (and flattened head) with two faint, burnt-orange lateral stripes just below the head. Also, Brushy Lake is a little too far north for a cottonmouth, but not for its cousin, the copperhead.

Rescue index: Had I been in doubt about the snake, I would not have taken any chances. If you sent for help with a phone call from one of the houses up around the Pine Torch Church, it would take 30 minutes for help to arrive. Take extra precautions here.

Land status: This is National Forest land.

Maps: Acquire the map of the Bankhead National Forest. Although parts of this trail are leftovers from its time as a motorcycle route, no trail shows up on the map. The map in this book is made from notes gathered on the ride and use of the Bankhead National Forest map. The Grayson quadrangle topo map (7.5 minute series) would also be helpful.

Finding the trail: After turning right onto Brushy Lake Road, look for the first house on your left. Back up 20 yards and look on your left. There's a single-track coming into the road. You can pull off the road enough so traffic can get by. Or if you want to make it a longer trip, park at Brushy Lake and ride back up.

Sources of additional information:

USDA Forest Service
2946 Chestnut Street
Montgomery, AL 36107-3010
(205) 832-4470

Bankhead National Forest
P.O. Box 278 (South Main Street)
Double Springs, AL 35553
(205) 489-5111

Notes on the trail: This trail is tricky to stay on. The first time I tried it, I went straight when I should have turned left. I wound up having a great ride anyway, with an adrenaline rush from thinking I was lost. But here's the scoop.

Because there are few markers other than where tires have beat down a path, it is important to watch the trail. The first turn after beginning at the single-track on Brushy Lake Road is a right onto the rutted double-track. At the bottom of the hill, a road with a Forest Service marker goes off to the right, but you continue straight. Approximately .5 mile farther, look for an initially wide trail on the left that closes down quickly to single-track. If you miss the turn, you'll soon have to carry your bike over a deadfall. In addition, Brushy Creek at the bottom of the hill will be too large for you to cross easily, and the extremely rutted, narrow single-track on the other side of the creek cannot be ridden. So turn around, head back uphill, carry your bike over the tree again, and look to your right. You'll see it this time.

The rest of the trail is easy to stay on. It dead-ends at FS 257. Take a left toward Pine Torch Church to make a loop using the gravel roads and left again at the church. You should recognize the first gated road on your left where the first section of single-track comes into the road. Turn left, go around the gate, and right back onto the short section of trail leading back to Brushy Lake Road.

RIDE 44 OWL CREEK HORSE TRAIL

Part of the package for constructing new trails in the Bankhead National Forest includes new horse trails. As mountain bikers, we know the impractical side to riding heavily used horse trails: big potholes and muddy, chewed-up track overall. But as time goes on, and no horses use them, the trails do heal enough for a mountain bike to take over. And that's exactly what's in store for the old, closed horse trails in the Bankhead, such as Owl Creek, nearly six miles of physically demanding loop accessed by taking Forest Service Road 245 about a mile east from Brushy Lake Recreational Area.

The National Forest Service has closed these old horse trails and does not plan to maintain ones such as Owl Creek; however, an invitation is being extended to any groups or individuals to keep these trails clear for mountain biking. Unless a tornado comes like the one that hit the western section of the Bankhead in 1973 (it tracked for over 40 miles in constant contact with the ground), trails usually don't require much labor to keep them open.

With this in mind, 30 miles of single-track lie in Bankhead, open only to foot travel and mountain bikes. Frequent junctions with Forest Service roads make possible many different lengths of trail, depending on how much time and energy is available. This inheritance from the equestrians (and Uncle Sam) stands to become one of the more popular trails in Alabama.

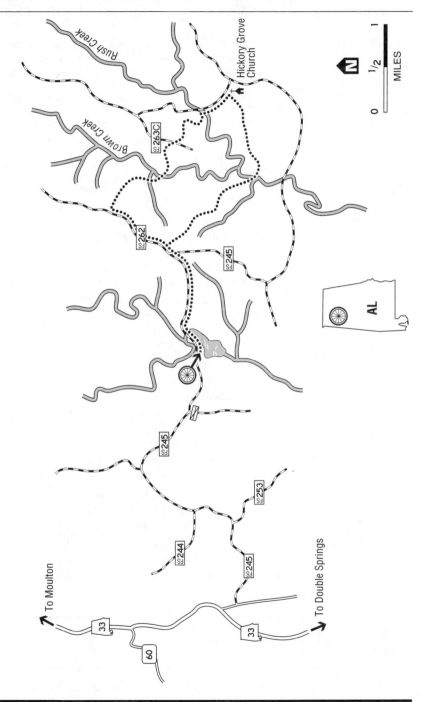

General location: This trail lies east of Brushy Lake in the Bankhead National Forest.

Elevation change: The rugged elevation changes found just west of here in the Sipsey Wilderness stretch east enough to affect this section of trail. You will find yourself in overdrive on Owl Creek more than once before you put the bike up on the rack for the drive home.

Season: One of the wonderful qualities about living in the Deep South comes from its temperate climate. Few days in either the winter or summer become too extreme for biking. Slick 'Bama clay, however, can be as unforgiving as a spinster and should therefore be avoided in wet times.

Services: Head back to Double Springs for supplies.

Hazards: Since the horses no longer tread these parts, the trail should improve dramatically and quickly. But until then, be alert for rough sections and deadfalls.

Rescue index: You'll probably wind up asking yourself before you get back to your vehicle, "Is there a more remote trail in Alabama?" I doubt it.

Land status: This is trail located within the Bankhead National Forest.

Maps: The 1985 Bankhead National Forest map has this trail fixed on it. After 1995 and the proposed trail changes take place, this loop will not be included on official National Forest Service maps.

Finding the trail: Leave Brushy Lake Recreational Area's parking lot and turn right. At the top of the hill on FS 245, FS 262 comes in from the left, although it looks like FS 245 continues straight and a different road comes in from the right. The trail lies just left of 245 at the junction, heading southeast. This is where a counterclockwise route begins.

Sources of additional information:

> Bankhead National Forest
> P.O. Box 278 (South Main Street)
> Double Springs, AL 35553
> (205) 489-5111

Notes on the trail: Traveling counterclockwise, begin the 6-mile loop by riding parallel to a small creek that empties into Rush Creek as you ford across Rush Creek. Climb the hill up to Hickory Grove Church at the junction of FS 255 with FS 262. Then head northwest and cross FS 263-C. After crossing Brown Creek, make your way back up to FS 262. Left leads back to Brushy Creek Recreational Area.

RIDE 45 *MULTI-USE TRAIL IN THE BANKHEAD*

At the heart of why a big national forest like the Bankhead has no officially designated mountain bike trails may be the unofficial attitude of the National Forest Service in the district. As I was doing research on this proposed 25-mile

RIDE 45 *MULTI-USE TRAIL IN THE BANKHEAD*

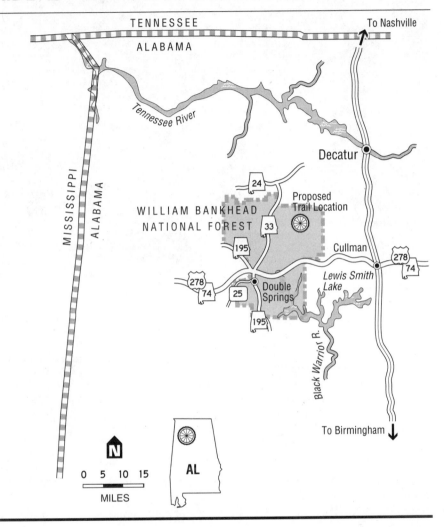

loop, which promises to be full of demanding sections, I spoke with an official who told me he was surprised at the support and desire for constructing designated mountain bike trails. "With all the Forest Service roads open for mountain bikes," he said, "mountain bikes already have a lot of backwoods mileage to ride."

I was talking to a person who—in all honesty and sincerity—thinks it is just as good traveling on a rocky, wide, shadeless Forest Service road as it is riding on a tight, winding, shady single-track. Unless they've been undisturbed for many years, most Forest Service roads lack the intimacy of a green canopy overhead, something I've always needed for the communion to begin.

Bankhead National Forest, Alabama.

General location: The proposed location is in the northeastern section of the William Bankhead National Forest.

Elevation change: The Bankhead has radically angled terra firma, all the way to cliffs. While some may prompt a check to see if you have a flat back tire, most are manageable for the intermediately conditioned biker.

Season: Avoid periods of heavy moisture on the track. Otherwise, enjoy!

Services: You may want to consider setting up an account with your favorite Double Springs merchants. They are the closest ones who can provide more than the basics.

Hazards: The greatest hazard to this trail would be for the funds not to be appropriated by Congress, thereby putting on hold plans to construct nearly 60 miles of various trails.

Rescue index: The northeastern section of the Bankhead, the proposed location, is the most remote.

Land status: This is national forest.

Maps: So far, no name has been given this trail system. It is referred to as the "25-Mile Multi-Use Trail."

Finding the trail: This is yet to be determined by the Forest Service, but the location may make it more feasible to approach from the north, off Highway 157 out of Cullman, instead of using Highway 278 from the south.

Sources of additional information: There is a Bankhead Trails Coalition, whose representative—Roger Blalock—will be glad to pass on information he has concerning any trail construction in the Bankhead. Roger can be reached at (205) 734-8668.

Bankhead National Forest
P.O. Box 278 (South Main Street)
Double Springs, AL 35553
(205) 489-5111

Notes on the trail: Following a satisfactory environmental impact assessment to be completed, a 25-mile loop allowing hikers, equestrians, and mountain bikers will be constructed. Primary input for the project has come from the Bankhead Trails Coalition and Birmingham Urban Mountain Pedalers.

Birmingham Area Rides

If Birmingham bikers are a bit more steely-eyed than some other Southern cyclists, they came about it naturally. This city, partially built into the fingertip of Red Mountain, has more than just a name in common with its English counterpart. Both have traditions surrounding the smelting of iron ore. However, the most surprising similarity is that Birmingham, Alabama, is also a port of entry via the Mobile River, Tombigbee River, and Black Warrior River, the last of which has only a nine-foot canal.

Visiting bikers bent toward taking in the city's sights will want to make it atop Red Mountain where Vulcan, the world's largest iron statue at 55 feet tall, sits above a 124-foot observation tower. A similar sculpture, a miniature Lady Liberty, overlooks a bend in Interstate 459 near the Cahaba River. This body of water flows near the north boundary of Alabama's premier state park, Oak Mountain, which also is home of the mountain bike trail that many claim is the finest in the state.

Birmingham's cultural roots encompass more than mountain biking and iron sculpture. In fact, first-timers to this northern Alabama city of more than a quarter-million will see many examples of a diverse community. The Alabama Jazz Hall of Fame, Museum of Art, and Botanical Gardens provide alternatives to mountain bikers who consider themselves aesthetes. For the athletes, the Alabama Sports Hall of Fame, Birmingham Barons, and the New Birmingham Race Course give thrills not found in the Birmingham Zoo and Riverchase Galleria, a mall of epic proportions for those who think they've walked them all.

The sciences and arts have also been drawn to this busy city. The Ruffner Mountain Nature Center (over 500 acres of sanctuary eight miles from downtown) and the Robert R. Meyer Planetarium cater to the micro- and macro-ends of the scientific recreational scale. If medicine interests you, plan a trip to the Alabama Museum of Health Sciences—no appointment necessary between 8 A.M.–5 P.M., Monday through Friday. Birmingham is also home to international publishing houses, such as Menasha Ridge Press, without which there would be no *Mountain Biking the Deep South* nor many other fine books.

For more information:

Cahaba Cycles
3120 Cahaba Heights Plaza
Birmingham, AL 35243-5221
(800) 846-9829

Crestline Cycles
#11 Dexter Avenue/Crestline Village
Birmingham, AL 35213-3703
(205) 879-6255

Alabama Cycle & Equipment Company
9107 Parkway East
Birmingham, AL 35206
(205) 833-1122

Bob's Bikes
1410 Montgomery Highway
Birmingham, AL 35216
(205) 979-3460

Cycle Service Company
4908 Gary Avenue
Birmingham, AL 35064
(205) 780-9261

Dr. Joe's Bikes
1001-B Tuscaloosa Avenue, SW
Birmingham, AL 35211-1620
(205) 780-1950

River Oaks Cycle
3704 Lorna Road
Birmingham, AL 35216-6206
(205) 988-0930

Baker Bicycle Company
2217 West Meighan Boulevard
Gadsden, AL 35290-1705
(205) 549-1200

Scott's Bikes
109 Ladiga Street
Jacksonville, AL 36265-2631
(205) 435-2453

RIDE 46 *OAK MOUNTAIN*

The Birmingham Urban Mountain Pedalers (BUMP) set a goal to construct and maintain the finest mountain bike trail in Alabama. They succeeded. Approximately 15 miles of trail, most of which is single-track, makes a loop

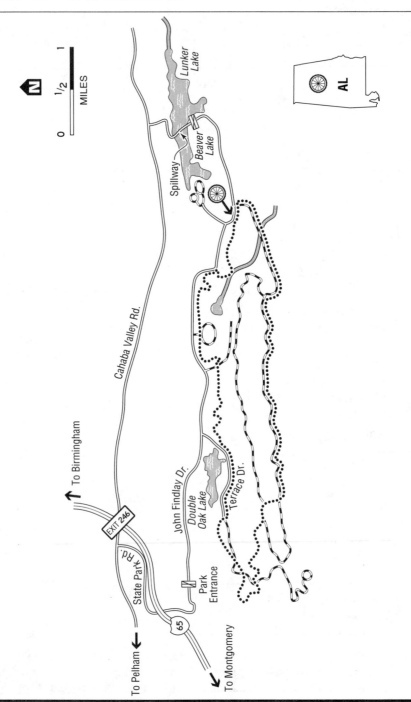

as it climbs ridges and falls into valleys near Double Oak, Beaver, and Lunker lakes in Oak Mountain State Park. Alabama's largest park and its 10,000 acres of mature, mixed hardwoods draw out-of-state bikers on a regular basis to ride its moderately challenging track.

One such biker, a young guy from Dekalb County, Georgia, sat in the back of his pickup one cold day in February and told me, "Oak Mountain is the first trail I ever rode." Despite living two to three hours away, he still manages to return to Birmingham at least once a month. Sometimes, he takes a day off work to ride when it's not as crowded, as he did that Monday afternoon. No doubt, he told his boss he was "unable to come in to work" that day. What he probably didn't tell his boss was that he was suffering from that uncomfortable feeling, *cyclus bellus interruptus,* and unless he rode the Oak, he would pop.

Even though it is heavily used by a large Birmingham contingent of cyclists, in addition to mountain bikers from Montgomery who consider it their trail as well, you will not find a better maintained track anywhere. One of the best uses of old car tires has them buried on slopes, half the tread showing and stretching across the treadway. When rain runs down the slopes, it hits the exposed tread and is diverted down the mountain before it becomes an eroding torrent. Although the resistance you meet when riding over them uphill is consequential, it is not enough to prevent reaching the top. Compared to riding in a rut, there's no comparison. Way to go, BUMP!

It's been nearly six months since I've been back to Oak Mountain. If I told the boss I was going would he really mind? Hey, Bob, last one there buys lunch.

General location: This grand trail is in Birmingham, Alabama's Oak Mountain State Park.

Elevation change: There is no elevation change so dramatic that an old poker like me can't take it all the way, at least on my good days.

Season: There would probably be a revolt if this trail ever closed. Ride it and love it.

Services: Birmingham is capable of satisfying a diverse and varied clientele. Oak Mountain State Park provides all the amenities found at the best parks.

Hazards: You share the trail with hikers, who have the right-of-way. Parts of the trail go on asphalt where motorized vehicles lurk.

Rescue index: Unless you ride the trail late into the day—or into the night—you should be part of a large group enjoying this trail and, therefore, subject to quick discovery should a mishap occur. Still, a good whistle shrilly blown ought to be loud enough to be heard by a patrolling ranger on the road below.

Land status: This is another Alabama State Park.

Maps: A map of the entire park—including the numerous trails—can b picked up at the entrance station where you'll have to pay a token fee to inside. Topo maps in the 7.5 minute series, Chelsea and Lena quads complete geographic data of the area.

Finding the trail: Exit Interstate 65 onto State Park Road and go straight at the gate until you reach Terrace Drive. Turn right and go to the parking lot; the trailhead is at the end of the road on the right. Another trailhead can be found by taking the Cahaba Valley Road exit off I-65 and heading east on Highway 119. Turn right at the sign and enter the park. You'll have to cross a spillway between Beaver and Lunker lakes, which is fun, but this entrance closes at 5 P.M.

Sources of additional information:

Oak Mountain State Park
P.O. Box 278
Pelham, Alabama 35124
(205) 620-2524

Birmingham Urban Mountain Pedalers
Contact: Barry Hair
(205) 987-8510

Notes on the trail: Many markers lead the way for bikers new to this trail. Just remember that the red blazes point out the 15-mile loop open to mountain bikes. While the majority of the trail goes on single-track, some old wide roadbeds and paved roads have been incorporated into the length. I was told that the section paralleling Findlay Drive offered a great chance to spot wildlife (deer, in particular). I had almost forgotten about the chance when I was suddenly aware of a sound—half-snort, half-honk—coming down from the ridge on my right. I stopped and looked up just in time to see a many-pointed buck shake his rack at me before bounding off. I sat for a moment watching his huge white tail disappear into the brush and wondered if I had interrupted something important, like the deer's own run down the trail.

RIDE 47 *LOOKOUT MOUNTAIN TRAIL*

When the Alabama Appalachian Association was organized in 1983, it set a goal "to design, administer, and build" 125 miles of trail. Beginning in Gadsden, Alabama, it was supposed to cut across northwestern Georgia and ⌐d in Point Park, Chattanooga, Tennessee. Another group, the Lookout ⌐n Trail Association, was also formed to help bring about completion

⌐he trailhead in Gadsden, I followed the paved highway ⌐r so. Across the street from some apartments, I saw the ⌐, blocked now by felled trees, going up the mountain. ⌐section of the Lookout Mountain Trail, or the John F. ⌐e call it, is involved in some sort of litigation. It appears

RIDE 47 *LOOKOUT MOUNTAIN TRAIL*

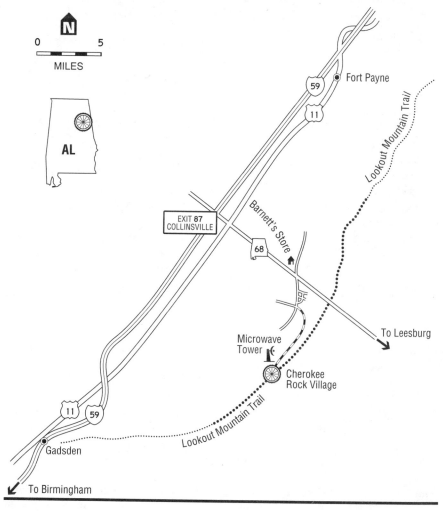

a landowner built his home smack dab in the middle of the trail close to Gadsden, forcing users to either trespass or make a very inconvenient detour.

Consequently, the Gadsden trailhead is not the point of choice for beginning this ride. Most people start the northeastern roll of approximately 25 miles on an out-and-back (50 miles total) from a nationally known place for rock climbers and spelunkers, Cherokee Rock Village. The striking sha of boulders 200 feet high scattered about the apron of stone makes quit impression. Other impressions—caves and crevices—offer miles of terranean thrills for those who partake in that pastime.

Back topside, the extremely physically demanding bike trail provides cyclists a path along the ancient routes of the Cherokee who followed the ridges on trading trips to other villages. Now, all types of vehicles are just as likely to be seen bouncing along the rugged track with hikers, horseback riders, and climbers. The promise of turning this historical area into a throughway for the entire 125 miles has not been fulfilled.

General location: This trail roughly parallels the Lookout Mountain Parkway, northeast of Gadsden.

Elevation change: You can travel so fast going downhill, you run the risk of suddenly being airborne—sometimes unintentionally. Several mandatory opportunities to hike up the other side lie in wait for you here.

Season: No season should prevent you from riding this trail.

Services: Go to Gadsden or Fort Payne for more unusual items; otherwise, you can pick up the basics as close as Barnett's store, on Highway 68 right across from the right turn you take to Cherokee Rock Village.

Hazards: Some of the smaller "buildings" from Cherokee Rock Village find a place in the trail and require evasive action or super suspension. Locals, or 'Necks' as we call them where I live, have been known to be a trifle unruly and trash the parking lot. Keep this in mind if you prepare a solo trip. You might find yourself on the receiving end of a question like, "Say, where'd you git them purty shorts?"

Rescue index: You could squeal like a pig for a long time and no one would hear you.

Land status: The 20 miles you can ride from Cherokee Rock Village north belong to Cherokee and Etowah Counties and a paper company. And, as the pending court case suggests, some private landowners feel they have an inalienable right to the trail.

Maps: You can request the Lookout Mountain Trail map that shows the general layout from the Lookout Trail Association or BUMP. Also, for those who collect topo maps, the Gadsden East, Keener, Leesburg, and Portersville 7.5 minute series quads give complete topographic information of the area where most riding takes place.

Finding the trail: Take Interstate 59 leaving Gadsden headed northeast and exit onto Highway 68 toward Leesburg. Just before getting to Leesburg, a store on the left where Sand Rock School Road intersects Highway 68, 's sits facing the right-hand turn you need to take. After making this at the bottom of the slight hill (the fourth paved road to the left the road) and travel only a short distance before it turns ep going straight on this road until you pass the right. Parking is past that. The trail begins behind,

Sources of additional information:

Lookout Mountain Trail Association
P.O. Box 1434
Gadsden, AL 35902

Baker Bicycle Company
2217 West Meighan Boulevard
Gadsden, AL 35902
(205) 549-1200

Birmingham Urban Mountain Pedalers (BUMP)
Contact: Barry Hair
(205) 987-8510

Notes on the trail: This trail lends itself to an overnighter or two. Taking the trail out and back makes it nearly 50 miles of hard riding. If you enjoy the challenge of taking on rough terrain while carrying a full load, this is definitely the place to try. While you're out there gazing at Weiss Lake and the eagles screaming overhead, try to imagine what it was like many years ago when the Native Americans trod this trail.

RIDE 48   KENTUCK ORV

As the name suggests, you will have to share this trail with some of our motorized brethren, although on the days I rode, I neither saw nor heard anyone else on the trail. You may be tempted to forego this 15-mile loop simply because of the possibility of getting run up on by motorcycles or four-wheelers. Resist this urge and experience one of the finest rides anywhere. And, yes, this trail is open and legal to mountain bikes. Despite the possible absence of signs at the trailhead, other signs are posted farther in that corroborate the legality of this moderately strenuous ride for mountain bikers.

Evidence of wildlife is everywhere. Buck scrapes were numerous, and I even saw what looked like where a bear had clawed up the side of a tree, more to mark its territory than anything else. Later on down the trail I saw remnants of a yellowjacket nest strewn all over the ground where something (the bear?) had discovered it and gotten to the pupae and honey. If you're fortunate enough to ride on this trail during the week when there's not much traffic, a wide variety of birds and small mammals flit and skitter about.

Make sure you bring a snack on this ride and plan to spend the better part of the day enjoying the overlooks of creeks and distant mountain ridges. While there are some ATV trails I would not be caught dead on, this trail is among

RIDE 48 *KENTUCK ORV*

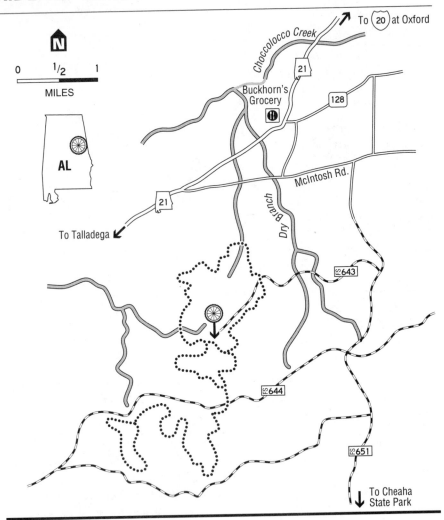

the most scenic and well maintained trails anywhere. Do yourself and every other mountain biker a favor, though, and listen for oncoming motorized riders and accommodate them by getting off the trail. This trail was built and is maintained by these people in conjunction with the National Forest folks. I'm sure you'll agree that what they've done is worthy of more than a little respect.

General location: This route runs through the Talladega National Forest.
Elevation change: Kentuck is characterized by the ups and downs common to mid-Alabama mountain chains. If you're up on a ridge, it won't be long before

"Carry my bike to ole Kentuck."

you're going back down to one of the many creeks and springs along this trail. Although there are some steep sections, they are relatively short, and if you're having a good day and the track is dry, you will be able to pedal all the way without taking a hike.

Season: I would recommend this as a weekday trail. Weekends have many motorcycles and quadrunners coursing about. Of course, if this does not inhibit your enjoyment, ride on. Wet, slick mud slopes can pose problems. Give the trail a day or two to dry out after a good rain.

Services: The store at Cheaha State Park can provide basic foodstuffs and such; otherwise, Anniston, north of Interstate 20, is your closest purchase point for specialty items.

Hazards: Motorized vehicles use this popular trail; however, I only saw 1 group of motorcyclists the 3 times I rode Kentuck, and they were just unloading their bikes.

Rescue index: You get pretty far removed at times from the saving grace of civilization. You could shoot a .44 all day in some places and not have too much said about it other than, "Was that thunder?"

Land status: This is national forest.

Maps: Request the Kentuck ORV Trail map from the National Forest Service, Talladega Ranger District. Riders who also tote topo maps will need the Ironaton, Munford, and Oxford quadrangles in the 7.5 minute series for complete coverage.

Finding the trail: Find this trail by getting off I-20 at Oxford (Exit 185) and going southwest on Highway 21 toward Talladega, which is the Creek word for "town-border." This is the area of the boundary between where the Creeks lived to the east and the Natchez to the west. After passing the Anniston Airport on the left and crossing the Choccolocco Creek, look for County Road 128 (Buckhorn Road—across from Carter's Grocery) coming in to Highway 21 from the left. Take it straight until it dead-ends. Turn left onto McIntosh Road and go a couple of miles, past Antioch Church on the right, where there should be a sign directing a right turn to Kentuck ORV trail. The pavement ends before the sign giving the right turn onto Forest Service 643. This road dead-ends, but not before the gated road to the left leads to the parking area for this trail.

Sources of additional information:

Cheaha State Park
Route 1, Box 77-H
Delta, AL 36258
(205) 488-5111

District Ranger, Talladega District
National Forest Service
1001 North Street (Highway 21 north)
Talladega, AL 35160
(205) 362-2909

Notes on the trail: I started off in a clockwise direction, although I saw no signs indicating you had to begin in this way. Go nearly to the exit by the outhouses and park. You'll find the signs to the trail off to your right. If you want the other leg to be the beginning, it's on the opposite side of the loop. Any way you ride will lead to some mighty fine trail.

I rode this trail just after rain had fallen the day before. Water was still standing in some low spots, but I was able to navigate without getting too muddy if I got off before crossing the obviously sticky spots. The tan clay that sometimes shows on the worn spots of this trail are not to be ridden wet unless you want to be sliding sideways going downhill or getting incapacitating gunk on the chain. It's formidable stuff and worth avoiding.

RIDE 49 *MUNNY SOKOL PARK*

To most Alabamans, Tuscaloosa means only one thing: Crimson Tide Football. Spring training, Bear Bryant, fall games, Bear Bryant, summer recruiting, Bear Bryant. It's a never-ending cycle, and a surprise to find a close second to

RIDE 49 *MUNNY SOKOL PARK*

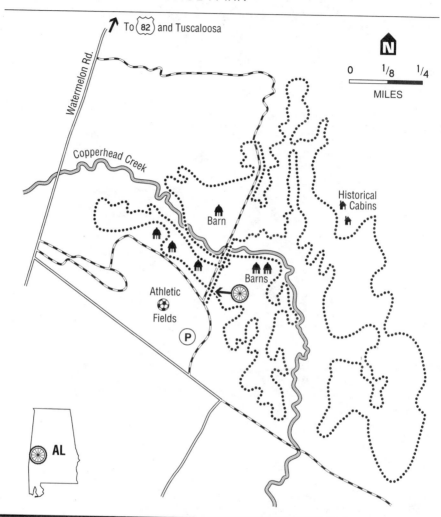

Birmingham's Oak Mountain Trail here where the passion for pigskin keeps the population pumped up. But a better trail will be hard to find.

My first ride on this 11-mile configuration of loops-within-loops came on a wintry, blustery Sunday afternoon. I caught up with two riders who had brought their tagalong beagle that possessed trail savvy beyond his years, which was good because some sections require pretty technical skills. The four of us rode an abbreviated four-mile section of the trails, staying south of the main access road, rolling through a surprisingly old oak and pine forest where

Bikers and beagle at Munny Sokol Park (dog's hind leg
behind tire of backmost rider).

two old homesteads (registered with the National Historical Society) still
stand.

Munny Sokol Park has its own unique history. A former farm run by
patients from a mental hospital, it was used to raise fruits and cows. In 1970
the experimental farm folded and Tuscaloosa's Parks and Recreational
Authority (PARA) purchased the property with the help of longtime PARA
board member, Munny Sokol.

General location: This park is found in north Tuscaloosa, a few miles east of
Highway 82.
Elevation change: The rather tame elevation changes are not what you will
remember this trail for.
Season: Due to the exceedingly kind care given to the trail, you should be
able to ride this during all but the most extreme conditions.

Services: Tuscaloosa is a big-time college city and has all the amenities demanded by such an eclectic group. The park has water and rest rooms. Munny Sokol's hours are from 8 A.M. to 11 P.M., but if the gate is locked, you can easily put your bike over it and have a perfectly legal ride.

Hazards: You will need to keep a close watch on the trail ahead for the possibility for oncoming bikers. It's a popular trail . . . with no direction requirements. Some of the passes through trees and over logs barely admit your own handlebars, much less two sets.

Rescue index: You will find no trouble getting rescued here.

Land status: This land is owned, operated, and maintained by Tuscaloosa, Alabama.

Maps: The bulletin board has a chalk-drawn rendering of where the trails go. I used this for my model.

Finding the trail: Take Highway 82 out of Tuscaloosa headed north to the Black Warrior River. After crossing over the river, look for the sign at the intersection of Highway 82 with Water Melon Road and turn right. The park's entrance will be about a mile straight down this road. Parking is on the left below the athletic fields, in between the road and some long buildings where maintenance equipment is stored.

Sources of additional information: Tuscaloosa Parks and Recreational Authority can be reached at (205) 758-0342. Munny Sokol Park's directors can be reached at (205) 553-3671.

Cycle-Path
1221 University Avenue
Tuscaloosa, AL 35401-1629
(205) 345-3144

The Bicycle Shop
1408 University Avenue
Tuscaloosa, AL 35401-1634
(205) 758-4906

Notes on the trail: After talking with Jerry Belk, trail aficionado and Munny Sokol source of information, it was hard to imagine a more enthusiastic mountain biker. He spoke proudly of the trail's Physician Trail (where you are likely to wind up needing one if you aren't an experienced biker), Deer and Cabin Loops, Trik-Track-Trek, and Whoop-De-Doo. The single-track has been laid out in a challenging course of tight turns in the middle of drops and climbs as it goes through the forest. Portions of it go along wide-open hillsides offering views of the river valley.

Montgomery Area Rides

Since 1846, this middle Alabama city has been Alabama's capital. In 1861, it served as the short-lived Confederate States of America's first capital. Incorporated in 1819 and named for a Revolutionary War leader, Montgomery has off-and-on found itself in the middle of a great deal of activity. Ancient mound-building Native American civilizations settled here in the middle of the fall line from Tuscaloosa in the north to Phenix City in the south.

The great irony of Montgomery as a mountain biking community lies in the fact that although it boasts four bike shops, so far, no officially developed bike trails exist in the immediate Montgomery area. However, each direction out of Montgomery leads to bike trails where terrain of all sorts can be experienced.

Up in Tuscaloosa, a growing population has pushed football aside and taken to mountain biking. The city of Tuscaloosa—which means "black warrior," named for the river running through it—enjoys not only the advantage of being a big-name college town, but also the variety of lifestyle and goods from having access to the Gulf of Mexico via the Black Warrior River.

Most folks pop open a boiled peanut or fork off a chunk of sweet potato pie without the first thought of Tuskegee or George Washington Carver. However, without this man's experimentation in the lonely Alabama fields east of Montgomery, mountain bikers and others would have to settle for an inferior goober and an inefficiently produced yam. Not a pleasant thought for a Southern purebred like me. As a result, my ride in the Tuskegee National Forest held more the feeling of homage than mileage.

Finally, in what may be the strangest marriage of cultures, Montgomery has the only theater outside of England invited to fly the flag of England's Royal Shakespeare Company. The Alabama Shakespeare Festival produces Shakespearean plays all year long to international acclaim. For some, this smacks of much ado about nothing, but others can think of no better complement to a day's ride on the trail than a play by the man recognized as the greatest dramatist of all time. I've come to believe that if variety of ride be the spice of thigh, then roll on. You'll find plenty of variety in and around Montgomery to keep the wits nimble and the reflexes sharp.

For more information:

Cycle Escape
4501 Atlanta Highway and 5851 Atlanta Highway
Montgomery, AL 36109-3104
(334) 277-5288 and 277-5572

Mr. Bicycle
706 Forest Avenue
Montgomery, AL 36106-1005
(334) 265-4716

Montgomery Hobby & Cycle
703 Forest Avenue
Montgomery, AL 36106-1004
(334) 262-5945

Cloverland Cycle Shop
3656 South Perry Street
Montgomery, AL 36105-2203
(334) 265-9427

Montgomery Visitor Center
401 Madison Avenue
Montgomery, AL 36104
(800) 240-9452 or (334) 262-0013 or fax (334) 240-9290

RIDE 50 *CHEWACLA STATE PARK*

I wouldn't be at all surprised to find out that *Chewacla* is Choctaw for scalp-raising rocky descents. This former site of an Alabama NORBA State Championship has a full complement of trail challenges worthy of weeding out the rest from the best when it comes to mountain biking. The eight miles of steeply pitched and rocky course makes a loop between Moore's Mill Creek on the north and Chewacla Creek on the south.

You can easily get sidetracked and onto another one of the total of eight different trails at Chewacla. Deer Rub Trail and Mountain Laurel Trail both share treadways with the Mountain Bike Trail, and a moment without concentration can lead you down the "Trail of Tears," where an inexperienced biker should not enter. Along Chewacla Creek, where schools of large-mouth bass lurk in long, clear pools, unerring control and balance are a must. Any spill here leads either into rocks and poison ivy on one side or a bath with the bass on the other.

Rocks play another role at Chewacla besides being trail obstruction. The far side of Chewacla Creek has a quarry where wayward boulders rest on the bank above the water. Although I heard no such explosions, some dynamite thunder could accompany your passage through Chewacla. In any case, you'll think this is a dynamite trail. Chewacla? It means either Raccoon Town or Land of the Beaver.

RIDE 50 *CHEWACLA STATE PARK*

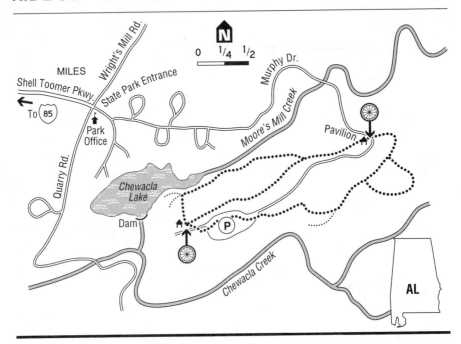

General location: The not-so-distant roar of Interstate 85's traffic outside of Auburn, Alabama, will not diminish enough for you to get too turned around.

Elevation change: The changes in elevation are sometimes extreme, but short enough for most bikers to ride.

Season: Chewacla holds up well to the extensive use it gets. No seasonal restrictions apply.

Services: Auburn is Alabama's other college town. As a result, it carries a wide range of supplies for your every need, academic and extracurricular.

Hazards: Being one who does not care for the rockier roads, I consider the number and size of rocks on this trail to be a significant challenge to my balance and enjoyment. Maybe my recollection on traveling (illegally but innocently) along the Chewacla Creek stands out too much. Maybe I should break down and buy those new shocks I've been wanting.

Rescue index: This trail sees many mountain bike tires daily. Help will not be too far away, nor will you ever get too far away from where you started.

Land status: The Alabama Department of Conservation and Natural Resources manages this park.

Maps: Maps of Chewacla State Park are available at the entrance. All trails, hiking and biking, are included. The Auburn topo quad in the 7.5 minute series details the trails at Chewacla.

It's a difficult ride down to the dam at Chewacla Lake, Auburn.

Finding the trail: Get off I-85 on exit 51; travel south on Highway 295 about 200 yards. Take the turn onto Shell Toomer Parkway which dead-ends at the park. Pay your entrance fee and get the map of trails. Continue on Murphy Drive until crossing the bridge over Moore's Mill Creek. Climb the hill and look for the pavilion on the left. You can park here and begin the trail by continuing uphill, or you can ride the trail clockwise by crossing the road and picking up the single-track directly across from the parking lot entrance.

Sources of additional information:

Chewacla State Park
124 Shell Toomer Parkway
Auburn, Alabama 36830
(334) 887-5621

Auburn-Opelika Convention and Visitors Bureau
P.O. Box 2216 (714 East Glenn Avenue)
Auburn, AL 36381
(800) 321-8880 or (334) 887-8747, fax (334) 821-5500

Notes on the trail: After beginning the trail at the pavilion on the right at the top of the hill, cross the paved road and bear to the right at the first fork. You can either turn right at the next split or continue straight; the horseshoe comes back in from the left shortly. Bear right at the next fork and climb up the hill; otherwise, you bump along the rocky bank of Chewacla Creek, which you don't want to do. Once you reach the paved road at the top, turn left onto the road, staying to the right at the loop leading to the other pavilion. Several trails at the pavilion lead down—and steeply—to the lake. Take the one farthest on the right. When you come to the bank above the lake, turn right and go .5 mile along the bank. Take the right fork back up to where another trail goes left (to the pavilion where you began) or right to the pavilion above the lake.

RIDE 51 *BARTRAM TRAIL*

You know how a song sometimes gets stuck inside the airspace between your ears and won't quit playing? The refrain of "All Shook Up" filtered in and played each time my frame rattled over a series of protruding roots on Bartram Trail, which is to say, it must've played a thousand times in the course of this eight-mile out-and-back (16 miles total). For techno-cranks who believe roots create biking happiness, your Shangri-la awaits a few minutes off Interstate 85.

The Tuskegee National Forest, a small one at 21 square miles, contains the entire length of the Bartram Trail, named for the famed explorer who made his way into several southern states while documenting wildlife and plant life. After the southern planters had basically eroded the landscape away through foolish farming practices, the federal government bought the land in 1938 during the Submarginal Land Program and wound up making it a national forest 20 years later.

The biking use on the trail has exceeded the trail's capacity to hold up under the many tires rolling through. Boardwalks have been built over the boggier spots, but long low-lying stretches have caused deep, squishy ruts to form. But enough solid ground remains in the deep hardwood forest where giant beeches grow for the trail-starved biker to enjoy.

General location: This trail lies just a few miles south of I-85, east of Montgomery, Alabama.

Elevation change: Some sections require some quick, forceful pedal stokes to reach the top of climbs. Other sections defied my attempts to ascend or descend them; however, I did see evidence of other bikers making their way through these more demanding draws.

Season: I rode this trail during a moderately dry period, but you couldn't tell it on the trail. Periods of heavy rain would make parts of this trail impractical for most bikers to ride for quite a few days following.

Services: All services can be obtained in Auburn, a few miles to the east.

Hazards: It may be that one biker's hazard is another's happiness, which most likely applies to the numerous roots and bogs found on this trail. A

Sunlight dapples the forest floor of Bartram single-track.

major highway (186) has to be crossed about midway through. Also, an innocent-looking stream—on the map at least—calls for a murky ford. It was with more than a little trepidation that I finally made my mind up to ride through the 15 feet of yellow water to the other bank, but only after having seen a lone tire track on the other side. I asked myself, "Now what would Bartram do?" My answer was something akin to a white-water rebel entry.

Rescue index: This trail never gets very far out in the boonies, although it creates a remote and isolated feeling.

Land status: This is a national forest trail.

Maps: The office has maps of the forest and the trail. The forest map is excellent, containing topo contour lines. I ordered my map ahead of time, and I was glad I did. When I got to the office, no maps were available other than the less detailed ones made by the friendly, helpful staff at Tuskegee National Forest. Ask for the Bartram Trail maps.

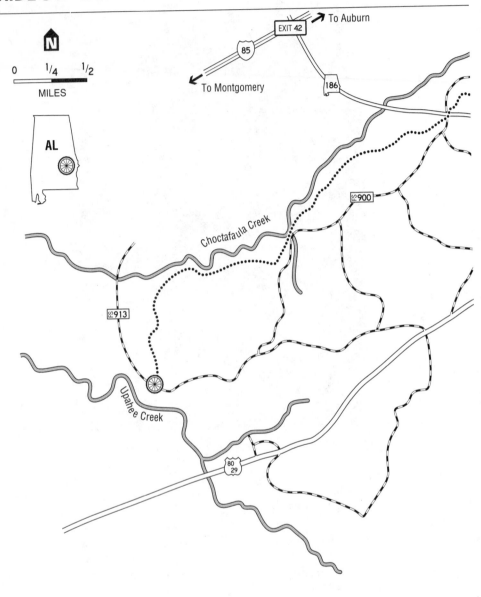

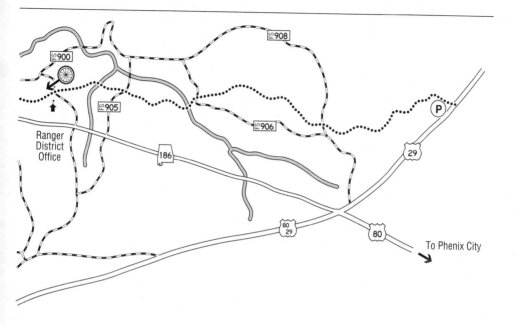

Ranger
District
Office

FS 900

FS 908

FS 905

FS 906

186

29

80
29

80

To Phenix City

Finding the trail: Exit I-85 onto Highway 186 south. This is exit 42. Turn left at the Forest Service sign a couple of miles down the road. I parked at the lot behind the ranger's office where the picnic area is, but—depending on what type ride you want—there are numerous spots to begin the trail.

Sources of additional information:

> Tuskegee District Ranger
> 125 National Forest Road 949
> Tuskegee, AL 36083-9801
> (205) 727-2652
>
> Supervisor's Office
> National Forests in Alabama
> 2946 Chestnut Street
> Montgomery, AL 36107-3010
> (205) 832-4470

Notes on the trail: The southwestern section of the Bartram paralleling the Choctafaula Creek is wetter than the part above Highway 186, which, for the most part, stays high and dry. A trailhead exists at each end of the 8.4 miles (one-way), and a good idea if you don't want to do a 17-mile there-and-back is to set a shuttle and ride one way. A loop can be put together on the lower section by beginning at the ranger's office and following the Choctafaula. After coming out at the Forest Service Road 913 trailhead, head east on FS 913. The fork allows you to choose the high road (FS 913) or the low road (FS 900) to the left. If you take the high one, the next left (FS 901) should be taken if you don't want to ride on busy Highway 15. The Forest Service roads are well maintained, have little traffic, and offer many miles of opportunities for exploration behind gated roads on both the upper (north of Highway 186) and lower ends of the national forest.

Mobile Area Rides

Alabama has the shortest saltwater shoreline of all the Deep South states with only 53 miles, but what a choice 53 it is! A series of radical creek ridges have formed by interaction of the coastal plain setting with the Mobile River pushing through its 34-mile-long channel. These ridges, such as the ones found streamside of the Chickasaw Creek, make for good mountain bike trails. Although Mobile was the site of the 1994 NORBA State Championship, its history has not been dramatically shaped by bicycles. Ships, and the people who made and used them, are what made Mobile an international city.

After De Soto, the original Deep South guide, explored Mobile in the mid-1500s, the city's future lay in the tranquil waters of Mobile Bay. Originally less than 6 feet deep, the bay now allows drafts of nearly 40 feet to clear the sandy bottom. The Alabama State Docks, built to accommodate this oceangoing commerce, are among the largest in the nation. The control of this seaport in 1864 by Admiral David Farrugut helped drown any hopes the Confederacy had for military victory in the Civil War.

A barrier island just southwest of Mobile, named appropriately enough "Ship Island," was chosen as a site where one of the many forts were to be built to protect the newborn country's shoreline. Fort Massachusetts was the result. Designed by a Frenchman, the structure has withstood onslaughts of many hurricanes since it was completed in the early 1800s. However, as Hurricane Camille cut through the island with a 35-foot tidal surge, it separated the long barrier into two islands. So effective is the fort's protection that two men, looking for the ultimate storm party, elected to stay on the island despite evacuation orders. They survived, but only after having to curl up inside the topmost section of the fort.

Back on shore, visitors not pedaling nearby Chickasabogue Park trails can amble along trails in Alabama's Bellingrath Gardens, a former Coca-Cola bigwig's location for a fishing camp; a more elegant fish camp you will not find anywhere. Gulf Shores National Seashore, a protected sanctuary, helps keep the interior waters calm as well as being a beautiful place to hike or bike along the road.

As a former "swabbie," I enjoyed touring the USS *Alabama,* a hulking battleship the people of Alabama bought and brought back to Mobile Bay after WW II. Farther inland, the entire family can find a special spot to explore when not astride a bike saddle. Hands-on science exhibits, such as the Weeks Bay National Estuarine Research Reserve and Dauphin Island Sea Lab Education Center, have been established in order to study and explain the delicate balance between land and sea.

Mobile's appreciation of the more refined side of life—outside of mountain biking, that is—can be taken in at one of the antebellum museums, like

205

Oakleigh and the Richards Daughters of the American Revolution (DAR) House. A collection of art from the last 2,000 years stays on display at the Fine Arts Museum of the South; relics there trace the history of the City of Six Flags from the days when Mobile was under Native American, French, Spanish, English, Confederate, and American rule.

This is a land shaped by many influences: rivers pouring soil down from the north, the ocean beating water against its doorstep on the south, and marshes joining the two. It is a place where worlds collide and create. Mobile . . . a good place to go mobile.

For more information:

> Alabama Gulf Coast Convention and Visitors Bureau
> 23479 Perdido Beach Boulevard
> Orange Beach, AL 36561
>
> or
>
> P.O. Drawer 457
> Gulf Shores, AL 36547
> (800) 745-7263
>
> Mobile Convention and Visitors Bureau
> (334) 433-6951
>
> Mobile Schwinn and Cyclery
> 4258 Cottage Hill Drive
> Mobile, AL
> (334) 666-3700

RIDE 52 *CHICKASABOGUE TRAILS*

Tucked away neatly in the Alabama coastal forest near Mobile Bay is a series of single-track maintained by Chickasaw County in Chickasabogue Park. Sharing boundaries with Chickasaw Creek on the north and Interstate 65 on the east, Chickasabogue offers sights and elevation changes along its trails that will bring to mind mountains more than the gulf coastal plain.

These trails are widely used by bikers of all levels of ability from many areas, including professionals who come here to train. The first time at Chickasabogue, I met Ron Hansen, the owner of Biloxi (MS) Bikes, who says it's the best place in the coastal area to ride. The three different loops—over eight miles combined—hosted the 1994 Alabama NORBA Championships.

The wide assortment of other activities at the park—a walk along an interpretative nature trail, a softball game at the sports field complex, boating or fishing on the Chickasaw Creek, or trying your hand at disc (frisbee) golf—

RIDE 52 *CHICKASABOGUE TRAILS*

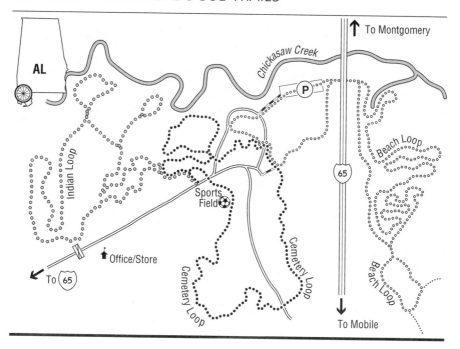

makes this a good place to stay for a few days. There are also camping spots to fit whatever mood or mode you're in, from primitive hike-in sites to asphalted pads for your big rig.

General location: This trail parallels I-65 as it heads into Mobile, Alabama, 13 miles away.

Elevation change: My previous expectations about sandy strands on the Gulf had been on the level, literally. Chickasabogue dispels that notion entirely. Prepare yourself for a challenge of both thigh and lung; you'll love it.

Season: Despite the fine job of maintaining the trails with boardwalks and bridges, there are still several places which become hardly worth riding when they're wet. Having said that, I realize some bikers relish the wet; they will love it year-round. You may be comforted enough to finish the trail on even the hottest, muggiest days with the thought that a swim in the Chickasaw Creek is only a shout away after doing a lap around Beach Loop.

Services: Mobile can deliver to you whatever the world sends to its ports. The park store has many items the biker may need.

Hazards: Roots, capable of throwing the unwary off balance, lie exposed on the steeper slopes. Sandy stretches, having lost their pine needle and clay cover, can quickly turn the front wheel of a speeding mountain bike.

Rescue index: While I rode—late morning on a weekday—I saw several bikers. I also saw the park staff out on adjoining service roads keeping an eye on things.

Land status: This is land operated by the Chickasaw County government. If each county maintained a park the caliber of Chickasabogue, the world would be a far, far better place.

Maps: Free maps showing the trails at Chickasabogue can be picked up at the park store and office. Just ask for the map of the biking trails.

Finding the trail: Take Exit #13 off I-65 and head west, following the sign, on Highway 158 (Industrial Parkway). Be ready for the quick turn onto Shelton Beach Road at the first light. Take a left onto Whistle Street and another left onto Aldock Road, which leads into the park. The Sports Field is the trailhead for both Indian and Cemetery Loop. The trailhead for Beach Loop can be found on the paved road directly across from the Sports Field.

Sources of additional information:

Chickasabogue Park
760 Aldock Road
Mobile, AL 36613
(334) 452-8496

Notes on the trail: For this ride it's "Notes on the trails." Here's a bit of information on each of them.

Cemetery Loop. This trail is listed as a moderate challenge for the average mountain biker, but I would say it is on the order of a moderately difficult trail to navigate. It starts off running along the ridges of pine forests and some hardwoods before dropping off into the draws of Chickasaw Creek tributaries. Just like flying a plane, it's the landing into and taking-off from these draws that provide the most need for concentration. Exposed roots and crude bridges, possibly rotting in places, give need to try out those technical moves. The less-experienced bikers may be better off doing a hike and bike on the descents as well as the climbs. My son did great on this trail until an especially tricky descent required him to abandon bike. He exercised a pedal-departure and wound up doing a perfect two-point landing in a boggy spot, landing up to his ankles in Mobile Mud.

We all got more excitement as we wound our way on the back side of the trail where the cemetery is located next to the interstate, just the other side of a stand of pines. We were off our bikes looking at the magnificent old live oak shading the headstones when we heard the boom of a truck recap blowing out.

Indian Loop. Indian Loop and Cemetery Loop share the same trailhead beginning at the parking lot across from the sports field. The trails are well marked at this point, so you should not have any trouble finding the extremely tight single-track that begins Indian Loop. I can't imagine anyone wanting to

My son Jared lets his mind meander on a bend in the Chickasaw Creek.

or being able to go very fast on the first half-mile or so of this trail. It nearly loops back on itself in quite a few places. Exposed roots 3 or 4 inches high, along with muddy spots, require finesse instead of speed. The trail changes character after the first mile or so after it dead-ends into a sandy section. A right turn leads to Chickasaw Creek. You can get up a good head of steam on this section, but be aware that the thicker sandy spots can write a mighty quick surprise ending to your forward progress.

This is the trail where all sorts of coastal wildlife can be seen if you pay attention: deer, foxes, beavers, rabbits, and other animals are frequently sighted on this trail. Also, as you make your way closer to the water's edge, you may also run up on various reptiles, most of which only want to get out of your way. The two possible exceptions to this rule are the cottonmouth and alligator. Both of these are used to getting their way, so don't try to mimic what you saw on an old movie and wrestle with either one. Save your energy for the trail.

Beach Loop. By far, the most difficult loop of the 3 is this one. Pick up the beginning at the cemetery and head for the noise of the interstate. There are few trails where you go under interstate overpasses, but that's what's required on this one. It isn't as bad as it sounds, although I confess I felt uneasy when I thought of what could happen if someone going 70 mph above me tossed out a bottle or some other missile. I stopped underneath and listened to tires sing for a few minutes before heading down the trail.

The backwaters of the Chickasaw Creek offer an especially beautiful, relaxing view where you should plan some time to watch before heading to the ridges above the creek. Once you start the descent from Turtle Ridge, the really challenging section begins and doesn't let up for about 2 more miles when the flatter piece begins near the interstate. Expect steep climbs (never mind that they are relatively short) up slopes that would be tough enough without having to pick your slots between the large roots supporting oaks, sweet gums, and pines.

RIDE 53 *CLAUDE KELLEY STATE PARK*

Lying slightly more than 75 miles north of the Gulf of Mexico, another Alabama state park contains a combination of single-track and service roads leading up to sandy Piedmont overlooks in the Little River State Forest. Two separate trails—Gazebo (a 2.5-mile section containing two loops, a larger one and the smaller one going around the gazebo) and the 1.5-mile CCC (a quarter-mile approach to a mile-long loop utilizing eroded double-track and service roads)—explore opposite sides of the Little River Lake, where many of this park's visitors swim and rent paddle boats.

If you're lucky, some of the park's year-round visitors might be encountered, such as a gopher tortoise out of the burrow and taking an unhurried hike along the underbrush looking for a snack . . . or a mate. Those who have made binoculars a part of their mountain biking equipment can scan the old growth pine in the park for the red-cockaded woodpecker.

The land within this river plain seems to have undergone a series of hiccups in elevation. In a matter of a few miles, the piney knolls double in height from the surrounding land. Granted, the change is not one to cause much physical exertion, but the contrast suggests significant summits are reached when you behold a view stretching out nearly to the sea across a washboard of green woods.

The gazebo, midway through the trail named for it, straddles Monroe and Escambia Counties. It was built with the labor of the Civilian Conservation Corps that has dotted so much of the American landscape. The large stones and timbers under the shake roof make for a meditation station worthy of the weightiest subjects.

General location: The park occupies 960 acres on Highway 21 northeast of Mobile, Alabama.
Elevation change: A few grades call for getting geared into the small ring, but as a rule you won't find much to exert thighs, calves, or lungs.

RIDE 53   *CLAUDE KELLEY STATE PARK*

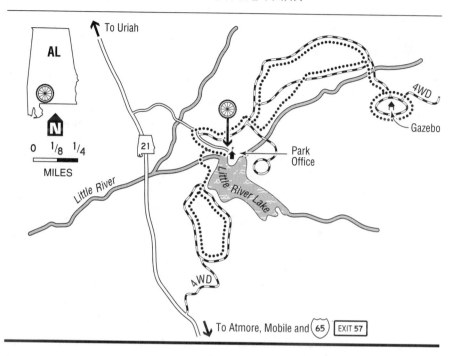

Season: Some of the clay—especially on the CCC Trail—takes a few days to dry out from a rain. Before it is sufficiently dry, clay outcrops pose a slick menace. But if you like to play in the mud, the ruts already there can't be hurt too much by your free wheeling.

Services: Mobile is the closest city where you can pick up specialty supplies; Atmore can supply the basics.

Hazards: There are few roots, rocks, or other traditional biking hazards to contend with. Keep alert also for the possibility of hikers on the trail.

Rescue index: You stay pretty much within shouting distance of the park's office.

Land status: This is a state park open for public use.

Maps: The office has a good map of the trail called "Claude Kelley State Park Trail System," which has incorporated a topo map of the area.

Finding the trail: Exit Interstate 65 at the Atmore exit and travel 10 miles north on Highway 21. Enter the park and begin your ride in the office parking lot near the bridge over the spillway below the lake. Turn on the first dirt road on your right heading out and follow it up to the Gazebo. The CCC Trail begins across the bridge and goes along an old roadbed.

Sources of additional information:

Claude Kelley State Park
Route 2, Box 77
Atmore, AL 36502
(334) 862-2511

Notes on the trail: The Gazebo loop begins by taking the service (gravel) road to the right headed back to the entrance. Another road on the right intersects about .25 mile later; this is where you'll come back in to the road after making a clockwise loop. Continue up the slight grade, taking the left fork where a service road splits to the right. Just before crossing the river on a bridge, the road forks again. The right goes back to the last intersection; the left leads to the gazebo. At the top of the hill, the road circles the gazebo where you'll want to stop and enjoy the view. On the way down take the left fork after crossing the river. Look for the single-track turning off to the left about .5 mile down. It dead-ends into a service road. Turn right and then left when it enters the gravel road. This is the approach you made from the parking lot.

The CCC trail begins by crossing the bridge at the spillway on your left headed toward the entrance from the parking lot. The eroded gravel road makes a short loop and climb up to the hill overlooking the lake and park. The road coming into the loop on the back side leads to Highway 21.

RIDE 54 *CONECUH TRAIL*

Back in 1976, when this 20-mile loop for hikers was begun by the Youth Conservation Corps, mountain biking was just a gleam in Gary Fisher's eye. It was with a similar gleam that I made my approach to this 80,000-acre southern Alabama National Forest. No fanfare preceded my discovery of this remote and scenic trail, only a biker's sixth sense that something wonderful lay in the longleaf pine forest and hardwood bottoms where stands of magnolia, American holly, and cypress grow.

Conecuh, (pronounced, "kuh-nek´-uh" and meaning "land of cane") has been traced back to the Muskogee Indians who lived in this land of plenty. Today, plenty of natural discoveries await the biker who plans to ride this loop. Because it's in Alabama's coastal plain, the Conecuh has grades hardly steep enough to make you breathe deeply.

You can keep your attention on the landscape where sightings of various wildlife—deer, mink, alligator, turkey, quail, heron, and more—keep the pulse high. I stopped by the National Forest office on my way out, talked to the district ranger, and checked facts. I told him I was nearly run over on several

The trails sometimes just stop, like this spur on the Conecuh Trail.

occasions by deer leaping over the trail. He got a kick out of hearing this because hikers had been complaining about some bikers nearly running over them on the trail. I guess a word to the wise is sufficient: Yield the trail to the hikers for whom this trail is primarily intended.

General location: As I was doing research for this trail, I discovered this national forest is approximately 90 miles from nearly everywhere: Pensacola, Mobile, Montgomery, and Dothan.

Elevation change: Even though little elevation change occurs, gentle rolls seem to be present constantly.

Season: Periods of heavy rain will make parts of this trail inaccessible. Of course, being situated less than 70 miles from the Gulf Coast makes this area prone to great heat waves and long growing seasons, which the insects love. If you have adapted to these conditions, you should always have a superb place to bike.

Services: Andalusia, 15 miles to the north, is the closest place where even the basics can be obtained.

Hazards: Few hazards exist, other than those associated with being in a remote environment, like running out of potable water.

Rescue index: Exercise caution on this trail. Only armadillos will hear your wails of want should you need rescue.

Land status: The trail lies inside the Conecuh National Forest.

RIDE 54 *CONECUH TRAIL*

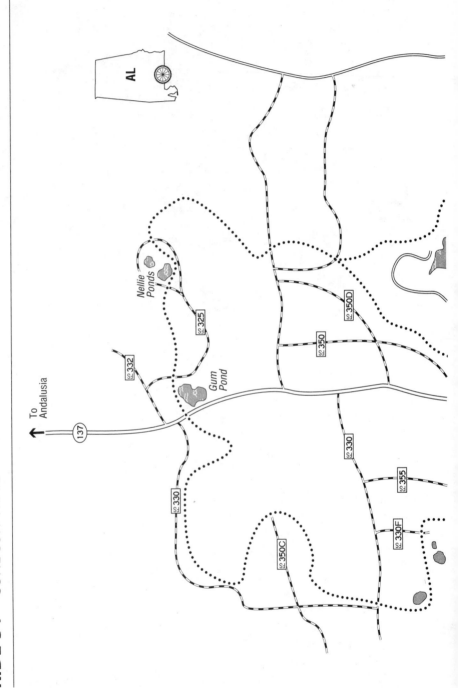

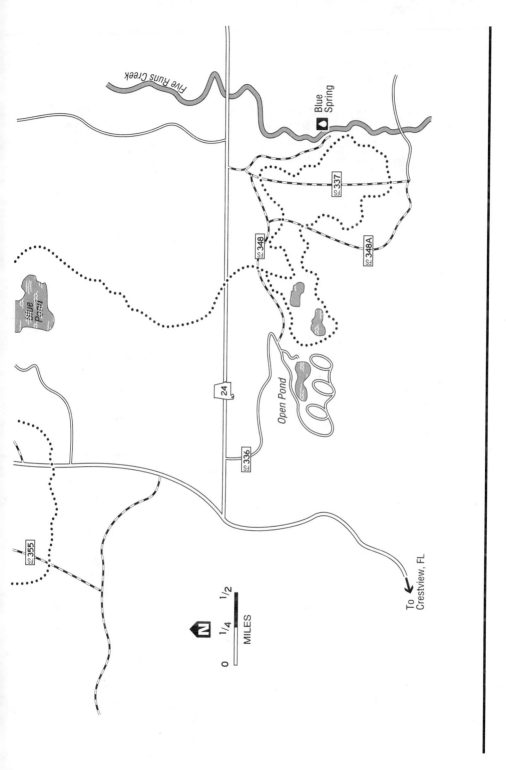

Maps: A good map—the Conecuh Trail Map—can be obtained from the National Forest District Ranger's Office in Andalusia, or the Supervisor's Office in Montgomery.

Finding the trail: From the north, exit Interstate 65 at Georgianna (birthplace of Hank Williams, Sr.) and head south on Highway 31 toward Andalusia. Leave this town on Highway 29 South, taking a left onto Highway 137. (Take note of the huge estates on the left; they are homes of people who have made their livelihood on the carnival circuit.) Begin your ride at either the trailhead at Blue Pond Recreational Area or Open Pond Recreational Area.

Sources of additional information:

> District Ranger
> Conecuh National Forest
> Route 5, Box 157
> Andalusia, AL 36420
> (334) 222-2555

Notes on the trail: Be careful to adhere to the signs allowing—or prohibiting—bike riding. I became confused and rode the trail down to Blue Springs, which is not open to bikes. Consequently, I got one of the nicest rides in the Deep South, remote and nearly blinding in its beauty. I also met some rangers from the state who were out on the trail setting up stuffed otter, bobcat, and wood duck for a group of children who were going to take a hike along this trail later that day. After talking to them for a few minutes and reporting I was headed for Blue Springs, a natural subterranean channel of clear water hitting the surface in the middle of Five Runs Creek, one ranger turned to me and said, "Be particular."

GEORGIA

A recent survey revealed that when most people think about the South, they think about Georgia. Call it the "*Gone with the Wind* Syndrome" or "*Deliverance*—itis." Those are two powerful images not easily plucked from the memory of a country. Most Georgians, however, do not deserve nor desire the stigma that remains as a result of these popular stories of the Deep South.

As I was growing up, I moved with my family to the North. After I left home, I traveled farther abroad. In each place, it was the same when I mentioned Georgia—questions and comments about hoop skirts with Scarlet prancing about, race riots, cotton fields filled with buck-toothed rednecks looking for one more swig of corn liquor. However, as Ferol Sams has written, "I was Raised Right"; I explained in as gentlemanly way as I knew that Georgia does not deserve the label of backwardness.

Georgia's beginnings, however, do little to remove this smudge of notoriety. King George released selected debtors from English prisons so they could colonize a foreign land in his name. The sons of these settlers predictably became blinded by what Georgia's earliest explorer, De Soto, had desired: Gold. Its discovery in the 1830s spelled doom for the peaceful Cherokee Indians who finally wound up on the Trail of Tears headed for reservations in Oklahoma.

Georgia, though, is a land of many natural resources. The tall trees that lined its coast were used to build ships. The fertile fields inland begged plow to turn it into cold cash. Indigo, rice, cotton, sugar, corn, wheat, tobacco, peanuts, pecans—there seemed to be no end to the ability of the land to create crops. But then the land wore thin. Sherman's torch was followed by carpetbaggers. Weevils moved in. It was not a pretty sight.

However, this land has potential that cannot be bottled up or torched. From small fits and starts, industry grew. The many creeks and rivers turned mills grinding grain, sawing lumber, and spinning fibers into cloth. Subsistence farming held communities together while big cities grew. Savannah commanded the Gulf Stream, Columbus the lower Chattahoochee, Dalton delivered textiles, and Atlanta became the hub of it all.

The northern section of Georgia has been largely set aside in one national forest, the Chattahoochee. Nearly reaching from the western border of the state beyond Rome, all the way across to its eastern boundary with North and South Carolina, the largest state east of the Mississippi has provided a wonderful playground for hikers, bikers, hunters, fishers, boaters, birders, campers, you name it. The true gold of Georgia's hills lies in its ability to touch those searching for a natural communion.

When I think of Georgia, I picture deep, dense stands of hemlocks hovering over cool waters rushing so quickly they give a chill even on the hottest summer day. I close my eyes and can feel the salt breeze off Cumberland Island and can hear the pounding hooves of wild horses running across its sand dunes, which are higher than houses. I climb the oldest mountains around and pitch my tent where I can see the sun set at my head and the sun rise at my feet. Whenever I grow weary of the wild (which isn't often), I head to the urban madness of Atlanta and its nearly three million people and celebrate with them the beauty of being in the South, of being in Georgia. Few places exist better suited to enjoying life. I'm not prejudiced; I'm just Georgian. After you stay here a while, you will understand the difference.

Albany Area Ride

Few people think of any place in Georgia south of the love-bug line as capable of having culture, let alone a mountain bike trail. All it takes, though, is a few days in this amazingly refined city to dispel such notions. Indeed, you have to travel many miles north in order to find a true mountain, or even a hill for that matter, but the culture . . . that's a different story.

Although Albany lies in an area where bass fishin' and quail huntin' form the true cultural centerpieces in many homes, the Albany Municipal Auditorium regularly produces plays, concerts, and (have you fainted yet?) ballet. The Theatre Albany also caters to those more esoteric needs you may have stirred up as you moseyed among the Albany Museum of Art and the Thronateeska Heritage Museum of History and Science. Radium Springs, Georgia's largest natural spring, remains a popular stop for many visitors who wish to soak it all in.

Albany even has its own magazine—*Albany*—designed to address the issues of dining, entertainment, business, and the arts. What brought this much money down this far south, this far west, this far east of so much? A quick trip through the countryside around Albany suggests an answer. Those trees growing in grove after grove are Georgia's answer to the black gold of Texas. Here, it's called "brown gold," and every year about November, pecans fall by the ton into trucks headed to market.

Closer to town, in the middle of a park that is home to exotic animals, mountain bikers will find true wealth in the trail named for people who arrived here long ago from the mountains. Chehaw Park has recently asserted itself as the focal point for many outdoor activities in Albany, including mountain biking. There's even a regular Thursday evening group that rides together in the tropical lushness of Chehaw's 700 acres.

It's true that Albany is an unlikely destination for those looking for an area to ride mountain bikes, but the fact remains that you can straddle your front fork on a trail that will make you say, "AW!" And when you're in town, be sure to stop by the bike shop that made it possible, Cycle World.

For more information:

Cycle World
351 North Slappey Road
Albany, GA 31701
(912) 431-0908 or (fax) 431-1678

Albany Convention and Visitors Bureau
225 West Broad Avenue
Albany, GA 31701
(912) 434-8700

Chehaw Park
Philema Road (GA 91)
Albany, GA 31701
(912) 430-5275

RIDE 55 *CHEHAW PARK TRAIL*

The unusual, but fun to say, name of this park in southwest Georgia comes from the Creek word meaning "people from the mountains." But don't look for any mountains here. However, if you're looking for a fun place to roll some knobbies, you won't have to go any farther than this 7.5-mile loop in the coastal plains.

Back in 1977, the Albany city government received a state park from the Georgia government, which was then developed into a multi-use park called Chehaw Wild Animal Park. Its collection of wild animals live in natural habitat exhibits based on designs by Albany native Jim Fowler of Mutual of Omaha's *Wild Kingdom* fame. RV, tent, and primitive campsites are available for the family or individual looking for a staging area for such activities as picnicking, fishing, boating, hiking and, of course, mountain biking.

The park provides the perfect answer to those families who have hard-charging mountain bikers and a less active family member or two. While the bikers are out on the trail spinning sand and spending endorphins, the others can cruise through the exhibits where bobcats, buffaloes, "electric-lined" zebras, colobus monkeys, elephants, and eagles can be viewed, for the most part, in a natural environment.

The catastrophic floods of 1994 in southwest Georgia hit Albany especially hard. Large parts of the park lay under water up to eight feet deep. Understandably, plans for putting in sections of single-track were shelved until the waters and weather moderated. In fact, it was March 1995 before trails could be cut in to connect with the already existing jeep track—officially termed a fire break in park parlance—and nature trails.

The trail had its ribbon-cutting ceremony on April 2, 1995, topped off by a race put on by Chehaw Park, The American Lung Association of Dougherty County, and Cycle World, whose owner, Jim Laue, has been the chief machete and ax wielder and designer behind making the trails. Jim presented the idea to the park's director, Steve Marshall, who saw it was a good deal all the way around. And, presto-chango, south Georgia off-road bikers have a sure 'nuff MTB trail.

The result brings drool to the lips of the avid mountain biker, or at least a good bead of sweat on the brow. Despite Chehaw Park's location on a fairly level flood plain, the slight elevation changes on the sandy uplands near the

RIDE 55   *CHEHAW PARK TRAIL*

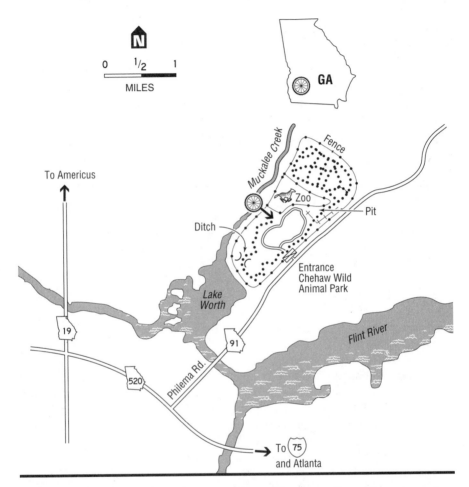

Muckalee Creek have been put into play with great effect. There is even a sandy ditch that will provide all the hill-climbing challenge most people can meet. Another drop of 10–12 vertical feet over approximately three horizontal feet will elicit an involuntary yip of excitement; however, a cheat chute exists to the left if you have a timid yipper. Plans are being considered for developing more of the area's vertical potential, which should satisfy most thrill seekers' search for the edge. In order to ride some sections of park trail legally, you will have to be a part of the regularly scheduled races.

General location: Most of the single-track lies on the 200 acres north of the zoo. The less technical family trails go throughout the park, utilizing jeep track and nature trails, some of which may not be open for everyday use. Be sure to check in at the ticket office and get permission before riding any of the unblazed sections.

Elevation change: The trail's slight overall change in elevation should not be misconstrued as "a ride in the park." While most sections do not have much to crank about, there are at least 2 areas that will positively flare your nostrils.

Season: The trail's sandy nature holds up well under wet conditions. The heat and humidity of south Georgia's summers, however, prove an impediment to all but the most avid of mountain bikers. Still, early summer mornings can provide an especially rewarding time for biking this trail without taxing your cooling system too much.

Services: All services can be acquired in the beautiful city of Albany.

Hazards: Heat and biting insects in the summer could be troublesome to some bikers; however, if you ride fast enough the bugs won't keep up. The heat is a bit more persistent. No other hazards will likely be found unless you accompany Jim Laue on rough-cut, virgin sections of new single-track he's putting in. Then prepare to find out how saw briar got its common name.

Rescue index: You seldom travel out of earshot should you need to yell for help, although at times it feels as though you are in the middle of a tropical forest.

Land status: All the trail falls within the friendly confines of Chehaw Park.

Maps: The trail is well marked and has as its perimeter a fire break that encircles the park. You can pick up a map of Chehaw Park at the ticket office on your way in. This map does not show the single-track; however, Jim Laue drew out the sketch and scale from which the map in this book has been developed.

Finding the trail: Exit off of the Liberty Expressway (520/82) onto Highway 91, Philema Road. Follow the signs to Chehaw Park and enter at the gate where you'll be asked to pay an entrance fee. Take the one-way road to the right and follow it nearly to where it joins back up with the main road. Look for Pavilion 10 and park there. The trailhead is through the fence about 100 yards to the left of the pavilion. Look for the sign. The trail is blazed with orange arrows that are 18 inches tall and on laminated paper.

Sources of additional information:

Chehaw Park
Philema Road, GA 91
P.O. Box 447
Albany, GA 31703-4801
(912) 430-5275

Jim Laue enjoys the fruits of his labor at Chehaw Park.

Cycle World
2401 Dawson Road
Albany, GA
(912) 435-1678 or 431-0908

Notes on the trail: The single-track portions of this course were literally hacked out of dense stands of pine and bluejack oak, saw briar, and sparkleberry shrubs. The shifts in elevation provided the direction for much of the trail. Jim Laue spent much time in looking at where the natural lay of the land would provide the most diversity and has left as much vegetation as possible. As a result, you will find a mostly unaltered sandy coastal plain sliding by as you pedal this quietly inviting and intriguing landscape. And slide by you must, at least while on the single-track. Saplings stand in an intricate maze of gates which require moves that suggest what a worm would do to the insides of an apple.

You'll be glad for the slower pace since you may see such majestic creatures as the great blue heron or the endangered gopher tortoise. Magnificent, looming live oaks spread their vast canopies over sinkhole springs where you should stop and catch your breath, which will be shortened more because of the natural beauty rather than exertion. The Creeks, who came south unwillingly from the Appalachians years ago and for whom the park is probably named, no doubt found out they had been done a favor.

Columbus Area Rides

Southwest of Macon—on Georgia's border with Alabama—seems an unlikely setting for grabbing the mountain bike off the roof rack and spinning some dirt, but a few days in the neighborhood should make a believer out of you. Two topographic features—Fort Benning and the Chattahoochee River—dominate the landscape. One you will want to stay fairly far away from; the other will beckon constantly.

Another remarkable natural feature found near here is Providence Canyon, a state park established to control a situation run amuck. The soil in this part of Georgia has a strong tendency to erode if not treated properly. After a certain barn was built in the early 1900s, its roof runoff began carving what quickly became the monstrous valley called Providence Canyon. After you see it, it is still hard to believe. No, you can't ride your bike there unless your name is Captain Hook.

This part of Georgia obtained presidential significance from the time when Franklin Roosevelt visited Warm Springs seeking relief from polio. He spent so much time here, a "Little White House" was built where he stayed during his frequent visits. Former President Carter's hometown of Plains, the town of 700 that became a National Historical Site as mandated by the National Park Service, continues the presidential connection. And while you're there, get a fist full of the prince of delicacies—the boiled peanut—which is grown by the tons nearby.

The lakes formed by the frequent damming of the Chattahoochee south of Atlanta—West Point, Lake Harding, Bartletts Ferry Lake, Goat Rock Lake, Lake Oliver, and Walter F. George Reservoir—are the shrines where bass are gods. An entire industry has grown up on the hundreds of miles of shoreline these lakes have created. If your idea of the perfect complement to a day on the bike trail is wetting a line and waiting for a big 'un to hit, come on down to Columbus.

And if your social life is in need of some high PSI, make sure to check with Bill Arnold at Arnold's Bicycle Sales and Service in Columbus, where the Lone Wolf Social Club gathers regularly. This pack of smiling cyclists gets together for a howling good time of biking, hiking, gabbing, and anything else they can dream up. You'll be glad to meet them.

For more information:

Columbus Visitors Center
1000 Bay Avenue
Columbus, GA 31902
(800) 999-1613

"Bike spoken here."

Providence Canyon State Park
Route 1, Box 158
Lumpkin, GA 31815
(912) 838-6202

Arnold's Bicycle Sales and Service
4613 Warm Springs Road
Columbus, GA 31902
(706) 568-1806

RIDE 56 *TINY TRAIL*

Bordered by two major highways, a subdivision, and a secondary road, this trail presents an unlikely setting for a rubber-tired foray into natural wilderness. The sight of a beaver pond, deer tracks, and a waterfall all suggest something you would find in a national forest rather than on the outskirts of a metropolitan area where fast food joints line the highway. Although the hum of traffic remains nearly constant, it does little to take away from the beauty this trail offers.

Although I was prepared for the possibility of finding wildlife on this trail, I was still surprised when I wound up playing tag with four deer. At first, they

RIDE 56 *TINY TRAIL*

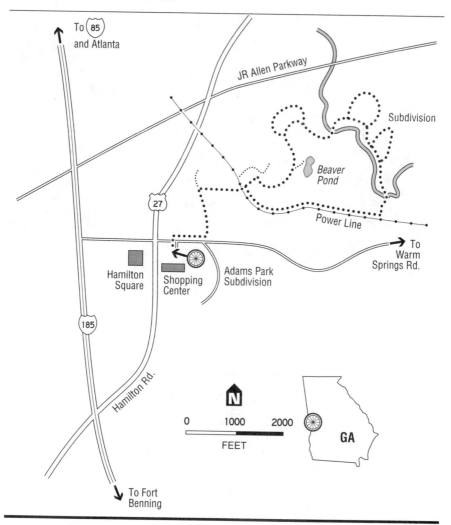

jumped one direction over the creek gurgling in the bottoms, and then again to the other side as I crossed behind them. They seemed to enjoy it, and it almost seemed they were waiting for me to follow along.

The seven or so miles (total) lying in this out-and-back-loop combo between highways also presents a surprisingly difficult section leading down to Ginger Creek. Although I made it down to streamside, I exercised discretion and walked across gingerly. Others, however, seem to have made it a habit of crossing pedal-bound, judging by the deep tracks on either side of the creek.

A beaver in the middle of suburbia did this on Tiny Trail.

General location: Situated among 3 busy thoroughfares in north Columbus, Georgia, this trail may be called "Tiny," but it is big on biking entertainment.

Elevation change: You won't have to adopt an intense pedal push to make most climbs, but some require full power to throttle up without interruption.

Season: Wet times hamper the enjoyment of this trail. Other than too much water, no seasonal restrictions should apply.

Services: Columbus has many facilities, among them the army base, Fort Benning. As a result, and depending on which side of the city you wind up, you can get anything from tattoos to licorice twists and everything in between.

Hazards: A couple of turns require total focus. Should you let your mind wander for a brief instant, you could find yourself head-over-heels for this trail.

Rescue index: The 4 sides to the trail are as follows: J.R. Allen Parkway on the north, US 27 on the west, Weems Road on the south, and Hillbrook Estates (a subdivision) on the east, all within the space of less than a square mile. This bodes well for those in need of assistance.

Land status: This land is not posted as being private, yet it has no signs suggesting otherwise. It seems to be in a dead-man's zone, partially owned by the power company, whose powerline runs lengthwise between sections of trail. The topography apparently has prevented development more than what has already occurred.

Maps: The map is made from my notes and the Columbus City Map.

Finding the trail: As you enter Columbus on US 27 from the north, stop at the first shopping mall, Hamilton Square, across from Weems Road and the Del Taco. Park behind the Del Taco and ride down Weems until you get to Adams Park subdivision on the right, approximately .75 mile. The single-track begins directly across from Adams Park entrance, up the bank on the left.

Sources of additional information:

Arnold's Bicycle Sales and Service
4613 Warm Springs Road
Columbus, GA 31902
(706) 568-1806

Notes on the trail: The trail begins in a depressingly trash-strewn manner. Asphalt shingles and concrete blocks from destruction projects lie in piles along the first section of trail. I must confess that at this point on my initial run, I felt let down. However, as you take the first single-track to the right, the trail begins to gain a credible character. The most confusing connection to make on this trail comes after crossing the powerline right-of-way: cross the opening and look for the barely perceptible right-hand turn. This single-track cuts off just after beginning the counterclockwise loop back into the powerline trail. Do not take a right turn after coming immediately into the powerline clearing: it takes you to some trails used by ATVs, which eventually wind up in some-one's backyard, away from where you want to ride. A small section of single-track goes to the right toward an acre-or-so pond made by a beaver, which makes for a nice hesitation station. The trail leads down to Ginger Creek, crosses it, and goes back into the powerline right-of-way. I suggest turning around at this point. On the way back, look for the single-track leading up the hill in 2 spots on the right, which loop back into the main trail. Disorientation coefficient on this trail is low; just follow your nose and you should stay between the highways.

RIDE 57 *FLAT ROCK PARK*

My first sighting of a mountain biker in Flat Rock Park came when a young man flew across the park road, hair blown back in a helmetless hairdo. Although I doubted the young man's sincerity about safety, I had no doubt he was enjoying himself as he followed his friends up the hill in this city park. It was dusk, and I could hear the yelps of excitement he and his friends let loose as they made their way down the other side of the hill to Flat Rock Lake,

RIDE 57 *FLAT ROCK PARK*

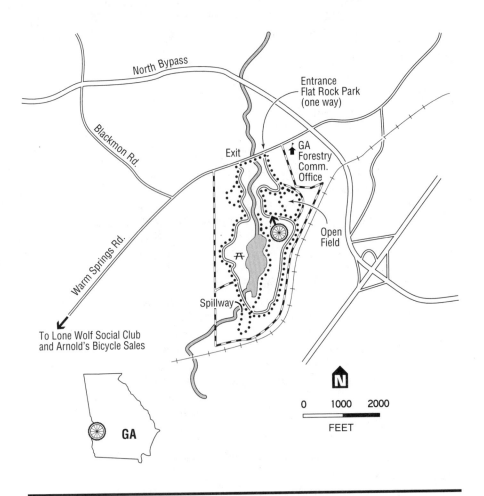

which is fed (naturally enough) by Flat Rock Creek. They were right in the middle of approximately four miles of a basic loop around the lake that runs on single-track, double-track, gravel service roads, and pavement.

This park's allure to bikers comes from its absolute lack of adherence to much structure at all. No blazes and no established single-track confines this course to a certain direction and distance. Many of the pathways are barely perceptible. If you want to climb up the bank covered by monstrous longleaf pines, so be it; you can. If you want to employ your amazing trials skills by

Tail-to-tail, a pair of muscovys observe morning at Flat Rock Park.

riding across a gas pipe above a creek, you can do that, too. The beauty of Flat Rock Park Trails comes as much from the freedom you can use while picking your route as it does from the stark outcrop of rock over which Flat Rock Creek flows.

General location: This trail is found within the city of Columbus, Georgia, in the northeast part of town.

Elevation change: A few hills provide an area where you can muscle up on some serious cranking; they are short and easily climbed.

Season: The park provides all-season terrain for mountain bikers.

Services: The bulk of developed businesses lies to the southwest of Flat Rock Creek Park in Columbus, Georgia.

Hazards: A few narrow and technical crossings exist lakeside. Other than that, I would not expect a moderately experienced biker to have any difficulty.

Rescue index: This park is open from 8 A.M. to 10 P.M. It is a popular place and not very large; therefore, it should be easy to obtain assistance should you need it.

Land status: This park is managed by the City of Columbus Parks and Recreation.

Maps: No maps exist, probably because few established, orthodox trails exist. This is a place where you can ride along pretty much wherever you want.

Finding the trail: Traveling on Interstate 185, north of Columbus, exit onto the North Bypass and head east. Get off on Blackmon Road and head south. When Blackmon Road dead-ends into Warm Springs Road, take a left and then the right into Flat Rock Park. The trail cuts across the road after passing the concession stand. Parking for the trail can be had on the left at a pavilion, above a rock bridge on the right of this one-way park road.

Sources of additional information:

Flat Rock Park
Warm Springs Road
Columbus, GA 31902
(706) 571-4895

Arnold's Bicycle Sales and Service
4613 Warm Springs Road
Columbus, GA 31902
(706) 568-1806

Notes on the trail: Use the asphalt as departure points for much of this trail. There is little danger in getting lost; keep the lake on your right as you ride in a clockwise direction around the park. Take your time and explore any ground that does not have a sign prohibiting entry.

RIDE 58 *CALLAWAY GARDENS*

Mountain biking purists will not see Callaway Gardens as the ultimate expression of off-road cycling. Its asphalt pathways and manicured shrubbery and flowerbeds present a less-than-rugged arena for your pedaling prowess. However, this special site is one that can satisfy your physical wanderings on a set of fat tires.

What this trail lacks in challenging hill climbs, it more than makes up for in scenery and mileage. Over 18 miles of trail loop various gardens. Roses, azaleas, rhododendrons, and annuals and perennials of all sorts have been planted to keep a full array of color before you year-round. Signs are posted on representative trees and in special areas to identify the many examples of flora found here.

As if that weren't enough, a butterfly garden houses a large number of various fluttering flyers dressed in exotic colors. The huge pane glass windows of the lepidopterium create a tropical atmosphere inside. Butterflies flit in the airspace around you while ground birds wander freely looking for food. This is a stop you'll want to reserve quite a few minutes for.

RIDE 58 *CALLAWAY GARDENS*

Note: *Ride is black-top, double-track bike path.*

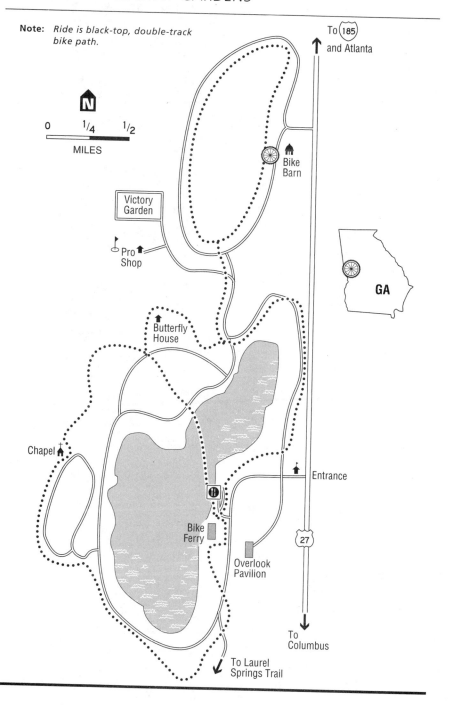

0   1/4   1/2
MILES

To (185) and Atlanta

Bike Barn

Victory Garden

Pro Shop

GA

Butterfly House

Chapel

Entrance

Bike Ferry

Overlook Pavilion

27

To Columbus

To Laurel Springs Trail

Part of the pampered trail at Callaway Gardens.

General location: This trail is found within the park boundaries of Callaway Gardens.

Elevation change: I saw some folks who had rented bikes huffing and puffing as they used their single-speed bikes to climb the gentle slopes.

Season: The asphalt makes this a smooth ride year-round.

Services: Columbus is the biggest city nearby. Quite a few businesses have been built up along this stretch of road to cater to the guests at Callaway Gardens and Warm Springs.

Hazards: This is a popular spot for tourists. Some of them will be on bikes when they should be on foot. Be aware of their aberrant on-bike behavior. In places, you will be tempted to ride faster than what is safe for you or others sharing the trail. Keep your eyes ahead and look for oncoming traffic.

Rescue index: Plenty of people, in the form of visitors and staff, remain visible in this attraction. If you are unlucky enough to have problems on this trail, it would not be long before someone would happen by and offer help.

Land status: This is land owned by Callaway Gardens.

Maps: The front gate has a map of the entire area inside Callaway Gardens, which you will receive with payment of admission fee. Call for details.

Finding the trail: Numerous intersections are marked by permanent signs. Park anywhere you want inside the park and ride the trail from there.

Sources of additional information:

Callaway Gardens
Highway 27
Pine Mountain, GA 31822
(800) 282-8181

Notes on the trail: The trail is easy to follow except for in the parking lot behind the lake. Ride through the parking lot and turn right onto the park road once you've left the parking lot. You'll notice an intersection soon. Turn left onto the asphalt double-track going up the hill.

Macon Area Rides

My first experience with Macon came at the tender age of seventeen as I followed my sweetheart down to Mercer University where I somehow managed to accrue a 1.4 GPA. My parents were unimpressed with my accounts of all the many distractions to be found by a Mercer University freshman: the terrific snowstorm of early February, which dumped over a foot of snow in less than 24 hours; a Jackson Browne concert in the university's chapel when Greg Allman showed up strumming a 12-string and singing "Sweet Melissa"; the huge magnolia trees just outside the history department building where I would go view the campus for hours as the wind rocked me high aloft in my perch. Ferol Sams might understand, but my parents did not.

Thank goodness that was before mountain biking, or I never would have graduated. But Macon has not changed in one respect despite the years: it still provides many opportunities for exploration and discovery that belie its apparent middle Georgia drabness. Spring is a wonderful time to visit Macon with its Cherry Blossom Festival and explosion of attendant color. The Ocmulgee River has long attracted people and civilizations to it, and the Ocmulgee National Monument commemorates the 1,200-year existence of Native American society along the banks of this river.

In the days when poetry was more widely memorized by school children, Sidney Lanier, a Macon native and widely known poet of his day, was partly responsible for many Georgia children entering lines of poetry into their lexicon, more or less willingly. My father still launches into the first lines of Lanier's "The Song of the Chattahoochee" whenever we cross that river. My favorite, though, is "The Marshes of Glynn."

There must have been a bit of the poet in the old man who saw me ascend to my usual magnolia nest one Sunday afternoon. Since he was the only movement on that quiet afternoon, I watched him as he ambled his way slowly along the sidewalk leading directly underneath the tree. I must have been 40 feet up in the boughs when the gentleman suddenly stopped by the trunk, looked up straight at me and croaked the riddle, "What's high in the elements, but not in the tree? I told you, now you tell me." Before I could answer, but not before my jaw dropped the full 40 feet, he trudged his way on down the sidewalk and disappeared. Such is the magic of Macon.

For more information:

> Bike-Tech of Middle Georgia
> 3003 Vineville Avenue
> Macon, GA
> (912) 741-8356

Breakaway Cyclery
3121 Vineville Avenue
Macon, GA 31204-2342
(912) 741-9090

Capitol Cycle Company
1090 Washington Avenue
Macon, GA 31201-6798
(912) 745-3946

Macon Welcome Center
200 Cherry Street
Terminal Station
Macon, GA 31208-6354
(912) 743-3401

RIDE 59 *THUNDER SCOUT TRAIL*

Centrally located Upson County marks the beginning of the Pine Mountain chain of ridges whose steep sides suggest the more northerly, mountainous regions of the Deep South. The mighty Flint River rolls through the valleys below on its way to merge with Georgia's chief river, the Chattahoochee, which is called the Apalachicola River as it leaves Georgia in the southwestern-most corner.

Here the mountain biker can ride 7.5 miles of single- and double-track combination looping through the Thunder Boy Scout Camp. The rocks and radical climbs make this a good workout for the experienced rider. The narrow, steep single-track down to the Flint River will exercise forearms and balance in a descent more daintily done by horse, but it was my favorite part of the trail.

The Flint flexed its muscles during the great flood of 1994 when it spread out for miles around, carrying downed trees so numerous and violently swirling, they reminded two young boys I talked to of an armada of alligators. Sand bars and scarred trees will no doubt remain for many years as a reminder of this waterway's dominion over the landscape it has helped form.

If you choose to set up camp in this wilderness either along the Flint's banks or in the more developed sites inside Camp Thunder, a sense of the region's unbridled nature will come creeping out from the dense woods and grab you as suddenly as a coyote's call. Or it may pad softly up to camp on the paws of panthers. Or it could just as easily roll up on the worn rubber tires of two country boys on bikes.

RIDE 59 *THUNDER SCOUT TRAIL*

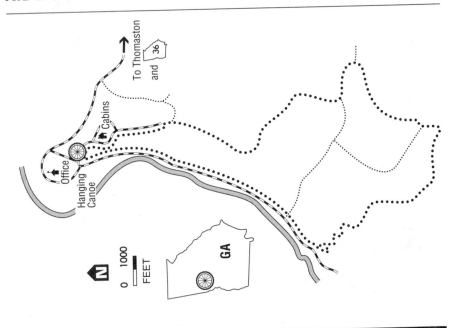

Justin and his brother, who lived in a house nearby, came to visit me as I was eating supper. "Hey, mister. You goin' fishin'?" one of them asked me. After I told them I was there to collect information on the bike trail and ride it the next morning, they started to give me the lowdown, but not before they took a look at my bike and said, "It looks like it's been through some stuff."

For the next 20 minutes, while dusk settled along the river bank, they described the good fishing and hunting to be had in these hills. They told me not to worry if I heard the sound of a woman being killed; it was just the sound of a panther screaming. As we slapped and rubbed at skeets digging in on our skin, the boys pointed across to the other side of the river where an obvious fire had happened and said, "Yesterday the smoke was so thick on the ridge it's a wonder there are any mosquitoes at all."

They also informed me that I could get good water dripping right out of the rock up on the bike trail. "That's where they get the name of the road from. There's rock steps leading up to it." With that, they rode back to their house.

That night, as I lay awake listening to the gurgle of the river and the mosquitoes whining outside my tent, I heard what I could have sworn was a desperate woman's scream far off in the woods. As I rode my bike alone up into the secluded mountains the next morning, my ears and wits were nimble with the memory of that sound.

They say panthers inhabit the mountains of Thunder
Scout Trail.

General location: The trail goes through property owned by Flint River
Council, Boy Scouts of America, east of the Flint River.
Elevation change: 800 feet of climbing for each 7.5-mile lap; most of it is
located in 2 sections, which made me yearn for a weenier gear.
Season: The dense shade provided by the forest keeps the sun off your back
in the summer, and except for the hottest days, this trail is suitable for year-
round riding.
Services: Wilson's Grocery on Highway 74 is a good stop for most basic
provisions. Water is provided at the scout camp.
Hazards: If you are a biker who is half mountain goat, this trail with its wide
assortment of rocks scattered all through the trail will roll you to ecstasy. The
switchbacking descent to the river has some twists and turns you will need to
finagle your way down.

Rescue index: You are in a mountainous, fairly remote area. It could take an hour or more to get help if you slip up on one of those rocks.

Land status: The 2,000 acres are owned by the Boy Scouts of America.

Maps: A detailed topo map of Camp Thunder showing the trails is available at the scout office. A copy of this map is also posted on the bulletin board under the hanging canoe.

Finding the trail: From the west, go to Woodbury and head east on Highway 74 for 4 miles and turn right at the Camp Thunder sign shortly after going through the intersection at the stop sign. The eastern approach calls for finding Thomaston and taking Highway 74 west for 13.5 miles and turning left not too far after passing Wilson's Grocery on the right. Turn right onto Dripping Rock Road at the sign about 200 yards. About another mile or so farther, you will see a soccer field on the left. Turn to the left on the dirt road up the hill. The trail begins on the road underneath the canoe, or you can start off on the other end of the loop by taking the first left on a gravel road, go 50 yards, and take a right on the service road past the cabins.

Sources of additional information:

Gerald I. Lawhorn Canoe Base and Training Center
P.O. Box 173
Griffin, GA 30224
(706) 647-6313
For camping reservations: (770) 227-4556
For Camp Thunder: (706) 647-9539

Thomaston Mountain Bike Association
1104 South Green Street
Thomaston, GA 30286
(404) 525-2373 or (706) 567-8970 or (706) 647-5199

Bicycle City
2905 North Expressway
Griffin, GA 30223-6497
(770) 228-7422

Mike's Bikes
3901 Miller Road
Columbus, GA 31909-4701
(706) 569-1875

Arnold's Bicycle Sales and Service
4613 Warm Springs Road
Columbus, GA 31909-5439
(706) 568-1806

Notes on the trail: Parts of the trail use access roads for the camp, but the majority follows single-track. The first section has a two-part climb: the first will test your endurance over a sustained climb of approximately 300 feet in .75 mile, and before you catch your breath, you'll see the ski slope to the right awaiting your throbbing thighs, which will take you up another 100 feet in about 200 yards.

Once on the ridge you will be treated to some fantastic views and relatively moderate climbs on the circle around Double Branch. The next 2 lefts go to Thundering Spring Road and Lake Ini-To, which will add approximately 4 more miles to your trip should you decide to ride them. The 7.5-mile loop is completed by taking the next right along Muddy Slash Ridge. The steep switchbacks will be found on this last section that begins nearly 1,140 feet above sea level. The descent to the rocky roadbed running along the Flint River will strain your forearms, as a loss of altitude of over 400 feet occurs in less than .5 mile.

The rock garden, masquerading as a road along the Flint River, will be a long trip without good front shocks. The flood of 1994 made this section worse as it was under water for much of the summer. You'll soon—but not soon enough—wind up at the gate where you began. Take a shower up at the bathhouse inside the camp if you want to and bask in your bike-worthiness.

RIDE 60   *THOMSON COMPANY TRAIL*

Macon, Georgia, has a classic trail located in an unlikely place—an industrial park. The six-plus miles in a series of loops developed jointly by NORBA expert racers Mitch Thompson and Chris McGee make their single-track way through a young pine forest. Chris also heads up L.H. Thomson Company's bicycle components department and had the trail built so that it would be demanding enough to simulate the toughest conditions known to bike.

This trail was completely hand-built using picks, shovels, weedeaters, and chainsaws in order to retain many special qualities as it winds through technical single-track so tight in places you have to inhale at just the right moment to squeeze through. There's a bit of something for every type of biker, provided you like handlebar-gripping excitement. But tug your chin strap tight and wear your goggles because features on this trail have caused company president Ronnie Thomson to remark, "Mountain bikers must be part masochist."

Plans are for developing up to six more miles of trails that can be used by anyone who signs a waiver prior to the first ride. Just check in at the front desk and ask to speak to someone about signing the waiver to ride. That's

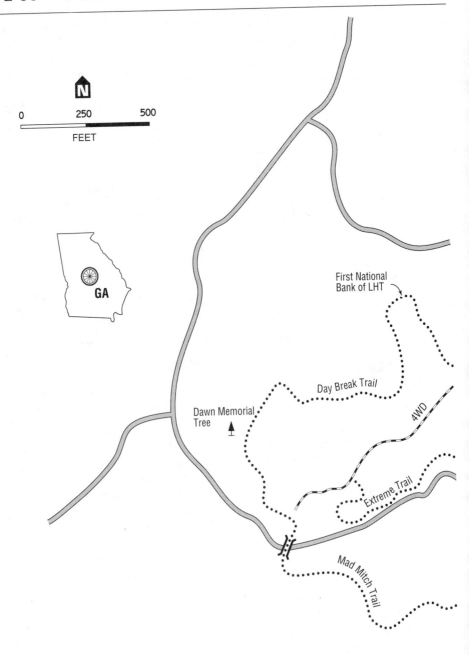

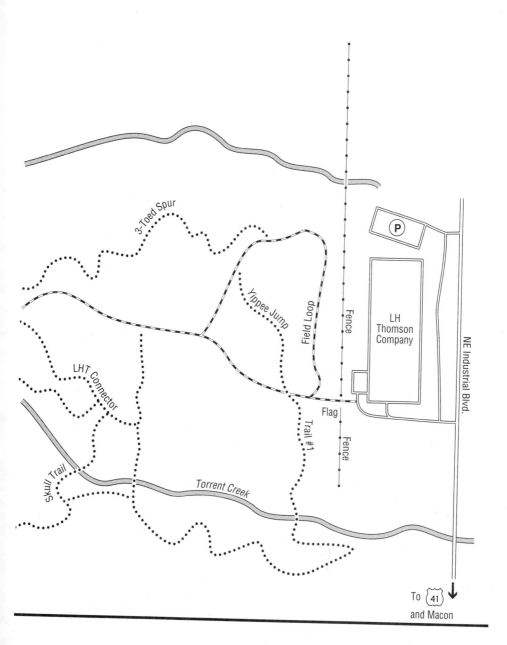

when you'll probably learn the company's policy for putting out an orange flag when the trail's in use, and you'll receive a map of the trail.

If you are planning your first trip to the trail after normal business hours or on a Sunday, call the company or write in time for them to send you a waiver. Otherwise, you'll be violating the generosity of a big supporter of mountain biking and putting at risk the availability of the trail. And I assure you, once you ride this trail, you will want to protect it as carefully as you would your water supply.

General location: The course is located behind the L.H. Thomson Company's building on the other side of a chainlink fence with an opening just wide enough for a mountain bike's handlebars.

Elevation change: Although no sustained climbs of much consequence are found on the trail, you will drop off banks that can cause your eyelids to catch air. Very little of the trail is level outside of the loop circling the field immediately behind the fence.

Season: As is the case with much of the Deep South, mid-summers can be painfully oppressive as both the heat and humidity can reach the mid-90s during afternoons. However, the trail—with its sandy soil and good drainage—can be ridden in all but the wettest weather. If you need to know the shape of the trail, ask. Remember, you're a welcome guest for now. Trashing the trail in any way can put riding it in jeopardy for the rest of us.

Services: All services can be obtained in Macon.

Hazards: Logs, switches, steep drops, and technical creek crossings can be a source of great fun and challenge, but use discretion with them if you are not very experienced.

Rescue index: Help is nearby, but don't forget to put out the orange flag to let the folks inside know the trail is being ridden. When you finish, put the flag up or check with someone inside to let them know you're finished riding.

Land status: Most of the trail is on property owned by L.H. Thomson Company, Inc. However, the trail does skirt and cross over onto land owned by another company and the county government, who have both graciously given permission for the trail. As a result, you are asked not to stop or do any exploring on foot. Keep moving and keep the trust.

Maps: Ask for the bike trail map at the front office of L.H. Thomson Company or ask for their map at one of the area bike shops.

Finding the trail: Take Interstate 75 south out of Macon and exit onto the Pio Nono/Warner Robins/41/247 exit. Head south on Highway 247 for 4 miles when you'll see a beer distribution center on your right. Exit onto the ramp for Highway 41 south (directly in front of the plant) and go a little over 2 miles. Look for the Trane Company on your left. Turn left onto the road (Northwest Industrial) immediately past Trane. Cross the tracks and turn right at the stop sign onto Northeast Industrial Boulevard. L.H. Thomson Company is the second building on your left at 7800 NE Industrial Boulevard.

Chris McGee rides part of the trail he and Mitch
Thompson designed at Thomson Company, Macon.

Enter the service road and park behind the right side of the building if this is
not your first ride. If it is your inaugural ride, park in front and go inside to
check in and sign the waiver.

Sources of additional information:

L.H. Thomson Company
P.O. Box 10158
Wilson Airport
Macon, GA 31297-0158
(912) 788-5052

Bike-Tech
3003 Vineville Avenue
Macon, GA 31201
(912) 741-8356

Notes on the trail: Very few trails in the Deep South have been built with the care and sheer artistry of this one. As mentioned earlier, no backhoes or big machines were brought in to do the dirty work. When Ronnie Thomson suggested bringing in dozers to make the job easier, he was greeted with, "What? And ruin the trail?"

As a mark to the enthusiasm guiding this trail's construction, a call was sent out to begin blazing the trail in the fall of 1994. Ten people showed up on a rainy, ugly day to lay the first routes through the woods. Their efforts resulted in such thrills as the "First National Bank of LHT," "Three-Toed Spur," "Mad Mitch Trail," "Yippee Jump," "Coyote Skull Skid" and more. Enjoy this one, folks!

RIDE 61 *HEPHZIBAH TRAIL*

Middle Georgia's lack of national forests has not been a deterrent to its development of mountain biking trails. They have, however, been located in some rather unusual sites. This is not to say they are inappropriate, just the opposite. The little over three miles looping through the creekside single-track in the forest near the Hephzibah Children's Home is a perfect example.

This institution has been serving middle Georgia since 1900 by providing complete residential care to children ages 6–17 who are primarily referred to them by the Department of Family and Children Services. The goal of Hephzibah is to provide the care and counseling necessary for the children to become incorporated back into a normal existence. Currently, there are 40 children in residence and plans have been made to bring the capacity to 120.

Part of the counseling program, of course, uses recreation, which has helped bring about the biking trails along the Colaparchee Creek. The trails, designed and developed by Macon's Bike-Tech owner, John Hall, are free of charge for the community's use as a support service provided by Hephzibah. The intent is to keep this trail open for public use as long as the scenic forest course remains free of debris.

Riding this trail during spring can be wonderfully distracting as you steer through some beautiful patches of painted trilliums, rue anemones, and Easter lilies scattered among mockernut hickory, buckeye, and maples. Hollies jut their prickly crowns over ferns growing along banks of springs trickling into the Colaparchee. Pay attention, though. There are some demanding maneuvers required in order to ride this one straight through.

General location: The trail loops and dips through a mixed hardwood forest just off of Zebulon Road west of Interstate 475 and west of Macon.

RIDE 61 *HEPHZIBAH TRAIL*

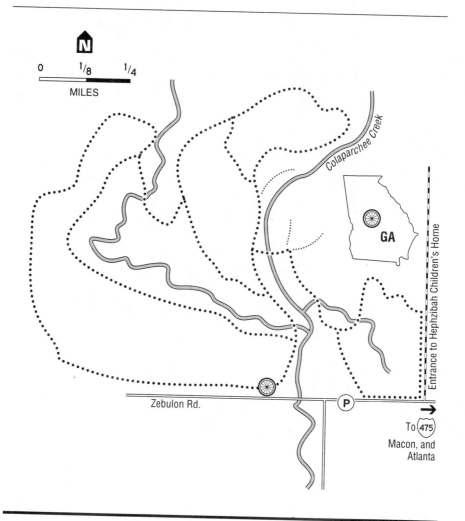

Elevation change: The steeper sections can be jaw-snapping in their degree of descent and near unrideable when you attempt the climb, but most of the trail can be characterized as gently rolling.

Season: The trail's location near the creek makes for some boggy spots in the wetter weather; wait for drier days. The creek, however, makes it awfully nice to drop your feet in and cool off on those hot summer days.

Services: All services can be found in Macon.

Part of the trail at Hephzibah goes along the Colaparchee Creek.

Hazards: There is one particularly difficult creek crossing that calls for a sharp turn to the right as a steep descent dumps onto a sandy oxbow of a small creek feeding the Colaparchee. A double dipsy-do alongside the creek, which is great fun, calls for care so that you don't hightail it and tumble down the creek bank.

Rescue index: This trail is fairly heavily used, and other users would soon pick up on any distress you might experience. You are less than a mile from either the entrance to Hephzibah or Zebulon Road.

Land status: This is land owned by the Hephzibah Children's Home.

Maps: This map was made from notes taken on the trail. The trail's relatively short length and looping nature make getting disoriented a challenge, but not impossible.

Finding the trail: Take I-475, exit onto Zebulon road and head west. The bridge at the bottom of the hill marks the trailhead on the right-hand side of the highway. Park on the shoulder of the road on either side of the bridge.

Sources of additional information:

Hephzibah Children's Home
Zebulon Road
Macon, GA
(912) 477-3383

Bike-Tech
3003 Vineville Avenue
Macon, GA 31204-2405
(912) 741-8356

Notes on the trail: A well-constructed bridge across the creek links 2 sections of trail on either side of the Colaparchee Creek. The northern loop drops down from Zebulon Road and goes along the creek for about .5 mile before veering off to the left in a couple of places. The first fork is a sheer climb which is better off left for riding down. The second fork to the left reconnects to the trail in .25 mile or less and serves to shorten the approach to the difficult creek crossing. The third fork to the left loops back toward Zebulon Road and picks up the second fork before crossing the small creek. After making this technical crossing, the trail splits. The right fork swings wide to go along the bank above Zebulon Road. The left fork comes back into the trail down the sheer drop mentioned earlier. This is a very amusing section of trail.

You'll notice the bridge across the Colaparchee Creek before taking the third left fork along the creek. By taking this bridge, you can ride another, shorter section of trail which dead-ends into Hephzibah's main entrance road. It did appear, though, that plans were under way to construct more single-track on this side of the trail. I sure hope so.

Athens Area Rides

To say that Athens, Georgia, would not be here if not for the University of Georgia might be a bit presumptuous . . . but only a bit. Since 1785, the University of Georgia has been the center of activities in and around the Athens area. Each fall thousands of new students come to this east Georgia city, not an insignificant population.

And when you think of Athens in the fall, you have to consider the day of the week you may be planning to come and ride any of the area's trails. A planned ride for the Saturday, say, of the Georgia-Florida football game between the hedges at Sanford Stadium will leave you snarled in a sea of Georgia red-and-black mixing insanely with Florida orange-and-white. You should not plan that day to get anywhere in Athens faster than your bike can carry you.

But on most days Athens is a wonderful, non-football city to visit. Its love affair with flora has deep roots sunk into the rolling hills where the nation's first garden club was begun. On the corner of Dearing and Finley Streets stands the "Tree That Owns Itself." This white oak was deeded eight feet of land on each of its sides by a former owner, university Professor W. H. Jackson. Also, the State Botanical Garden of Georgia is located in Athens on South Milledge Avenue.

One unusual creation found in Athens is a double-barreled cannon at City Hall at the intersection of College and Hancock Streets. This weapon was designed to fire two cannon balls tethered together by an eight-foot chain, whose effect was intended to clothesline approaching Yankees . . . but it did not work. That must have been a test-firing fraught with tension. They probably drew straws to see who would be the one to light the fuse, while the rest stood w-a-a-a-y back.

For those who would like to see more traditional forms of art, the Georgia Museum of Art (free and open to the public on the University of Georgia's campus) permanently houses over 7,000 items with exhibits changing 20 times a year. A visit to the U.S. Navy Supply Corps Museum on Prince and Oglethorpe Avenues will acquaint landlubbers with some extraordinary aspects of life at sea.

But life on the road via bike is a rewarding way to experience downtown Athens. Scenic routes are marked and easily traveled by mountain and road bike alike. So while you're in the area preparing to ride one of the great off-road trails nearby, cruise through this comfortable city. And if you want to fit right in, wear your red and black biking gear and chant "UGA–UGA–UGA" as you cycle along.

For more information:

University of Georgia
Directory assistance
(706) 542-3000

Athens Welcome Center
280 East Dougherty Street
Athens, GA 30603
(706) 353-1820

Dixons Bike Shop
257 West Broad Street
Athens, GA 30601-2899
(706) 549-2453

Sunshine Cycle Shop
294 West Washington Street
Athens, GA 30601-2756
(706) 548-6088

RIDE 62 *OCONEE FOREST PARK TRAIL*

This trail is actually part of a system of trails the University of Georgia in Athens constructed inside a 60-acre natural area administered by the University's Warnell School of Forest Resources. You will find trails for hiking only (clearly marked and monitored), trails for walking pets on a leash and off, and the trail for mountain biking. The mountain bike trail is not very long (a 1.2-mile loop officially, but I managed to rack up two miles meandering back and forth), nor is it very difficult, making it an ideal place for beginners to come out and test that new bike's handling on the combination of gravel road and single-track.

General location: Located on the University of Georgia's east campus near the intramural fields just off Highway 129 at the College Station Road exit.
Elevation change: Negligible but noticeable changes in elevation make this trail an ideal place for the very beginner to get a good start and feel for what mountain biking is all about.
Season: This is an all-season trail.
Services: All services can be found in Athens. Rest rooms and water are located on the right as you come in past the first set of fields.

RIDE 62 *OCONEE FOREST PARK TRAIL*

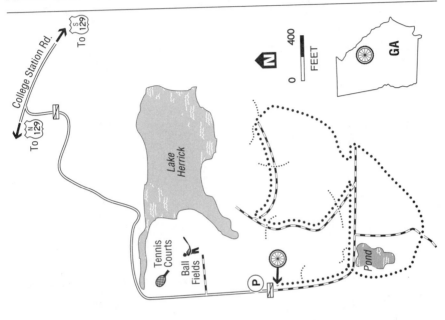

Hazards: The only hazards you may encounter would be other bikers going too fast or pets bolting out in front of you.

Rescue index: Every time I've used this trail, I've noticed a university truck just outside the gate manned by a driver who seems to be on duty to help with any assistance park users require.

Land status: This is land owned and managed by the University of Georgia.

Maps: Maps showing the entire Oconee Forest Park can be picked up for free at the gate.

Finding the trail: Exit off Highway 129 (Athens Perimeter) at College Station Road and take a left at the first light. After passing through the open gate, go past the barn on the left. Follow the paved road until it dead-ends at a closed gate. Take your bike and lift it over the fence by the gate. This is the trailhead.

Sources of additional information: Oconee Forest Park: (706) 369-5795 (park) or (706) 542-2521 (office).

Notes on the trail: Following the trail in a clockwise direction takes the biker on a flat warmup section before turning off to the left and beginning a gentle climb that's over before a mockingbird can complete its repertoire of songs. The last half of the trail is a wide single-track going up and around the

Oconee Forest Park Trail is short, but sweet.

off-leash area and a small pond. Before coming down from the ridge in autumn, stop and look down across the pond, where you may be able to pick out the largest scarlet oak tree in Georgia on Birdsong Creek's east bank. Its blazing red crown will be a beacon in this 100-year-old forest.

RIDE 63 *CAMP KELLEY YMCA TRAIL*

This private, single-track loop of 4.1 miles is open to only those who have registered as a guest and signed a waiver—this includes those riding in a sanctioned race like the Cactus Cup which was held here in the spring of 1994—or those who are members. Even at that, the trail is closed to mountain biking during the summer when the camp's Y activities are going full-swing.

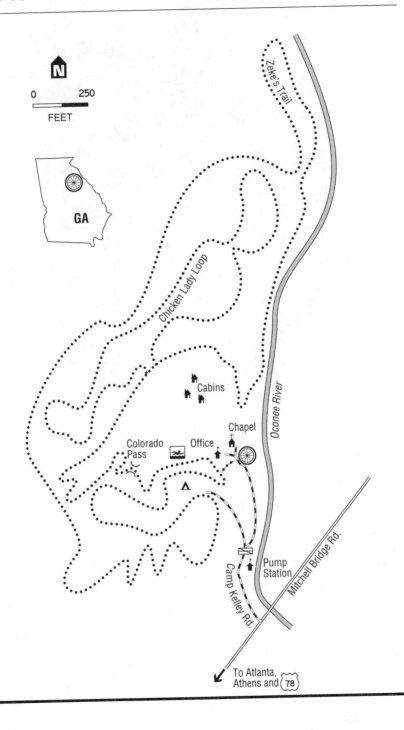

But despite the extra steps necessary in order to ride this course, it's worth the trouble. But don't take Junior for his first ride on this trail . . . unless he's been uppity and is in need of a dose of humility.

General location: This trail system is laid out on the steep slopes overlooking the Oconee River, and it is owned by the YMCA Camp Kelley. Failure to register as a guest or carry your membership card will invite prosecution as a trespasser.

Elevation change: You can get your uphill workout on this trail on several sections as the trail loops and goes up and down some radical ridges.

Season: The mountain bike trails are not open for use during the summer camp months.

Services: You can get what you lack in Athens.

Hazards: Steep hills with rocks outcropping in front of your wheels will send you skidding down without your bike if you aren't careful.

Rescue index: You are never very far from help, and you will be relatively easy to assist if you have a need.

Land status: This is private property and open to riders only by following proper registration procedures. Some bikers have broken into this facility and others have abused the registration procedure. As a result, plans are being considered to close this trail except by invitation only. Make sure to call ahead of time and check the current status.

Maps: You can pick up a map of Camp Kelley's trails at the office.

Finding the trail: Take Highway 78 west toward Atlanta out of Athens. Landmarks signaling your imminent turn are the K-Mart on your right, followed by the BMW dealership, also on the right. Take the second right after that at the light onto Mitchell Bridge Road. Watch for the sign and left turn into Camp Kelley just before you get to the bridge crossing over the Oconee River.

Sources of additional information:

YMCA
915 Hawthorne Street
Athens, GA 30606

Camp Kelley
Mitchell Bridge Road
Athens, GA
(706) 548-1322

Notes on the trail: After checking in with the front office and picking up the map of the trail, you'll get instructions on where to find the trailhead behind the area reserved for tent camping. The direction is clockwise only unless otherwise directed, which puts the climb up through "Colorado Pass" and into "White Oak Forest" first. "Chicken Lady Loop" finishes the first mile before the very fast downhill back to the river where the double-track road leads up to the climb at "Zack's Trail." The next section goes up above "Chicken Lady Loop" before the switchbacks down through "Pete's Path." The final climbs lead back to the start of the loop in the tent camping area. Most people will want to do at least a couple of laps before calling it a day.

RIDE 64 *TOWN CREEK ORV TRAIL*

This two-part ORV trail—two single-track loops (an eight-miler and a seven-miler) found at the Roberts Bike Camp in the Oconee National Forest in northern Greene County—accommodates motorized as well as the quieter cycles. Some bikers have a prejudice against motorcycles invading the woods because they leave the trails deeply rutted and mangled. Several trails in the Deep South in use by mountain bikes, however, have been built only because of the dedicated motorcyclists who supplied the necessary elbow grease to blaze the way.

Some off-road cyclists, like Jim Laue in Albany, got their start in mountain biking by riding a motorcycle. Others, like the guys from Minnesota I met at the trailhead at Town Creek one spring afternoon, take their mountain bikes along on trips when they take their motorcycles. Their mornings are reserved for riding the trail on the bikes and the afternoon finds them dressed a bit differently and using different fuel than what they burned in the morning. Different spokes but the same folks.

General location: This is a national forest trail found just north of Greensboro, Georgia.

Elevation change: There is no significant change in elevation other than some short stretches made more difficult by having to ride high and to the side to avoid ruts.

Season: This trail is noteworthy by being OFF-LIMITS DURING WET WEATHER. Signs are posted warning against riding during wet times. Most people have taken the sign at its word because the trail is in remarkable shape considering the type of traffic it gets. Don't cause someone to prosecute you by failing to keep off during wet days. If in doubt, stay out.

Services: Athens is just a few miles north, where most supplies can be replenished. Water bottles will have to be refilled in nearer Greensboro.

Hazards: Some low-lying parts are sandier than I prefer and will easily wrench the handlebars out of your grip if you aren't alert. Rocks and roots can jump right out in front of you in mid-turn. And, of course, the motor vehicles and riders that this trail primarily serves can come up suddenly. Yield the trail. Local riders also avoid this trail during hunting season.

Rescue index: You can get off into fairly remote territory on this trail.

RIDE 64 *TOWN CREEK ORV TRAIL*

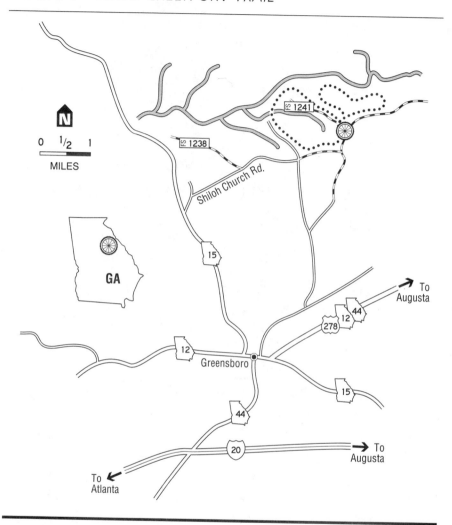

Land status: This 2-loop trail has been built in the Oconee National Forest.
Maps: Use of the Oconee National Forest map will help, but there was a map of both loops posted behind glass at the bulletin board. You can obtain the map of the Oconee National Forest by writing or stopping by the District Office in Monticello, Georgia, or, like I did, by writing the National Forest Supervisor in Gainesville, Georgia.
Finding the trail: Take Highway 15 south out of Athens for approximately 30 miles and turn left onto Shiloh Church Road. At the next intersection, an apparent dead-end, look for continuation of the road at about ten o'clock.

The single-track at Town Creek: home to bikes, motorcycles . . . and shagbark hickories.

Follow this road until you pass Forest Service Road 1241; the trailhead will be the next left.

Sources of additional information:

District Ranger
349 Forsyth Street
Monticello, GA 31064
(706) 468-2244

Forest Supervisor
508 Oak Street
Gainesville, GA 30501
(770) 536-0541

Notes on the trail: If you only have time for 1 of the 2 loops—both of which start at what appears to be an old homesite—I recommend the "A" Loop of 8 miles. The "B" Loop of 7 miles goes near the Penfield Camp about halfway through the ride; this could be a good staging area if you wanted to make this an overnighter and do both loops at a deliberate pace—one in the evening and the other the next morning.

I saw several deer snorting their displeasure at seeing me on this trail. They ran through this mixed hardwood forest where some fine examples of shagbark hickories live. Also, one of the earliest heralds of spring shows in the trumpet-shaped blooms of the Yellow Jessamine. Their yellow flowers can be seen on vines twisting high up small trees in the understory of the forest, though they are more commonly sighted in open areas. You won't have to stop to enjoy these plants, which have an unmistakably sweet aroma, but if you do stop to admire them, remember their leaves, roots, and flowers are poisonous to livestock . . . and mountain bikers.

Augusta Area Rides

After founding Savannah in 1773, General James Oglethorpe moved upriver and settled the largest inland cotton market anywhere in America. This city remained in tall cotton by serving as the state's capital from 1783 to 1795. Unconfirmed rumors still circulate that the reason Augusta fell out of favor as a political center was that politics and golf do not mix.

Augusta takes its golf seriously. I remember families who would speak in reverent, hushed tones whenever the Masters Tournament, held in Augusta the first full week in April, was mentioned. Tickets to this prestigious event have to be practically inherited unless you want to settle for getting on the year-long waiting list . . . for the practice rounds.

Golf is not the only thing Augustans consider important, however. The Medical College of Georgia, another institution where the waiting line is long, has one of the premier research facilities in the country. In fact, a member of my family survived a particularly tricky operation here under the steady hands of one of only two U.S. surgeons capable of performing the procedure.

For those who enjoy a good mystic experience, check out the Haunted Pillar, the only remaining part of a structure cursed by a visiting parson who was refused the chance to preach in the Market Place. (He probably was planning a sermon about the evils of golf.) A visiting cyclone in 1878, however, fulfilled the prophecy of destruction, leaving only the one pillar. Had the Confederate Powder Works still been in operation downtown, the disgruntled man of the cloth could have acquired some dynamite and set off a charge immediately.

It is said that despite its precarious perch on top of a smaller stone, the 15-ton Shaking Rock in nearby Oglethorpe County cannot be dislodged, but only see-sawed back and forth. I suspect if only a bit of the radioactive material from The Savannah River Site, where a nuclear reactor hums downstream from Augusta, were fused underneath it, the rock could be moved. But don't move through Georgia without visiting this old and beautiful city.

For more information:

Augusta-Richmond County Convention and Visitors Bureau
32 Eighth Street, Suite 200
Augusta, GA 30901
(800) 726-0243 or (706) 823-6600

Andy Jordan's Bicycle Center
527 13th Street
Augusta, GA 30901-1005
(706) 724-6777

Breakaway Cyclery
1904 Walton Way
Augusta, GA 30904
(706) 736-2486 or 868-6788

Martinez Bicycle Company
138 Davis Road
Augusta, GA 30907-2400
(706) 863-6862

Chain Reaction
Augusta Mall/Washington Road at Columbia Road
Augusta, GA 30907-2024
(706) 855-2024

Clyde Dunaway Bicycles
212 12th Street
Augusta, GA 30901-2145
(706) 722-4208

RIDE 65 *HORN CREEK TRAIL*

This loop allows the beginning biker to move up a notch in trail difficulty while passing through a forest of tall pines and old hardwoods. The six-mile single-track gradually climbs to the overlooks above gurgling Horn Creek in a wide loop. Massive beeches shade long lengths of this trail, which is bordered by trillium and ferns in many places. It is obvious to the first-time rider of this pathway that those who use it take good care of it.

The more radical creek crossings have sturdy bridges spanning them, projects undertaken by the local Boy Scout troop. Other areas—subject to washing during heavy rains—bear telltale signs that rakes and shovels are regularly used to control erosion. After seeing too many trails that have been abused and neglected, it is always enjoyable riding a course that has been pampered as this one has.

General location: Horn Creek is located in the Sumter National Forest in South Carolina, approximately 30 minutes north of Interstate 20 on Highway 230.

Elevation change: There are a few places on this trail that will tax your endurance and strength.

Season: I know hunters aren't supposed to be near a trail when they're loaded for bear, but it happens. For this reason, you may want to exercise caution on this trail during the hunting seasons.

RIDE 65 *HORN CREEK TRAIL*

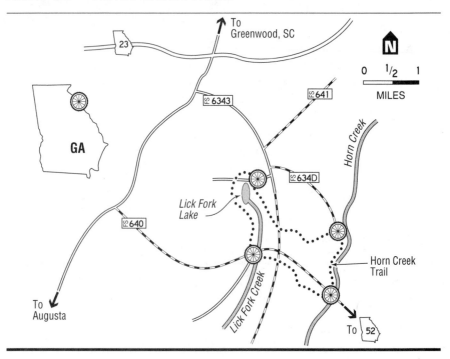

Services: All services can be obtained in Augusta, Georgia. Water and rest rooms can be found in the recreational area, which also allows camping.

Hazards: A narrow pass high above the creek calls for a quick burst of strength, balance, and luck to ride cleanly. Other than that, few roots and rocks pose problems to a safe trip. Hikers will be on stretches of this trail; remember to yield the trail. Wear an orange vest during hunting seasons and ring a bell or talk loudly if you expect hunters may be nearby. It is a bone-chilling experience to top a rise only to be caught in the sights of someone's 30-06.

Rescue index: This is moderately remote territory; however, the recreational area seems to get used frequently by both hikers and bikers.

Land status: This is part of the Sumter National Forest's 360,000 acres.

Maps: Ask for the Edgefield and Long Cane District map of the Sumter National Forest when calling, writing, or stopping by the Ranger District in Edgefield, South Carolina. The Colliers quad topo map (7.5 minute series) gives more detail.

Finding the trail: Leave Augusta on I-20 and cross into South Carolina. Take the Highway 230 exit and travel north for nearly 30 minutes. A relatively small sign on the right signals the right turn you need to make to Lick Fork. I saw cars parked at the camping area—the recommended spot—but parking

A beech home along Horn Creek, Sumter National Forest.

areas also can be found on Forest Service Road 634 and FS 640, which you will recognize as you cross them on your way around the loop.

Sources of additional information:

Edgefield Ranger District
321 Bacon Street, Box 30
Edgefield, SC 29824
(803) 637-5396

National Forest Supervisor
1835 Assembly Street
Room 333, Strom Thurmond Building
Columbia, SC 29202
(803) 765-5222

Notes on the trail: The loop is straightforward with no confusing turns or forks. The trail does intersect 4 times with roads: twice with County Road 263, once with FS 640, and once with FS 634.

As I finished riding the Horn Creek loop, I watched a station wagon park. Three pretty young girls and their parents got out. I don't normally like to stare, but what I saw tied down on the luggage rack tested my manners. A car bumper, complete with black rubber trim and caked-on red mud, was trussed up like an animal to market. The man, who had been driving, got out and noticed my bike in the back seat of my tiny car, surrounded by camping gear and dirty clothes (with things beginning to grow on them), and stared. He looked like he wanted to speak to me, so I said, "Hi." That was all it took.

For the next 10 minutes, he provided a discourse on his profession—scrapping. Yessir, this guy was a genuine scrapper who went around exploring sides of roads looking for items, such as abandoned bumpers, which he took home and salvaged the marketable aluminum, copper, steel—whatever he could sell. He nearly cried when I told him I had passed a large coil of heavy gauge copper wire back in Mississippi and didn't pick it up. I did, too, after he told me what copper wire sells for.

He told me he thought it would be good for business if he got him a mountain bike. That way he could cover more ground and tap part of the market in abandoned appliances. So if you see a guy riding a bike in the woods with a washing machine lid strapped to his shoulders, it might be the scrapper . . . or me.

RIDE 66 *STEVENS CREEK TRAIL*

This out-and-back single-track along the rather large Stevens Creek should not be ridden by novices. Its many technical turns, dips, slides, and climbs demand a full bag of bike handling tricks—in addition to front suspension—in order to ride it without having to get off and walk. Part of the enjoyment of riding this trail comes from being able to look down on this fast-flowing creek as it makes its way to Clarks Hill Lake.

It was on this trail where I had my most inconvenient mechanical failure while researching this book. I had begun the "out" portion of this out-and-back trail late in the afternoon, needing to cover the 12 miles total in a sprightly fashion in order to avoid being caught on an unfamiliar trail after sundown. I was riding well, coasting the descents quickly but under control while pounding the long pulls up to the gaps in a powerful rhythm. Stevens Creek bubbled over occasional shoals on my right as I made frequent crossings of feeder springs and freshets full from recent rains.

RIDE 66 *STEVENS CREEK TRAIL*

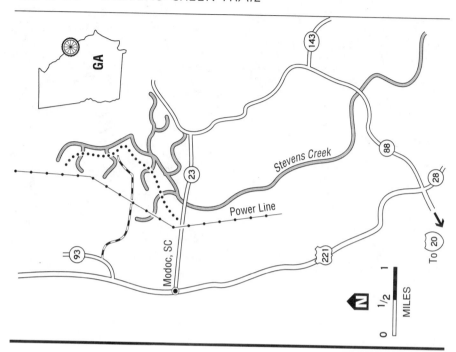

It was probably the repeated banging my back axle received as I landed too heavily on the saddle several times which caused it to weaken and then snap. I don't know when it actually gave way, but I noticed it first as I made my way away from the powerlines where the trail dead-ends. On the first climb, my back tire rubbed on the frame so much I thought a bullfrog was hopping along behind me. I could, however, ride downhill without the tire touching much. So that's what I did: push uphill and coast down as the sun set faster than I have ever known it to before.

Despite my aggravation and apprehension, it was a pleasant trip back as squirrels raced off ahead of me in the leaves, and the warbling song of the wood thrush ushered in the dusk.

General location: This trail is in the Sumter National Forest, just east of Modoc, South Carolina, which is approximately 5 miles north of Clark Hill Dam.

Elevation change: Long snatches of elevation constantly roll up and down above the creek this trail is named for. Unlike some trails built for hikers, this trail's gradients keep the limits of most bikers in mind; therefore, you will find few places where it's too steep to ride, unless your back axle goes.

You need to steer steadily at Stevens Creek Trail.

Season: The dense shade provided by the mature forest in this part of Sumter National Forest makes for a good year-long biking destination. Of course, the trail should be saved for times when it is not too muddy.

Services: Smaller stores line Highway 28 where you can replenish the simpler supplies. Augusta has whatever else you may need.

Hazards: Although this is a national forest, hunters do not seem to head to this neck of the woods. You may, however, wind up looking for your bike and your senses if you do not recognize the inherent dangers of some of the more technical sections. The steep slopes off the trail could roll a bike and biker a long way before they splashed into Stevens Creek. Narrow bridges—without the safety of rails—make some crossings more exciting than you want to experience. Hop off and walk across if you doubt your ability.

Rescue index: Forest Service roads 632, 632A, and 632B provide access for four-wheeled vehicles beginning about halfway through the trail. Still, effecting a rescue would be difficult.

Land status: This is a national forest.

Maps: Along with the Edgefield and Long Cane District maps of the Sumter National Forest, the USGS 7.5 minute series topo quads of Clarks Hill and Parksville will provide detailed data.

Finding the trail: Just shy of the South Carolina border on Interstate 20 headed east from Atlanta, exit onto Highway 28. Modoc, South Carolina, and Highway 23 lie approximately 30 minutes north. Turn right onto 23. A little over a mile away, trailhead parking is on the left before you get to the bridge crossing Stevens Creek.

Sometimes you have to pull over to take it all in.

Sources of additional information:

Edgefield Ranger District
321 Bacon Street, Box 30
Edgefield, SC 29824
(803) 637-5396

Forest Supervisor
1835 Assembly Street
Room 333, Strom Thurmond Building
Columbia, SC 29202
(803) 765-5222

Notes on the trail: As an out-and-back trail, you have the option to stop and turn around any place short of the end. My plan for riding this trail the first time was to go along until I felt sure I had enough daylight to make it back without hurrying and then turn around. Alas, the beauty of this trail is so compelling I kept telling myself, "Aw, just a little bit farther" until I wound up at the powerlines where the trail dead-ends. The trail seems to increase in difficulty the farther you ride. The first mile or so is reminiscent of the easy riding found at Horn Creek, but by the time you reach a particularly steep and rocky creek crossing near the end, many challenging maneuvers will be required to stay upright and bikebound.

Atlanta Area Rides

Considering all the good which has happened since the "unpleasantness" (as some Southern matriarchs still prefer to call the Civil War) occurred in the mid-1860s, Atlantans should erect a monument to Sherman in much the same spirit that Alabamans have honored the boll weevil. By having to reconstruct itself from the ashes left over from Sherman's March to the Sea, Atlanta has risen, phoenix-like, to become the center of a great many activities, mountain biking included.

Its metropolitan population of nearly three million will watch a different march in 1996 when the Olympic Games come to celebrate the centennial. And, for the first time, Olympic competition will include mountain biking, called cross-country cycling, whose venue lies southeast of Stone Mountain, the world's largest mass of exposed granite. The surface of Stone Mountain, carved a-la-Rushmore with the images of Confederate leaders Davis, Lee, and Jackson, also serves as the screen for summertime laser light shows.

In pre-laser days, Atlantans walked down Peachtree to the "fabulous Fox" theater, whose striking architecture—inside and out—provides as much entertainment as the movies which first showed there. *Gone with the Wind,* Margaret Mitchell's saga of the South, premiered here, and across the street a museum of its memorabilia is housed. Taking in all the sights just on Peachtree Street alone would take a month of Sundays, which is just one reason why Atlanta's metro area is one of the most rapidly growing areas in the country.

Coca-Cola, CNN, and Cyclorama have all made their homes in Atlanta, or Hot'lanta as it is locally known. Museums of science, discovery, art, politics, and all life forms—great and small, near and far—can be visited without driving outside the perimeter highway, Interstate 285. For those with subterranean tastes in culture and cuisine, a walk through Underground Atlanta showcases counter-trends and fashions. A leisurely stroll here goes past musicians looking to make their break performing for tips in an upside-down hat.

A trip to downtown Atlanta would not be complete without eating at The Varsity, described as the world's largest drive-in. It was here, just blocks away from Georgia Tech, that as a small boy I stood amazed watching Flossy, the legendary carhop, sashay from curbside to counter. It was all I could do to concentrate on finishing my chili dog. But finish I did, because after lunch I had been promised a trip to the newly opened Lenox Square, a shopping mall which still has no equal in ambience.

Across from Lenox, adults can enjoy the unusual environment of Dantes Down the Hatch where a wooden frigate mimics a port-of-call-turned-restaurant, complete with suggestions of Captain Hook as crocodiles lie basking in the warm moonlight. Eating does not have to stop at Dantes, either. Any dish can be found in Atlanta, from barbecue to baklava. Dust off your taste buds, put away your Powerbar, and sit back and say "Ah! May I have some more of those habanero grits, please?"

Did you say you like sports of all kinds? Then head to the Omni to catch a hockey match or some hoops with the Hawks, or indoor soccer. The Georgia Dome, site of football games as prestigious as the Super Bowl, is close to Atlanta Stadium, home of the Braves, where fans can cut loose with war whoops and wave tomahawks.

With all of Atlanta's fun things to do, getting tied up in the traffic as four major interstates bottleneck at Spaghetti Junction is not one of them. That's why you may want to consider riding Metro Atlanta Rapid Transit Authority (MARTA) rail or the bus line. It can make that trip back to Atlanta/Hartsville Airport, consistently one of the top five busiest airports in the nation, less frantic. But after you stay a few days in Atlanta and experience true southern hospitality, you may never want to leave. But if you do, "Ya'll come back now, y'heah?"

For more information:

REI—Recreational Equipment
  Incorporated
1800 Northeast Expressway
Atlanta, GA 30329-2005
(404) 633-6508

North Fulton Schwinn Cyclesports
10687 Alpharetta Highway
Roswell, GA 30076-1458
(404) 998-2550

Alpharetta-Roswell Bicycles
670 Houze Way
Roswell, GA 30076-1430
(404)642-4057

Ansley Schwinn
1579 Monroe Drive NE
Atlanta, GA 30324-5022
(404) 873-2451

Bicycle South, Inc.
2098 North Decatur Road
Decatur, GA 30033-5367
(404) 636-4444

Buckhead Bicycles
3165 Peachtree Road
Atlanta, GA 30305-1851
(404) 266-8480

Bikeways
4107 Lawrenceville Highway
Tucker, GA 30084
(404) 934-2002

Gwinnett Schwinn
3502 Satellite Boulevard
Duluth, GA 30136-5820
(404) 476-8158

North River Cycle
8807 Roswell Road
Roswell, GA 30350-1846
(404) 998-1672

Sandy Springs Schwinn
220 Johnson Ferry Road
Roswell, GA 30328-3820
(404) 252-2453

Vinings Schwinn
4335 Cobb Parkway
Atlanta, GA 30339-3811
(404) 952-7731

Dunwoody Schwinn
4480 Chamblee-Dunwoody Road
Atlanta, GA 30338-6201
(404) 455-3171

Pedal Power
1944 Rockbridge Road
Stone Mountain, GA 30087-3309
(404) 498-2453

Outback Bikes
1125 Euclid Avenue
Atlanta, GA 30307-1925
(404) 688-4878

Free-Flite
1950 Canton Road
Marietta, GA 30066-5471
(404) 422-5237

or

210 Pharr Road
Atlanta, GA
(404) 233-4103

Southern Off-Road Bicycle Association
P.O. Box 671774
Marietta, GA 30067-0030
Organized Ride Information: (404) 565-1719
North Georgia Race Information: (404) 565-1732
Scheduled Trail Maintenance & General Information: (404) 565-1795

RIDE 67 *SOPE CREEK*

Located a pulse away from the heart of downtown Atlanta, this urban recreational area established by the National Forest Service has nearly four million visitors yearly. What a thrill it was to discover a mountain biking trail of significance in the midst of a metropolis! I rode the loop of five miles or so at a slow pace, more to enjoy the wide single-track than out of caution. Several spots require a biker to deliver steady handling and powerful pedaling.

The Sunday afternoon I rode Sope Creek was in the middle of prime recreational time for Atlantans. Walkers, joggers, and doggers accompanied me on the trail that skirts the ruins of a former paper mill on the rocky ledges high above the Chattahoochee River near Cochran Shoals. Television and movies remain a poor substitute for the snatches of social drama played out on this trail. I stood under a huge sycamore near the Chattahoochee River and listened discreetly while two young financiers discussed their careers in terms of floating mortgages.

Sope Creek was named for a popular Cherokee man who spent many hours teaching youngsters what he knew about the land, plants, and animals. As the trail goes through large oaks, gums, and pines where woodpeckers cackle their jungle-like call, it is easy to imagine a group of boys following a man walking slowly and explaining such things as what fish bait to use, or how to make darts and blowguns from the river cane growing along creek banks.

This area also saw a critical event played out during the Civil War. General Sherman had been stymied by heavy rains and the Chattahoochee in his attempt to capture Atlanta. Confederate General Johnston, believing the

Union troops would try to ford the river at Peachtree Creek six miles south, left Sope Creek lightly defended. After a reconnaissance determined a suitable ford at Sope Creek—despite its steep banks—a stealthy movement across the wide Chattahoochee followed. And, as the saying goes, the rest is history.

This is a land where much change has been wrought. Yesterday spins into today, much like the tread of a mountain bike's tires picks up parts of the trail and sprinkles it over itself. The simpler days seem farther removed after leaving the forest behind and turning onto Johnson Ferry Road, where million-dollar homes have sprung up like saplings. Welcome to Atlanta.

General location: This recreational area is found near Sope Creek's merger with the Chattahoochee River north of Interstate 285 and Atlanta.

Elevation change: Once down on the creek banks, very little elevation change occurs; however, getting back on the ridges above Sope Creek will put you in a lather. I wondered on my way down if I could make the climb back up what resembled a dry creek bed in places. Fortunately, I have in my bag of tricks the "Kisatchie Hills Kick." I was able to ride ever-so-smugly past the speed demons who, moments before, had skidded past me on the slopes.

Season: Periods of heavy rainfall stopped Sherman's advance and they'll stop your bike riding on this trail as well.

Services: Atlanta's reputation has been built largely on its ability to provide whatever services the human condition may require; this includes services for those necessary toys—like mountain bikes—we play with.

Hazards: Most trails have enough rocks and roots to put the yellow light on; this one is no exception. Bikers scream down terrain in a loose interpretation of being under control, which poses hazards to those who ride more responsibly. This type of reckless riding can eventually result in this trail's being off-limits to biking as are other Atlanta area trails, such as Vickery Creek and Kennesaw Mountain.

Rescue index: A complete hospital staff could probably be assembled several times over by collecting those who are on the trail at any given time. Ditto for mechanical, legal, financial, and travel assistance.

Land status: This is a unit in the Chattahoochee River National Recreation Area.

Maps: All maps for the CRNRA can be picked up at the headquarters on Island Ford Parkway during normal business hours. The map for this trail is called Sope Creek and Cochran Shoals.

Finding the trail: Exit Highway 400 on Abernathy Road and head west toward Roswell Road, which you cross before turning right onto Johnson Ferry Road at the next light. After crossing the bridge, turn left onto Paper Mill Road at the next traffic light. Pass by Atlanta Country Club Estates on the left and cross the bridge. The entrance is a short distance on your left.

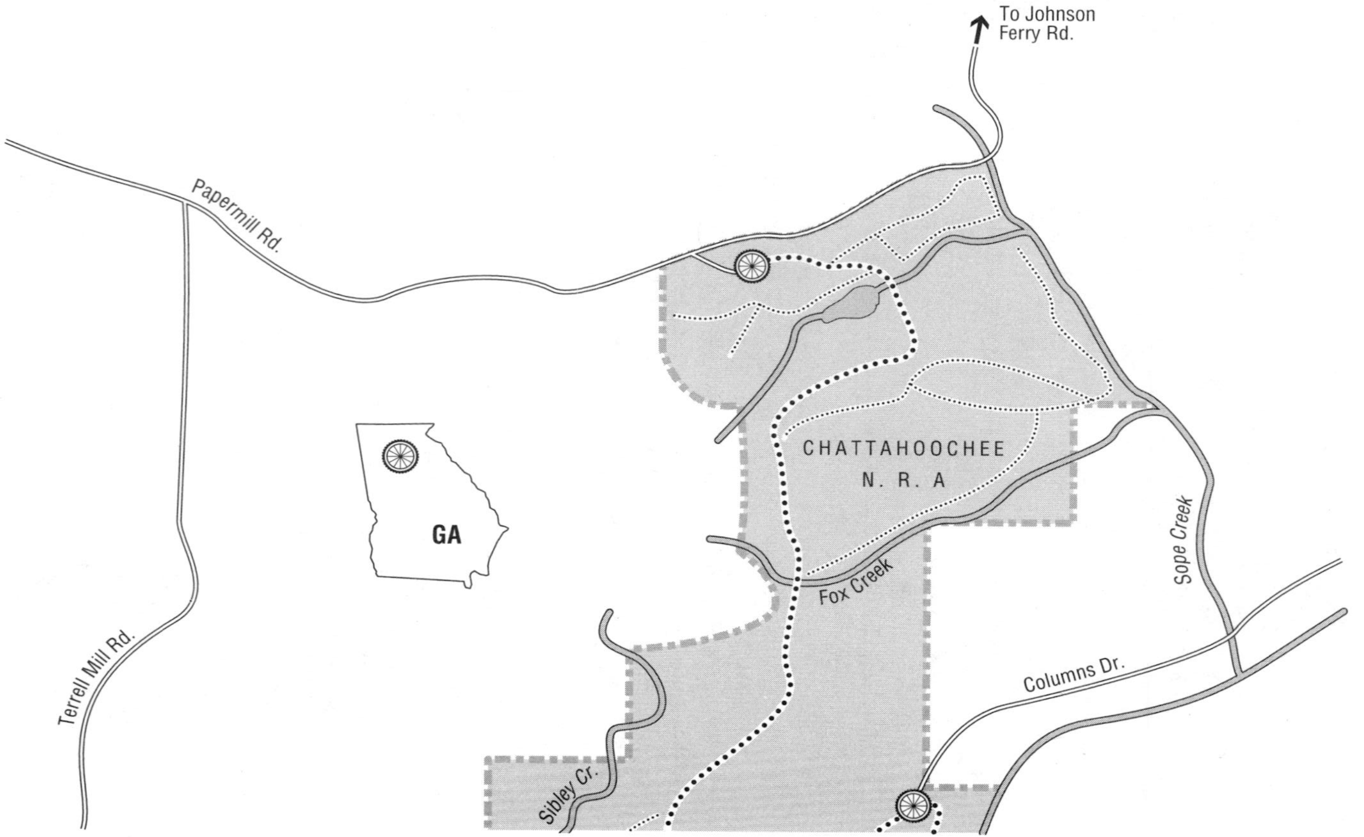
To Johnson
Ferry Rd.
Papermill Rd.
Terrell Mill Rd.
GA
CHATTAHOOCHEE
N. R. A
Fox Creek
Sope Creek
Columns Dr.
Sibley Cr.

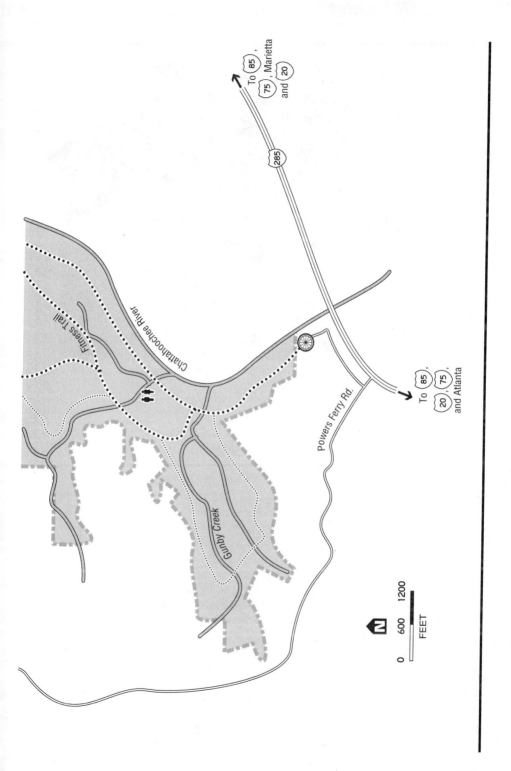

Part of the millions who use Atlanta's metro Chattahoochee each year.

Sources of additional information:

Superintendent CRNRA
1978 Island Ford Parkway
Atlanta, GA 30350-3400
(404) 399-8070

Notes on the trail: This is a combination of double- and single-track looping around Gunby Creek. Another gravel loop called the "Fitness Trail" completes it circuit down by the river. Several loops by Sope Creek, and on the slopes above it, provide the bulk of wide single-track for mountain bikes. Trails where biking is prohibited are conspicuously marked. The trails have been graded by difficulty, allowing various combinations of challenges and length. It is possible to rack up close to 10 miles without doing much doubling on previously ridden trail. Be sure to check for any recent changes in trail protocol whenever you check the bulletin board at the parking areas. One condition for riding inside the CRNRA is that your bicycle must be registered. If you aren't registered, stop a ranger the first time you see one and do the paperwork. Although it may be an inconvenience, such registration has allowed recovery of stolen bikes. This trail has also been the focus of Southern Off-Road Bicycle Association's maintenance projects. I hope involvement with this group will ensure this trail can be kept open to bikers; however, the trend has been for these urban trails to be closed due to irresponsible overuse.

RIDE 68 *LITTLE RIVER TRAIL*

It used to be that the only trails in the woods near Woodstock, Georgia, were the ones made by children crisscrossing their way to the river to fish and swim. Many of them were, no doubt, taking time off from chores on the farm where they still used mules and horses to plow and tote goods back and forth to town. It was the era of the general merchandise store and local mills grinding corn—and spinning rope.

Today on the slopes overlooking the river valley where an old rope mill was built, mountain bikers can ride a total of just over 15 miles of single-track originally designed and still used by motorcycles and horses. The three sections of out-and-back run along river banks, railroad tracks, and to the falls of a creek, depending on which leg you take.

If you sniff the air when the wind's right, you can smell what brought about the demise of much of the way life was lived back in the first half of this century. No, it's not a factory or plant belching out smoke or fumes. It's water. Big water. The 12,000 acres of Allatoona Lake were backed up by Georgia Power when it closed the locks on the dam January 1, 1950, near Cartersville, ten crow-miles away to the northeast. This created over 200 miles of shoreline, all owned by the Army Corps of Engineers, many of which have biking trails cutting through where eagles, deer, turkeys, goldfinches, and plant communities all live.

While there are trails to ride on both sides of the river, the most enjoyable—and most protected from future development—are the ones across the old bridge on the northern bank. Crossing this bridge by bike can be an exciting experience in itself. The mounds of bulldozed dirt on either end prevent large vehicles from crossing the narrow passageway above Little River as it slides by 20 feet underneath.

A series of trails leads upriver where single-track courses have been laid out up and down the sometimes radically pitched hills. This will seem like a gross understatement as you contemplate some of the downhill sections, like "Train Trestle," which seems more like a spot to take off with a hang glider than a bike route.

Another section taken on the northern side of the river ends at a beautiful 30-foot-wide falls where Blankets Creek crashes into an otherwise peaceful cove of Allatoona Lake. Two steep sections on the way to the falls prompted my guide for this trip, Rob Abbott, to remark, "I heard 'If you aren't hiking, you aren't biking.'" We did some biking that day.

General location: This rather large section of trails is found north of Woodstock, Georgia, on the slopes above the banks of Little River.

RIDE 68 *LITTLE RIVER TRAIL*

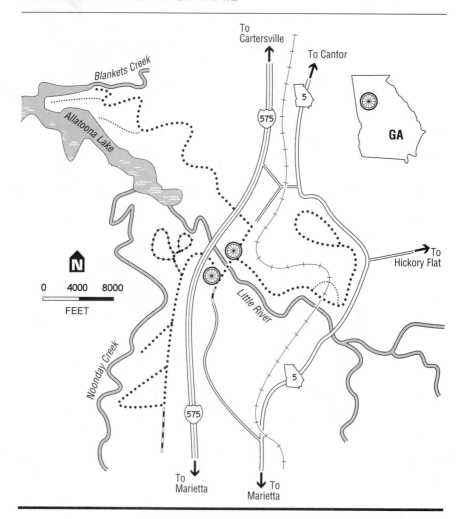

Elevation change: No really long climbs to make, but you will be hard-pressed to find steeper sections anywhere. Downhillers will love the short but sweet route near the train trestle which falls nearly 40 feet down a rocky 30-yard slope.

Season: The trail can be red-clay messy in some areas during wet weather. Following the river is sandy, but rideable, due to the flooding in early 1995. If the heat and humidity don't put an end to your biking in the summer, this is an all-season place to ride.

Services: Many services can be found in nearby Woodstock, part of metropolitan Atlanta. And if you can't find it in Hot'lanta, you ain't looking.

Hazards: Rocks, ruts, and sticks can all put an upsetting end to your day. My derailleur met its demise on an innocent looking section when a short, but stout, pine branch got jammed into it. Although this is primarily a bike trail, evidence of horses and motorcycles riding the trails can be seen.

Rescue index: You are very close to civilization for the most part, and a good yell or maybe even a bike bell should bring help, but ride with a buddy, especially if you put "Train Trestle" on the itinerary.

Land status: Most of the trail falls on the land serving as public right-of-way managed by the Army Corps of Engineers.

Maps: A topo map might be fun to use while on this section. However, you'll need to piece together 2 different 7.5 minute series quads in order to cover the entire trail: Kennesaw and South Canton. A map of Cherokee County will give other access points. Also, the U.S. Army Corps of Engineers map of Allatoona Lake can provide good info. The map of the bike trails was made from my notes.

Finding the trail: Depending on the side of the river you want to park on, you can take 2 approaches to the trailhead. The southerly approach requires making a trip through Woodstock on Highway 5. Just before crossing the railroad tracks, look to the left where Rope Mill Road forks off. Travel until the road dead-ends at the river, park out of the way, and stay on this side of the river for the less technical, less scenic, and less protected trails (construction on a future subdivision has been going on). You will notice the beginning on the left just as the pavement ends.

Cross the bridge and pick your bike up and put it on the other side of the low cable fence on the right for the more extensive series of single-track, which starts off heading upriver and should be quite noticeable.

Sources of additional information:

District Engineer, Mobile District
U.S. Army Corps of Engineers
P.O. Box 2288
Mobile, AL 36628

Allatoona Lake Information: (770) 386-0549

Notes on the trail: The trail system on the south side of the river, although making up a considerable network of loops, is in a construction limbo for the most part. Still, you can enjoy a 7-mile trip ending at a fairly large creek. From the south trailhead, take either a left or right fork after riding underneath Interstate 575 and climbing the hill on the other side of it. The right fork will dead-end on what is currently a red-clay road, but it shows every indication of being developed into an asphalt subdivision road. The left turn heads toward

Wrapping up a ride at Blankets Creek Falls, near the Little River.

Woodstock. The first road to the right toward Woodstock leads down to Noonday Creek. Before getting to the creek—about halfway down—look on your right for single-track. Although it is short, it is fun to ride.

The northern section of trails has 2 main directions: upriver past the ruins of the rope mill where bales of cotton (salvaged from the fairly common gin explosions and resulting fires) were converted into rope and sold in area hardware stores for use with farm animals, or you can continue straight up the road on the other side of the bridge and check out Blankets Creek Falls.

Look for a single-track entrance on the left off the dirt road about a .5 mile up the road if you want to go to the falls. Two sets of hills, which feel like mountains before you reach the top, occur before coming to the single-track on the right at a clearing. The road continues straight down to the lake, but turn right on the single-track. You have to work for them, but 3 more exciting downhills are found on this connector to the falls. (Don't feel bad if you have to get off and hike. In fact, if you can crank up these grades, give me a call; I should be able to find a sponsor for your NORBA competition.) Turn right, uphill, at the dead-end where it gets wider and take the next single-track to the left. You should be able to hear the wonderful sound of water splashing on a rock ledge. Get your lunch out and let your mind wander. Afterwards, take a rest and a dip in the large pool at the base. Ahhh!

Rome Area Rides

From Georgia's canyonland boundary with Alabama, to Ellijay's more eastern elevations blooming white with apple blossoms, the key word here is "mountains" and plenty of them. The Cohutta range's bulging biceps flex along summits extending from north of Dalton to diminish—but only slightly—by the time they reach Rome. Mighty rivers like the Coosawattee, inspiration for James Dickey's *Deliverance,* and the Conasauga flow together to form the Oostanaula. It and the Etowah join currents in Rome to become the Coosa along whose banks ancient Cherokee built a civilization influencing a great deal more than just names of waterways.

Chatsworth, Calhoun, and Cartersville were centers of the Cherokee Nation where leaders such as Chief Vann and John Ross negotiated treaty after broken treaty with the gold-greedy government of the United States. Another leader, Sequoyah, invented an alphabet for his language and published the bilingual newspaper, the *Cherokee Phoenix.* This voice was squelched in 1838 by the forced removal of the Native Americans to reservations in Oklahoma. Extensive measures had been taken for years by the U.S. government to identify and register "all indigenous people." Still, a significant population escaped "underground," setting up hidden camps in places like Amicalola, where they lived undiscovered for years. After the Civil War and Reconstruction became the common denominator in domestic dealings, no one seemed to care when the Cherokees came out of hiding.

For the mountain biker or family interested in visiting scenes of great importance in the Civil War, this section of Georgia provides site after site where pivotal battles were fought, most of which were lost by the Confederates. The following period forced many towns and cities to rebuild and establish an economy based on more than just agriculture. Dalton grew to become a giant in textile production. Berry College in Rome developed as a leader in education and academics, growing out of the simple one-room schoolhouse Martha Berry established at Possum Trot. Tate's marble production is exceeded by none, as mammoth chunks come out of the world's largest open marble pit. Crafts and arts—from Smithsonian pottery to sidewalk gourd shops—help fuel Georgia's multi-billion-dollar tourist industry.

Indeed, recreation remains the biggest reason to head northwest in Georgia. The Chattahoochee National Forest, three large lakes, state parks, and rivers ensure the outdoors' allure. So load up the boats, tents, and bikes to find the gold that was left behind. There's a wealth awaitin'.

For more information:

Greater Rome Convention and Visitors Bureau
P.O. Box 5823
402 Civic Center Hill
Rome, GA 30162
(706) 295-5576

Doug's Cyclery
315 B North Tibbs Road
Dalton, GA 30720
(706) 278-3775

Mountain Outdoor Expeditions
Highway 76
Ellijay, GA 30540
(706) 635-2524 Jay Srymanske (706) 635-2726

Bob's Cycle Shop
2203 Shorter Avenue
Rome, GA 30165
(706) 291-1501

Pullen's Ordinary Bicycle & Plain Outdoors
105 Broad Street
Rome, GA
(706) 234-2453

RIDE 69 *BERRY COLLEGE*

Imagine a school campus where you can turn off a busy highway and view a large pasture on the right where over 20 deer graze undisturbed, and on the left see a pine forest where several turkeys strut. The backdrop to it all is buildings hewn out of local stone and built into a shape reminiscent of castles and the chivalrous days of knights throwing capes over mud puddles. This, and more, awaits the mountain biker who schedules the basic 7.5-mile loop along the gravel service roads and pavement of Berry College. A wide assortment of rides—from the challenge of mountain stream fords to the calm cruise down a country road—can be enjoyed in this section of northwest Georgia in the foothills of the Appalachians. Much of the college campus, with its asphalt roads where the classrooms and dorms are located, seems better suited for 1.25 or 1.5 slicks than knobbies. But a survey of the bikes parked in front of these buildings shows more mountain bikes than road bikes; the temptation to go off-road is just too great.

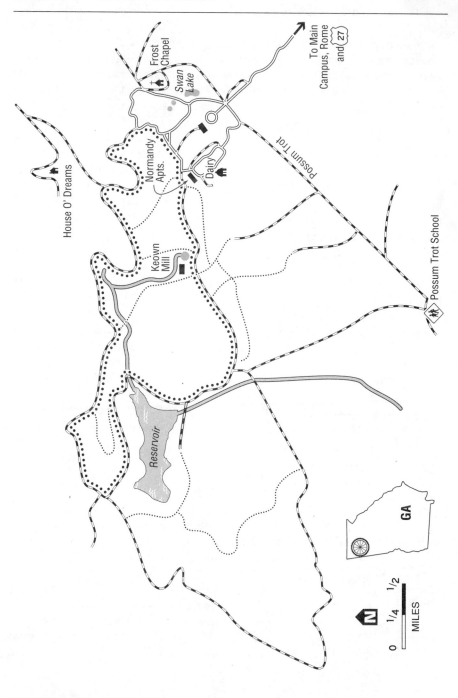

This biking paradise got its start earlier this century when a remarkable lady named Martha Berry began a school where children who lacked advanced social opportunities could acquire both a practical and academic education. The magnetic personality of Ms. Berry attracted such notable personalities as Henry Ford, whose partnership resulted in the magnificent buildings seen on the hill as you enter the school grounds. The Keown Mill at the trailhead for the basic 7.5-mile loop (Mountain Goat Trail) is another structure symbolizing Martha Berry's acquaintances with the rich and influential.

Slightly more than three miles from the college campus on a section called simply, "The Stretch," bikes can explore the 26,000 acres of the Berry Wildlife Refuge, the largest college campus in America. As the pavement ends, you can turn left and ride down "Possum Trot" to what is the first site where Martha Berry began her school. More of the architecture that casts such a magical spell is found where WinShape Center is located. Frost Chapel, where Berry Academy commencement used to be held—and many weddings now take place—is on the right if you take the counterclockwise tour of the campus. Take the detour and peek inside Frost Chapel. You can almost hear the shuffle of Academy students' feet on the stone floor as they filed in to Sunday evening chapel services.

The former academy dorms, Friendship Hall and Pilgrim Hall, which now house participants in Camp WinShape, sit on opposite hills facing the chapel. The road between them continues down the hill toward the Old Mill, where you'll pass the homes of Berry Schools employees. The Normandy Apartments lie above an expansive dairy farm, home to hundreds of cows, heifers, and calves as part of the work program offering students the chance to earn an education, a tradition Martha Berry started over 90 years ago. The tradition you'll begin after visiting this spectacular setting will be mountain biking.

General location: Berry College is north of Rome, Georgia, on Highway 27. The trails begin back in the foothills, 3 miles down "The Stretch."

Elevation change: Moderate climbs and descents ease their way along the shoulders of Lavender Mountain.

Season: A remarkable feature of the sandstone base of this trail allows biking during the wetter days. Except for the noon hour, shade keeps this trail as cool as possible year-round. Occasionally, snowfall will prevent your riding.

Services: Rome, Georgia, has supplies enough.

Hazards: Few hazards exist. As a wildlife refuge, hunting is not normally allowed; however, times do occur when special hunting seasons are arranged.

Rescue index: This is fairly remote terrain. Its frequent use should have someone coming along at regular intervals, especially on weekends. If your car is not removed from the parking space at the Keown Mill by nightfall, security guards will begin a search.

The trailhead at Keown Mill, where—when it still turned—students would hang on and do 360s.

Land status: Berry Schools owns the land while the Georgia Department of Natural Resources manages the refuge.

Maps: The map of Berry College showing the trails can be received from the school's administrative office or from one of the area's fine bicycle shops, like Bob's Cycle.

Finding the trail: Head north out of Rome on Highway 27. Turn left into Berry campus. Turn right up to the magnificent Ford Buildings. Go past them and continue down "The Stretch" for 3 miles until a speed bump. Bear to the right past Frost Chapel on the right. Turn left toward Friendship Hall, going past it and down the hill to the old mill. The trail begins behind the gate on the road leading up to the reservoir.

Sources of additional information:

Berry College Switchboard
2277 Martha Berry Boulevard
Mt. Berry, GA
(706) 232-5374

Notes on the trail: Although the basic loop of 7.5 miles stays on seldom-used dirt roads, single-tracks cut off and onto the road above the reservoir in

Guess which biker's from Florida.

several spots. Give yourself all day to explore these possibilities and you can string together upwards of 15 miles. But the basic loop is traveled as follows: After beginning the rolling trip up to the reservoir, a couple of signed sections of trail go off to the left, entering the road again above the reservoir. Follow the road along the picturesque lake that gravity-feeds the water needs of Berry Schools 5 miles away. As you cross the small creek, the road bends to the left and up. In the elbow of the turn, notice single-track making its way among boulders. At the top of the climb, in the gap where 4 roads intersect, take the gated road to the right. This section has obvious single-track coming in and going off to the right, down the mountain. After the road dead-ends, take a right downhill to Friendship Hall; the left at the dead-end goes up to Martha Berry's hideaway, the House 'O Dreams, high atop Lavender Mountain.

RIDE 70 *BEAR CREEK*

Records do not indicate whether or not the Gennett brothers, Andrew and N.W., owners of this land during the Depression, could have spared enough money to buy a bike. But their foresight at having spared one of the largest trees in the Chattahoochee National Forest today has its payoff for mountain bikers. The Gennett Poplar, with a girth of 18-feet near the bottom, is the most remarkable feature on this trail. An outdoor supply store in Atlanta, REI, restored this single-track in a 1992 project . . . with help from its many friends.

REI knows how to pick them. Both the 2.5-mile out-and-back single-track (five miles total) and loops (a three-miler and a longer seven-miler that use some double-track and gravel roads), which can either be combined or ridden separately, present the best of a north Georgia mountain bike ride. Hemlocks and wild grape vines hang over the treadway so thickly it suggests an underground experience. If it weren't for the occasional wildlife opening, the spell would remain intact the entire length.

My guide for Bear Creek, Noah Harris, took me on a variation of the traditional loop and up to Potatopatch Mountain where an overlook shows the Cohutta Mountain Range to the north, west, and east. It's worth the short, steep section and occasional traffic on the Forest Service road to reach this point. Along the way, we saw—lucky for us—an ominous-looking feline shape lurking in the tall grass where Bear Creek Trail comes into Barnes Creek Road. It turned out to be a skunk taking an evening feed at—where else?—Skunk Gas Pass.

As we made our way up the road, switching back often, Noah stopped at a corner and waited until I caught up. "A flock of large birds ran up the bank into the woods. If we hurry, maybe we can surprise them," he told me. Sure enough, as we approached the next bend, several turkeys flew over our heads, looking like bowling balls with wings. Wild turkeys infrequently take flight. When they do, it is an unforgettable sight of grace and beauty which defies their ungainly shape.

General location: This is one of many trails located in the Cohutta Wildlife Management Area of the Chattahoochee National Forest in between Chatsworth and Ellijay, Georgia.

Elevation change: Put your "Yee-Haw!" on alert. This is rugged mountain track that provides thigh-burning, lung-bursting climbs in one direction, and as quick a descent as you can handle in the other direction. It took 90 minutes to make the 4.5-mile climb to Potatopatch—I had to rest some ("C'mon, Noah, let's take another picture here.")—and only 30 minutes coming down.

RIDE 70 *BEAR CREEK*

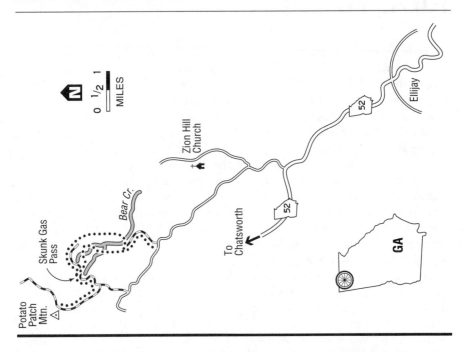

Season: Periods of high water may make the stream crossings in the Cohuttas more daunting than true safety can accommodate. No season seems better suited than another; however, it does get bitterly cold here occasionally.

Services: You're about as remotely situated as northwest Georgia can provide. Either Chatsworth or Ellijay will be the closest destination for supplies, although basic goods can be got at Fort Mountain State Park.

Hazards: Some rocks jut up into the trail with sharp noses, which can break yours if you land on them. Similar rocks lie under the water on stream crossings. Also, expect others on the trail and sing out when you approach them: "Bikers! Two more behind!"

Rescue index: You are accessible, but it would be more than difficult to get to you.

Land status: This land is part of the Chattahoochee National Forest, close to the Cohutta Wildlife Management Area.

Maps: Anyone wishing to explore the Chattahoochee National Forest should invest in the map covering the area, which goes all the way across north Georgia. In addition, contact the Forest Service for its publication, "Mountain Bike Trails—Cohutta Ranger District—Chattahoochee National Forest." Topo maps are a good idea if you plan to take any paths off the beaten ones. For Bear Creek, acquire the Dyer Gap quad (7.5 minute series).

Noah Harris is dwarfed by Gennett Poplar; horizontal lines mark holes left by sapsuckers.

Finding the trail: Leave Ellijay, Georgia, on Highway 52/2 heading west. A little over 5 miles from the square, look for a sign on the right announcing Zion Hill Church and turn. Just after crossing a small bridge, a Forest Service sign for Bear Creek Campground to the right should be seen; it's a steep cutback, so take it easy and look for oncoming traffic before swinging wide. Signs point the way to the trail. You can park at the trailhead or at the campground. Parking at the campground adds about another mile one-way.

Sources of additional information:

Cohutta Ranger District
National Forest Service
401 Old Ellijay Highway
Chatsworth, GA 30705
(706) 695-6737 or 695-6736

Notes on the trail: The trailhead starts both Bear Creek Trail and Bear Creek Loop. A bulletin board has a map of the area and information on the "trail opportunities." Basically, Bear Creek Trail is an out-and-back of slightly more than 5 miles total. Another two loops—a longer 6.7 miles and a shorter 3-miler—are completed by taking right turns at signs along the way. The shorter loop's right-hand turn is found just past the Gennett Poplar. This single-track dead-ends into Barnes Creek Road where another right turn takes you back to the parking lot. The longer loop has its right turn at the junction with Barnes Creek Road at Skunk Gas Pass. Ride this for about 3.5 miles before turning right onto the trail for the last .5 mile.

To reach the overlook at Potatopatch Mountain, turn left at the end of Bear Creek Trail onto Barnes Creek Road. After it dead-ends at the normally closed gate, turn right and do a "grind-and-groan" for a shorter distance than it seems. The large mountain chain of the Cohuttas disappears into the blue smoke of the northeast, home of the Great Smoky Mountains.

RIDE 71 *RIDGEWAY*

This nearly six-mile loop in Ridgeway Park, high above Carters Lake, got its beginning from one of the most dynamic forces in north Georgia mountain biking: Doug White. He got together with a ranger who also rides mountain bikes and they laid out the path for this course, which has held regular NORBA races since 1993. Using an old, abandoned double-track in places, the trail has been added to regularly in the form of more and more single-track through forest protected as a part of the U.S. Army Corps of Engineers property.

I showed up at Doug's Cyclery in Dalton to get trail information early one Monday morning and I hadn't been in the shop five minutes when a gentleman walked in with his bike needing some minor repairs and said, "Riding Ridgeway is such a wonderful way to start your day." After the repairs were completed, the man asked Doug how much he owed. The bill came to $13. The man asked Doug, "You been doing some more work out there on the trail?" Doug said yes. "It just keeps getting better and better. I sure do appreciate it." With that, the man gave Doug considerably more than he owed and said, "Keep the change."

General location: This trail is located at Ridgeway Park on Carters Lake off Highway 282/76, approximately 8 miles west of Ellijay, Georgia.
Elevation change: According to Doug, "You can't put a baseball anywhere on the trail and not have it roll off." I don't know about that, but I do know that there's more than one section where I had to push my bike up. But, hey, this is north Georgia, and you expect a trail to be like this.

RIDE 71 *RIDGEWAY*

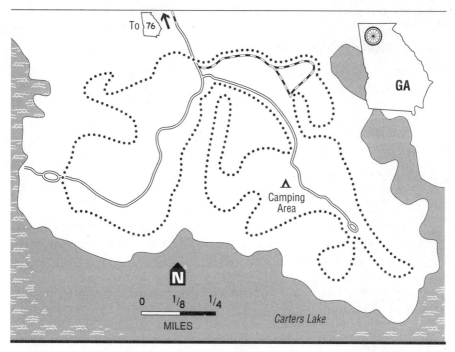

Season: You wouldn't want to ride this after too much rain or after a sheet of ice formed on the trail. You could start sliding and not stop until you got to Ellijay.

Services: Ridgeway Park has camping pads developed for tents, and water can be obtained by using the hand pumps located in several locations.

Hazards: Beginners need to be comfortable riding down steep sections of rocky trail before trying to ride all the way on this one. This trail has been designed with one approved riding direction only, so oncoming bike traffic should not pose a problem.

Rescue index: Although it would take more than minimal effort to get back to them, the trail does not get much farther than a mile away from one of the paved park roads. However, you are fairly removed from civilization. It takes approximately 10–15 minutes to get back to the highway from the camping area.

Land status: This is land managed by the U.S. Army Corps of Engineers.

Maps: A map of the bike trail is posted on the bulletin board by the boat ramp. Area bike shops may also have copies of the map, Ridgeway Mountain Bike Trail.

Finding the trail: Turn off Highway 282/76 about 8 miles west of Ellijay at the Ridgeway entrance sign. It's only a little over 3 miles to the camping area, but the gravel road should be driven slowly, so it takes about 10 minutes to reach the pavement of the park. One trailhead occurs just before the turn to the boat ramp. Another trailhead is at the boat ramp, and another one is at the camping area.

Sources of additional information:

> Carters Lake Resource Office
> U.S. Army Corps of Engineers
> P.O. Box 96
> Oakman, GA 30732-0096
> (706) 334-2248

> Doug's Cyclery
> 815 North Tibbs Road
> Dalton, GA 30720-2948
> (706) 278-3775

Notes on the trail: After finding the trailhead, you will find it easy to stay on the trail. Orange markers have been placed at all intersections where you might find an alternate route to take. Stay on the trail and follow the recommended direction.

Although not part of the Ridgeway Park, mountain bikers have got a big thrill in store for them when the proposed—and approved—42.5-mile multi-use trail gets put in place going from Dalton to Floyd State Park. The entire trail will fall within the boundaries of the Chattahoochee National Forest, Armuchee District.

RIDE 72 *RICH MOUNTAIN WILDLIFE MANAGEMENT AREA*

This combination of single-track and rough gravel road leading into the Wildlife Management Area provides mountain bikers with an opportunity to experience some riparian rolling along the Cartecay River. Although this area was ridden for several years by area bikers before it was officially turned into a six-mile loop, the state of Georgia now has a 30-year lease with Georgia Power to manage this land, part of the maintenance including an off-road trail which gives even the experienced biker need for caution.

The maniacally steep descent to the Cartecay is where, as Jay Srymanske of Mountain Outdoors Expeditions puts it, "Brakes do no good. You're either on your bike or off." As a result, and a favor to first-time riders, three orange blazes announce the radical section. Once down, the single-track follows the Cartecay for a half-mile, passing by one of the river's technical drops for paddlers, Clear Creek Falls.

RIDE 72 *RICH MOUNTAIN WILDLIFE MANAGEMENT AREA*

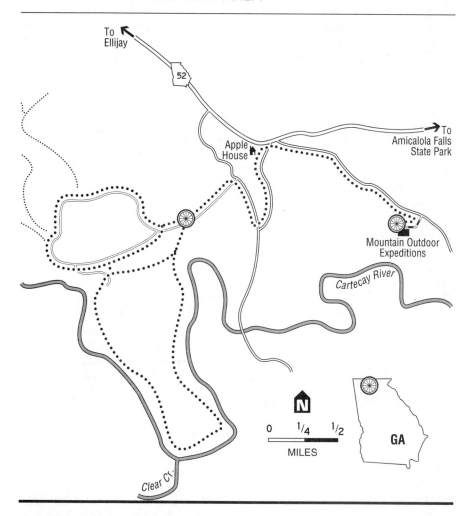

General location: This trail is located off Highway 52, about 5 miles east of Ellijay.

Elevation change: If you had wings, you could fly on some descents.

Season: Hunting does go on in these woods, especially during the fall and spring, deer and turkey seasons. If you must ride here during these times, wear orange and make lots of noise.

Services: Mountain Outdoor Expeditions on Lower Cartecay Road comes highly recommended as a safe zone for vehicles, as well as providing current information on a wide variety of subjects. Known as MOE, it has catered to outdoor needs for many years, even offering a place to stay at the MOE-tel on the property.

Hazards: Leaving your vehicle unattended for a long time at the gates closer to the single-track "is a day-to-day thing" according to Jay at MOE. "A lot of people just blow the additional mileage off and park with us," which is free unless you opt to purchase the copy of the map showing bike trails in the Rich Mountain WMA. The trail has at least 1 steep spot where some people may be more comfortable walking.

Rescue index: Some locations on this trail could be difficult to effect a rescue. Largely, though, gravel service roads and home construction along the Cartecay make this area easily, if not quickly, reached.

Land status: This property is leased to the Georgia state government from Georgia Power Company.

Maps: Go ahead and invest the buck or so for a map at MOE. You'll get more than your money's worth of information and friendly assistance.

Finding the trail: To find MOE, turn on Lower Cartecay Road, east of Ellijay on GA 52, and look for all the canoes on the hill to the right about a mile down the road. Beginning your ride here makes a lot of sense, but if you want to park closer to the single-track, turn at Oak Hill Apple House and go down the road until it dead-ends and turn right. Go a short distance and turn left at the Rich Mountain WMA sign. A gate that is closed from October 1 through the opening of trout season (usually late March) can be a parking spot, or you can go on a short distance to where there's another gate on your right and park in the wide spot in the road. You can, however, continue until the road dead-ends at the single-track about another mile down the road, but it's rough and better ridden on a bike. The white-blazed single-track begins at the end of the road, going up the hill over some roots by a large white pine.

Sources of additional information:

Mountain Outdoor Expeditions
Lower Cartecay Road
Ellijay, GA
(706) 635-2524

Notes on the trail: Beginning with the single-track, watch for the triple orange blazes indicating the steep descent. Walk it first to see if it is something you want to ride. After making it to the riverside, the trail goes for approximately .5 mile before leaving the river. The fork to the right leads back to the gravel road you came in on if you're having a difficult time of it, or if you just want to make a shorter ride. The trail continues in a wider loop with white on top of red blazes marking the way. Three trails go off to the left: the first one leads to an overlook and dead-ends, the other 2 are overgrown in summer and lead down to the river and a beach. The 6-mile loop is completed back at the second gate. Returning to MOE (and riding the 2.5-mile approach trail out-and-back from there, 5 miles total) makes the trip almost 11 miles.

Dahlonega Area Rides

No one could have predicted when Ben Parks stubbed his great toe on a chunk of exposed gold while hunting in 1828 that Dahlonega would become the destination for those looking for a golden mountain bike experience. But that's exactly what Dr. Matthew Stephenson unwittingly prophesied when he urged locals to stay and mine the "millions" in them thar hills.

With a large part of Lumpkin County designated as national forest, recreation has become a mainstay for it and other north Georgia counties. The mountains, which form the lower end of the Appalachians, have sometimes been cursed by those wanting to develop its breathtaking scenery into another two-bit manufacturing site. There are some things you can't move, though. The mountains remain, while bumper-to-bumper traffic crams Highway 400 leading from Atlanta, 60 miles to the south, with carloads of sightseers. Locals learn to take backroads or stay home on weekends around the peak seasons when "leaf-lookers" snake along curvy roads in seemingly endless caravans.

More and more, vehicles headed mountainward have been carrying contraptions with them, the sight of which would have caused grandpa to put a nervous hand on the shotgun. Bicycles, of course, is what they are. Thin-tire aficionados, as much as fat-tire pedalers, arrive to ride the inclines, passing by Trahlyta's Grave, where a solemn stack of stones commemorates a Cherokee maiden's death. The destination sought by bikers using only pedal power is also a popular route for motorcyclists, who can stay a night or two at T.W.O., a Suches, Georgia, resort for "Two Wheels Only."

Farther east, the National Off-Road Biking Association has developed a similar meaningful relationship with mountain bikers by holding its National Finals in the former logging town of Helen—now turned Bavarian. You can sometimes forget you're in America when international cyclists glide by shop owners dressed in lederhosen. It's just part of the mountain mystique you will want to hash out over a cup of coffee at The Goofy Rooster or Yonah Burger outside of town.

The Chattahoochee River, which begins as a tiny spring along the Appalachian Trail a few miles above Helen, flows south to Gainesville where it has been dammed to form the gigantic Lake Sidney Lanier—site of Olympic rowing and kayaking—named for Georgia's most widely recognized poet. Another Georgian poet, Byron Herbert Reece, is the central character in what has become an annual production of *The Reach of Song*, a celebration of mountain life, which can be watched at the Georgia Mountain Fairgrounds in Hiawassee.

Back in Gainesville, the largest city in northeast Georgia, a monument of a chicken perched on a pedestal draws attention to this city's importance to the poultry industry, whose houses are a frequent sight along backroads in north Georgia. Another important activity has been responsible for putting Gainesville on the national map. Road Atlanta, site of NASCAR racing, entertains throngs of passionate fans of motor racing, a topic that will heat up an argument around here as quickly as politics or religion. Perhaps it was religion that caused an anonymously funded project resulting in the Guide Stones in Elberton. These unusual spires of granite stand alone in a field, sentinels bearing a message of peace chiseled in 12 different languages.

Peace may not have been the entire motive behind Union County's decision to secede from the Confederacy during the Civil War. The people who live in these hills value their independence, sometimes more than their alliances. The natural boundaries formed by the towering peaks made defining friend and foe simpler in those days. Now, the mountains serve to bridge the gap between yesterday and today, urban and rural, as strangers meet in woods of green shade and find they have a lot in common.

For more information:

Dahlonega-Lumpkin County Chamber of Commerce
101 South Park Street, Department M
Dahlonega, GA 30533
(800) 231-5543 extension 10 or (706) 864-3711

Gainesville Hall Convention and Visitors Bureau
830 Green Street
Gainesville, GA 30501
(770) 536-5209

Mountain Adventures Cyclery
GA 400 and Highway 60
Long Branch Station
Dahlonega, GA 30533
(706) 864-8525

Bike Town USA
1604 Dawsonville Highway (GA 53)
Gainesville, GA 30501
(770) 532-7090

Alpine Helen Convention and Visitors Bureau
City Hall Building
Chattahoochee Street
Helen, GA 30545
(706) 878-2181

RIDE 73 *AMICALOLA FALLS STATE PARK TRAIL*

Georgia's most popular state park lies in the rocky region that serves as the unofficial Deep South trailhead for hikers beginning the Appalachian Trail trek up to Maine. For those who have hiked the eight miles to Springer Mountain (the official AT southern terminus) from Amicalola Falls, the strenuous terrain awaiting on the bike trail—actually a combination of jeep, ATV, and hiking trails—will come as no surprise. If this marks your first ride on north Georgia's physically demanding landscape, plan on spending the greater portion of the day negotiating the 14-mile loop of mountain bike trail laid out on the sometimes very sharp, rocky spines of the lower Appalachians, America's oldest mountain chain.

Although the information available at the park's Visitors Center sets the time for making this loop at 2–6 hours, it will probably take closer to the upper end than the lower for most bikers. Scenic overlooks along the way will be as responsible for slowing progress as will the hike-and-bike sections. Also, if you fail to make the turns at Nimblewill Gap and wind up at Nimblewill Church, it could be next Sunday before you make it back.

After riding this trail, rest and relaxation can be found by using one of the tent or trailer camping spots at the park. If, however, a different stretch of the legs is called for, several trails—some with camp sites along them—can be walked, offering various views of the land surrounding the largest falls east of the Rockies, the 729-foot Amicalola Falls. A lodge is also available for those who have had enough of the outdoors or who need a good home-cooked meal to stoke the biking fires.

Amicalola, which means "tumbling waters" in Cherokee, was the site of a different tumble back in the days of Prohibition. Bootlegging has always had a checkered reputation among the hill communities of north Georgia. For many farmers, it was the only way to get the corn they grew to market and still make enough profit to live. One such man, being hotly pursued by the authorities, failed to negotiate the turn by the falls. His car's bumper is still rusting on a ledge by the falls' viewing platform.

On the way back to larger communities, make a quick stop in Dawsonville at the Dawsonville Poolroom to check out the collection of Awesome Bill from Dawsonville's NASCAR racing memorabilia. Or for a slower pace, just down the road a short piece from Amicalola Falls Park, Burt's Pumpkin Farm offers hayrides for the family from September 1 through December 30—pumpkin season.

General location: The trail is found within the Chattahoochee National Forest, near where Lumpkin, Dawson, Fannin, and Gilmer counties meet.

RIDE 73 *AMICALOLA FALLS STATE PARK TRAIL*

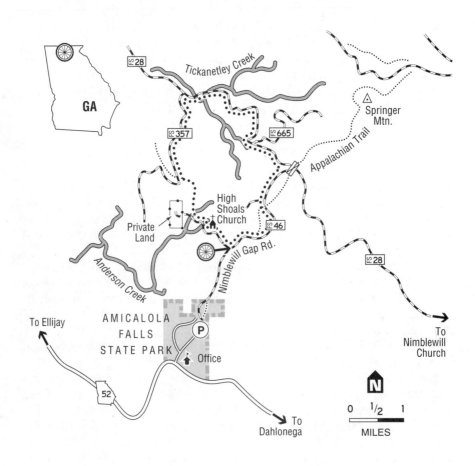

Elevation change: From the trailhead at the top of the falls (2,220') to Nimblewill Gap on Forest Service Road 28 (3,049'), several significant ups and downs occur. This is not a trail for those who do not relish climbs and descents. A steady, steep 4-mile climb from Tickanetley Creek on FS 28 to Nimblewill Gap—a gain of nearly 300 feet each mile—will make your brow sweat and chest heave.

Season: There are times during the winter months when the trail and park will be closed due to ice and snow. Call ahead for local conditions if in doubt.

The best views can be had when the leaves are off the trees, but these same leaves of the dense hardwood forest provide much appreciated shade during the summer months.

Services: Most services can be had in Dawsonville or Dahlonega.

Hazards: Vehicular traffic like jeeps and ORVs will be occasionally seen, especially on weekends. Rocks, roots, and deep ruts in some places can cause unintended dismounting. But perhaps the biggest hazard is straying off the trail and winding up miles from where you need to be and having to climb the 25% grade 1.5 miles back up to the falls from Highway 52. Ouch!

I spoke briefly with Ms. Kincaid at Kincaid's Grocery about riding the bike trail at the park. The first thing she wanted to know was if I had gotten lost, "A lot of people get lost on that trail." The park office has a map they reproduced and hand out. A word of advice: don't bother with it. It does not relieve the confusion at some intersections. Use the map and directions found in this book.

Rescue index: Depending on the day of the week, you're more likely to find a bear than another human. Act accordingly and carry emergency provisions for a backcountry trip.

Land status: The bulk of the trail is on national forestland and roads, although access to the most convenient trailhead requires entering the state park.

Maps: The topo maps (7.5 minute series) of the Nimblewill, Noontootla, Tickanetley, and Amicalola quads would be a help, but without the map of the Chattahoochee National Forest, the lack of recent topo revisions will cause critical junctions to be shown incorrectly. The best bet is to use the map reproduced in this book. Other sources of the trail's directions have been sorely lacking; many misdirected bikers will attest to this fact, as will Ms. Kincaid at the grocery outside the park's entrance.

Finding the trail: Enter Amicalola Falls State Park from Highway 52 and pay the parking fee (unless it's Wednesday when entrance is free or unless you tell the gate attendant you'll be going through to the national forest above the park) and take the first left up to the top of the falls. The paved road turns into a gravel road leading up to High Shoals Church. Pull off and park at any of the unimproved national forest camping spots on the right or left before getting to Nimblewill Gap Road (FS 46) coming in from the right. Begin the clockwise loop from the junction of FS 46 and High Shoals Road.

Sources of additional information:

Amicalola Falls State Park
Star Route, Box 215
Dawsonville, GA 30534
(706) 265-8888

Notes on the trail: The first mile or so leads up to High Shoals Church. Go past the church and down the rocky road, crossing first a small creek, then the larger Anderson Creek before making a short climb. Look for the narrow ATV trail shortly on the right, cutting between high banks as the gravel road continues to the left .25 mile, dead-ending at private property and a gate. The ATV trail intersects with FS 357 at what is a very confusing junction. The gravel road goes left and right; the ATV trail goes straight. Turn right and ride 2 miles down the hill until FS 357 dead-ends into FS 28. A pasture behind a fence is in front of you. Turn right, cross a bridge over a small creek before crossing the larger Tickanetley Creek twice in a valley with some houses. Get out your weenie gear. You're going to need it in the next hour and for the next 4 miles as you make the rocky ascent to Nimblewill Gap, the most troublesome intersection of the trail. Some landmarks to look for: about a mile from the top, FS 665 (a long dead-end road) goes off to the left, and the frequent switch-backs stop just shy of the gap, providing 2 long straight stretches. At the gap are several conspicuous landmarks: a set of log steps come down the mountain from the right; the road levels off and widens; a trail goes off to the left toward Springer Mountain; a large tree lies on the ground on the left; a gate (probably open) is in the middle of the right turn of the road you've been climbing; and finally, a rocky road lies to your right (taking you up another 150 feet or so in the next .5 mile). It is this rocky road (FS 46) to the right which you must take. While you're here, take a break and contemplate all the through-hikers who have trod this intersection in early April every year as they make their way up to Mount Katahdin in Maine over 2,000 miles away. After the final climb up FS 46, it levels out before another intersection: a right up to Frosty Mountain. Take the left; you've done all the climbing required. The rest of the trail goes down 450 feet over an extremely rocky roadbed for nearly 2 miles before coming back into High Shoals Road at the bottom. A left leads back to Amicalola State Park. Taking a right begins another 14-mile lap.

RIDE 74 *BULL MOUNTAIN*

This 14.5-mile loop around Bull Mountain nearly reaches this mountain's summit of 2,340 feet above sea level in one fell swoop, or maybe it just feels like it. Following a combination of double-, single-track, and gravel Forest Service roads, the high point of the trip actually comes on an unnamed peak west of Bull at an altitude of 2,480 feet. The lowest elevation occurs over 700 feet below on a bank somewhere along Jones Creek, the Chattahoochee National Forest's premier trout stream.

Jones Creek originates from one of the large springs gushing out of the southwestern flank of, naturally, Springer Mountain. This mountain serves as the official lower trailhead of the Appalachian Trail, and the point from which many hikers begin their "spring up the trail into Maine," ending in that state's Mt. Katahdin over 2,000 miles away.

RIDE 74 *BULL MOUNTAIN*

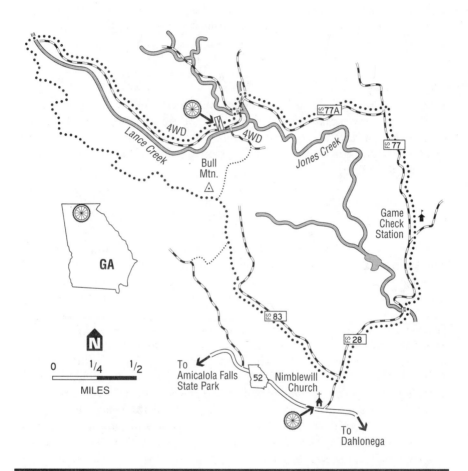

Lance Creek, the other major tributary of the Amicalola watershed and whose source pours from Springer's side as well, provides sights and sounds to accompany the trip up as the trail hugs its banks. The trail got its start earlier as an old logging road, and its double-wide nature allows bikers to travel side-by-side for much of this section, although mountain bikes have been wearing a single-track smooth.

The trail's length and difficulty make it an all-day affair for many bikers, although you will find those on the trail who spend only a couple of hours to make the trip. At any rate, covering the entire course with only two water bottles, especially during the summer, may require an unhealthy rationing of the H$_2$O. Try to pack at least another bottle or two, or consider investing in a back bottle. Don't be fooled into thinking that the fresh running stream coming into Lance Creek can be immediately put into your bottle. There are some springs in the Chattahoochee National Forest I would bury my face in and drink from without hesitation; however, I've seen too many signs of unsanitary habits up on Springer to use this water without first bringing it to an extended boil.

This trail gets a lot of use, especially on weekends when upwards of 80–90 bikers zoom around it in one day. You get all kinds. This is a popular destination for Atlanta area mountain bikers, and you can do a fairly reliable survey of current biking fashions by taking a break and watching the traffic pass. It's also a popular area for fishermen and turkey hunters in the spring, some of whom have other game in mind. I found out one day how hard it is to refuse religious literature when the person offering it is dressed in camo and carrying a .410 shotgun.

General location: This trail utilizes old, converted logging roads found in the mountainous region where Lumpkin, Fannin, Gilmer, and Dawson Counties come together just east of Amicalola Falls State Park.

Elevation change: Departing from the basic Deep South tradition of "short and steep," this trail provides ample opportunity to climb hill after hill. Although there is a tendency for one half of the trail to be generally ascending as a net gain of over 700 feet is acquired, significant portions of it are gained and lost several times.

Season: This trail is ridden year-round.

Services: Most services can be obtained in either Dawsonville or Dahlonega, although both these towns have limitations and are fairly far off the trail.

Hazards: This is a well-maintained trail. Besides not having immediately safe potable water, a section of approximately 3 miles incorporates Forest Service roads that can see traffic traveling at speeds greater than the law allows. There will also be bike traffic coming from either direction, and some of it will be on the narrower single-track sections. Hunters in search of quarry of all sorts may be marching through the woods.

Rescue index: You will be riding on some remote pathways, but because the trail is heavily used, you will no doubt be seen soon should you need help. Getting you out and to some place where you can get first aid—for either you or your bike—is another story.

Land status: This is land entirely located within the Chattahoochee National Forest.

Maps: You can obtain a map of the trail at Bull Mountain from the Forest Service office in Dahlonega, or you can pick one up at Mountain Adventures Cyclery on Highway 400. A topo map of the Nimblewill quad (7.5 minute

Riding on one of Georgia's most popular biking destinations—Bull Mountain.

series) will show the trail in its basic shape; there are some sections of single-track recently made that will not show up on the topo. Another good map to invest in is the Chattahoochee National Forest map, also available at the National Forest Service office in Dahlonega.

Finding the trail: Pick your favorite way to go to Amicalola Falls State Park and continue on Highway 52 headed north if you have a southerly approach. After passing where Highway 136 is accessed on the right, the county line is crossed. Take the left toward Nimblewill Church and park at the church. If arriving from Dahlonega, take Highway 52 as it splits from Highway 9, and head toward Ellijay. Look for the white building on the right and the sign for the church about 7 miles after making the turn onto 52. Park at the church and take Forest Service Road 28. The trail goes clockwise onto FS 83 or counterclockwise by continuing on FS 28. See the trail notes for further important turns.

Sources of additional information:

Mountain Adventures Cyclery
Long Branch Station
Highway 400 and 60
Dahlonega, GA 30533
(706) 864-8525

Chestatee District Ranger's Office
National Forest Service
1015 Tipton Drive
Dahlonega, GA 30533
(706) 864-6173

Notes on the trail: After taking the right fork keeping on FS 28, take the next left on FS 77. At the bottom of the hill, turn left onto FS 77A to Jones Creek. Take the right turn onto the gated road and miss the ford. The climb along the right bank of Lance Creek is pleasantly strenuous, but nothing compared to the steep grade awaiting you on the other side of Lance Creek. Turn left up the hill until you reach the ridge where the trail dead-ends. Turn left here and watch for the steep descent going off to the left which dead-ends into FS 83. Take a right onto this road and right again after it joins FS 28. The church will be on your right after coming up to the blacktop.

RIDE 75 *TURNER CREEK LOOP*

After the March 13, 1993, blizzard leveled huge tracts of white and yellow pines in the north Georgia mountains, it took nearly two days to open back up primary highways. The Forest Service roads in the Chattahoochee National Forest remained closed for months. The scale of devastation made finding a place to go off-road with a bike as difficult as locating a set of still jaws at a Talkers Anonymous meeting. Yet, out of the destruction came one of the finest trails anywhere in the woods.

The leadership of the Southern Off-Road Bicycle Association (SORBA) met after the blizzard with the rangers at the National Forest District Office in Dahlonega and agreed on plans to construct a mountain bike trail. By February 1994, single-track had been built that combined gated logging roads and current Forest Service roads, ridden either by itself in a 5.5-mile loop or put together with the longer Bull Mountain Trail.

Wildlife of many types can be spotted in these woods by the sharp-eyed, silent biker, especially during the bookends of daylight. It was on this trail late one spring afternoon when a friend and I took a detour to a wildlife opening. As soon as we arrived, we were greeted by the sight of an obviously agitated turkey hen flying in an erratic, mock-broken-wing circle around the perimeter of the clearing. Before we could get off our bikes, a chirping broke out at our feet. Two turkey chicks scooted away through the shin-high grass, but as we looked closer, another chick was found still motionless and unharmed less than three inches from the back tire of my friend's bike.

We backtracked while the hen flew ahead of us in awkward circles trying to draw us away from her newly hatched family. After we had retreated a couple

RIDE 75 *TURNER CREEK LOOP*

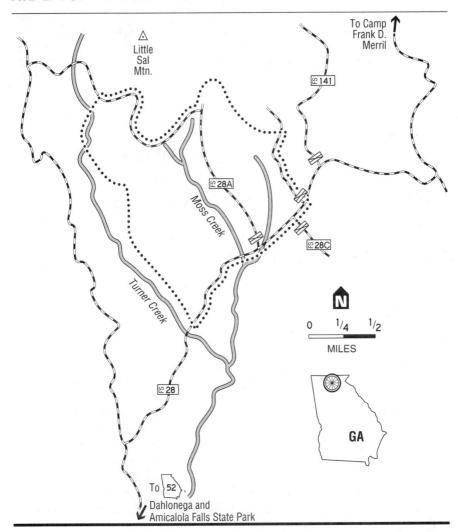

of hundred yards, the turkey finally peeled off and returned to the clearing in an iridescent glide of brown. It must have been such a display that prompted Ben Franklin to suggest this magnificent bird as our national emblem.

General location: This spectacular trail is located northwest of Dahlonega, Georgia.

Elevation change: There are at least 3 significant climbs lasting from .5 mile to a mile; 200 feet or more will be gained on each climb.

Season: Although this trail holds up well during wet weather, it is best left alone a day or so following rain. Riding on this surface after a thaw from a hard freeze will be especially destructive to the surface.

Services: The nearest services are found in Dahlonega or Dawsonville.

Hazards: Oncoming bikes on the single-track, automobiles on the Forest Service road, some rocks, limbs, and roots all present manageable hazards. During hunting season—especially the first few weekends—you would do better to try a different trail if you plan on riding either early or late in the day. Wear your orange vest and make frequent noise if you must get out in the remoter sections of national forests during any hunting season.

Rescue index: You are in a fairly remote area. Take note of the nearest houses as you make your way in to the trailhead. You could wind up walking more than 2 miles back to your vehicle, as a friend had to do once . . . toting his 85-pound bee-stung boxer.

Land status: This is land owned by the federal government and included in the Chattahoochee National Forest.

Maps: Stop by Mountain Adventures Cyclery in Dahlonega and ask for a map of Turner Creek. If you want to do some exploring of the area, topo quads in the 7.5 minute series—Campbell Mountain, Nimblewill, Noontootla, and Suches—give info on where you go on this trail. The map of the Chattahoochee National Forest is a wise investment.

Finding the trail: Pick your favorite way to go to Amicalola Falls State Park and continue on Highway 52 headed south. After passing where Highway 136 comes in from the right, the county line is crossed. Take the left toward Nimblewill Church at the sign.

From Dahlonega, leave town on Highway 52/9 toward Dawsonville. Follow the signs to Amicalola Falls State Park, but before you get to the park and after crossing the Etowah River (a large ostrich farm is on the left), look for the white building on your right where a sign for Nimblewill Church has been placed and turn. Take FS 28 to the right just before getting to the church and take the right fork when you get to the game check station. About .75 mile from there a culvert carrying Turner Creek goes under the road; directly after crossing it, the end of Turner Creek single-track comes out from the left onto FS 28. Just past this, gated FS 28A goes off to the left; you can park here and start, or go on to the next gated Forest Service road (unnumbered) on the left and park. It just depends on whether you want to begin your ride on FS 28, end it on this road, or go uphill first.

Sources of additional information:

Chestatee District Ranger Office
National Forest Service
1015 Tipton Drive
Dahlonega, GA 30533
(706) 864-6173

The white cascade of Black Falls on the Etowah River.

Mountain Adventures Cyclery
Long Branch Station
Highway 400 and 60
Dahlonega, GA 30533
(706) 864-8525

Notes on the trail: Although there is nothing prohibiting riding this trail in either direction, I recommend taking the trailhead at the unnumbered Forest Service road and riding in a counterclockwise direction. But for the very reasons I may give to go counter, you may decide to ride clockwise.

This is some of the most wonderful scenery anywhere in the system of north Georgia trails. The golden stretch of broom sage on your left as you make the first climb (from the unnumbered gated road) marks a good place to take a gander south across the valley. Finish the climb where an old roadbed comes in from the left and go straight. Look for the well-worn single-track splitting off to the left and take it to lose some of that hard-gained elevation. Turn right onto FS 28A and begin another climb. Look for the brown fiberglass marker indicating the trail's turn to the left onto more single-track.

The section from here until it dead-ends at FS 28 can get tight in a few places. You'll ride up above Turner Creek for much of the way, first on your left, then on your right after crossing a well-constructed bridge. The single-track dead-ends into FS 28. Take a left to reach the trailhead at the unnumbered, gated road.

RIDE 76 *LITTLE SAL MOUNTAIN LOOP*

The Little Sal Mountain Loop trail follows nine miles of Forest Service roads making a loop in a seldom visited part of the Chattahoochee National Forest. It could just as easily be called the Etowah Headwaters Trail, since it winds its way up and down the ridges surrounding the major mountain tributaries of the Etowah River. It's good to remember that nearby a military base (Camp Frank D. Merrill) trains army special forces. On more than one occasion I've heard the rapid popping of small-arms, grenades exploding, and choppers flying, causing me to check the cinch on my helmet. For the most part, though, it's easy to forget you're near such a place when you enter the woods of the upper Etowah River and enjoy a pleasant, moderate workout.

It was on this trail that I stopped one day listening to dogs baying in the distance. I had just dismounted my bike when I heard hooves galloping toward me. It was a deer on full run away from the dogs . . . and toward me. It rounded the bend and was 15 feet away from me before it noticed the trail was blocked by a wide-eyed mountain biker. After stopping full and looking back, it charged straight up the bank and disappeared into the mountain laurel. I took the deer's cue and also disappeared down the trail, away from the dogs. Although domestic dogs present little concern to peace-loving mountain bikers, feral dogs are a different story, and occasionally they show up looking for lunch.

General location: This trail takes you through the Chattahoochee National Forest north of Dahlonega, Georgia.

Elevation change: Little Sal has a few places where an intense pedal rhythm is almost reached, but you will not remember this ride for its change in elevation.

Season: Fording the Etowah River, small as it is at this point, and the Montgomery Creek at levels other than mid-summer's drought will probably soak your shoes. At especially high water, attempting to ford either of these by bike is not advised.

Services: Many services can be obtained in nearby Dahlonega.

Hazards: You may see a few motorized vehicles on the stretch from the ranger camp to Camp Wahsega, and even fewer on the road to Montgomery

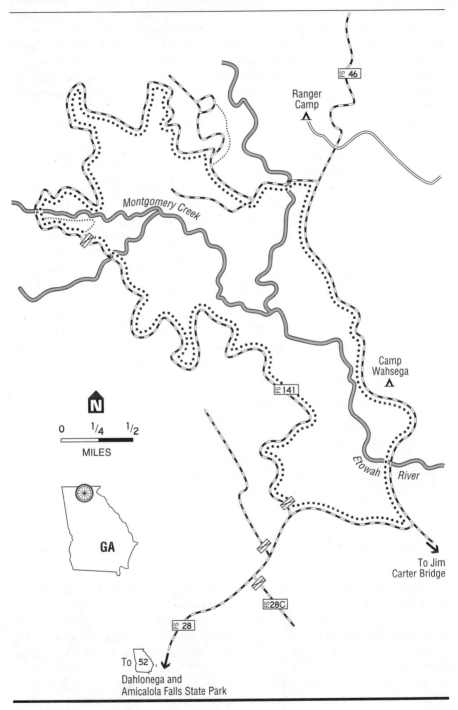

Creek. Hunters—in season—will park vehicles at junctions where they have most likely walked down to bag a buck. Choose another trail in the area.

Rescue index: You're in luck here in the backyard of Camp Frank D. Merrill where the rangers specialize in mountain maneuvers. However, it is remote and difficult to conduct any rescue, no matter how good or close help may be.

Land status: It looks as though you would be on Camp Merrill, but this is still part of the Chattahoochee National Forest.

Maps: Acquire the 4 topo maps in the 7.5 minute series—Campbell Mountain, Nimblewill, Noontootla, and Suches—for total contour coverage. The map of the Chattahoochee National Forest should be sufficient in most cases, however. The map in this book was drawn using these 2 map sources.

Finding the trail: From Atlanta, follow signs to Amicalola Falls State Park. After crossing into Lumpkin County and traveling about 3 miles, look for a sign announcing the left turn toward Nimblewill Church. Turn onto Forest Service Road 28 just beyond the church. Take the right-hand fork of FS 28 and drive past 1 gated road on the left as a creek passes underneath the road. You'll make a long climb, level out, and then begin a descent, passing another gated road on the left. The next gated road (on the left), normally gated FS 14, is one trailhead; you can park here.

From Dahlonega, head north on Highway 60 to Suches. Turn left at the sign for Camp Merrill approximately 3 miles north of town. Camp Merrill is nearly 10 miles down the road. At the three-way stop, turn left. Take the second right at the gym. Either park across from the gym or ford the Etowah River in your vehicle and park on the right side of the road.

Sources of additional information:

Chestatee District Ranger's Office
National Forest Service
1015 Tipton Drive
Dahlonega, GA 30533
(706) 864-6173

Camp Frank D. Merrill
Camp Wahsega Road
Dahlonega, GA 30533
(706) 864-3367

Notes on the trail: If you park across from the gym and elect to ford the Etowah, bring a change of socks if you want dry feet, especially if it's been raining. Big river stones—bike stoppers extraordinaire—can be hit if you're not careful on this ford. I favor the upstream path, but rocks move after big rains, so I try to scout it first. You can also walk across the foot-bridge behind the swimming pool.

After crossing the river you'll dry your spokes out with the uphill climb ahead. The first fork in the road offers what makes this loop exciting to ride—

Little Sal Mountain.

choices. The left fork leads down into the area above Black Falls, which has only recently been cleared of most of the trees downed by the fierce blizzard of March 1993. You will see much evidence of this "ice storm," as some locals refer to it, all along this region. Huge white pines lie uprooted—some with root balls 10 feet across.

After the diversion down to Black Falls, you'll come back up to the main road, take a left and continue on and up for about .5 mile until another fork: a road heading off and up to the right splits with a gated road (sometimes locked) leading down and to the left. The road up and right requires a steep 0.3 mile climb with a convenient spot to take a breather about half-way, but if you feel cranky, take it all the way to the top and pat yourself on the back. At the top, stop and turn around and look to the south. Campbell Mountain sits off by itself almost completely encircled by the Etowah River deep in the Chattahoochee National Forest. You can continue downhill to the dead-end another 0.3 mile where evidence can be seen of the rangers using this point as a start for wilderness exercises. Watch out for the barbed wire on the eastern side of the gap if you leave the trail.

The gate is sometimes closed on the road down to the left, but usually it's open and the occasional pickup can be met on this section. The rolling terrain down to Montgomery Creek ford provides food and habitat for many deer, and you're just as likely to meet 2 or 3 deer bounding off across the trail ahead as you are anything motorized.

Some days I use the Montgomery Creek ford as a stopping point for the day's ride. It's about 3.5 miles down there, and back makes a good 7-mile trip, about 90 minutes of travel time if you're there to check out the scenery. The creek banks are flat and accessible for quite a ways in both directions, and it's worth the time to explore.

Continue on to complete the loop. A washed out culvert has dammed up a small creek on the right, which you'll probably have to carry over. From this point to FS 28, the loop goes over the shoulders of Little Sal Mountain. Once you dead-end into FS 28 (this is the other trailhead), take a left up the hill at Camp Wahsega and ride FS 28 until the gym on the left.

RIDE 77 *HELEN'S UNICOI TRAIL*

When NORBA's competition director, Brian Stickel, began searching for a Deep South venue for its National Championship Series, he wound up talking to Don Hoche at Unicoi State Park. Despite the lack of a trail for mountain bikes at the time, Stickel was impressed with Hoche's proposal to install a trail where the best of the best can compete in cross-country cycling. A deal was struck, and plans went ahead for incorporating the existing double-track with some new single-track into a loop of approximately seven miles to be used for NORBA's opening race in April 1994. Racers and spectators were so happy with the track, arrangements were made to return for the 1995 Finals.

Unicoi (pronounced "oo-nee' ko-weh'" in its native Cherokee tongue, meaning "where the white man goes") was first established in 1954 as a small 250-acre park lying mainly north of present-day Smith Lake. In the late 1960s a major reconstruction brought in 750 more acres where most of the bike trail climbs and falls in woods grown up since the Helen logging operations of 50 years ago ceased.

Racers paying too much attention to the scenery, which is magnificent, may wind up wrapped around some of the hemlocks, rhododendrons, and river birch lining the course. Spectators—and those who bike with less intensity—will enjoy the dense shade of most of the course. After fording Smith Creek for the second time, a ride through pasture lined with autumn olive and river cane provides a contrast to the green-lighted forest ahead and behind.

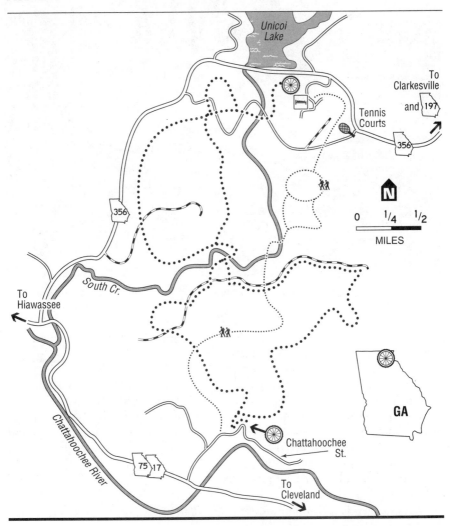

Mountain bikers had to stay off the course in between the race in 1994 and 1995, but after August 1, 1995, courtesy of Georgia's Department of Natural Resources, riders made Unicoi a permanent addition to their trail stops. A World Cup race takes place here in June 1996. Those who follow the racing scene will probably want to mark it on the calendar. A rather large field of international bikers should be here for this one as final preparations are made for the Olympics in Atlanta the following month. In addition to that event, Brian Stickel has remarked that the Helen venue is the best anywhere in the

When my son Jared leans into a turn, thoughts of being a future champion spin inside his mind.

world for spectators. This bodes well for keeping this trail on the international and national circuit for many years to come.

General location: Helen, Georgia, is nestled in the mountains 70 miles northeast of Atlanta; a portion of the trail cuts behind the Helen Library downtown.
Elevation change: Although a change was made from the first course layout which called for a backbreaking climb right out of the gate, long ascents will still have to be made by pedal or push. Yes, if you're serious about it, you can hoist your bike over your shoulder and run up.
Season: No seasonal restrictions should apply here except during deluges and ice storms.
Services: Helen is a community that has made its living since the late 1960s by catering to the needs of tourists; therefore, with the exception of a bike shop close by, all services can be found here.
Hazards: Until the proposed bridges across Smith Creek are completed, fording it can be an upsetting experience if maximum biking velocity meets a submerged stone at the wrong angle. Hikers will be found at some intersections during normal, non-race times. Signs will be posted warning the biker to yield when appropriate. Some roots and rocks on the tread demand extreme care. Some sections are steep enough to cause your cheeks to be wrapped around your ears if you do not brake.

David Juarez leads the race, driven by the cadence of his childhood dreams.

Rescue index: Most portions of the path can be reached fairly easily . . . once you're discovered. A walk out of no more than 2 miles—if you know the trail—is available if you can't fix your bike's gripe.

Land status: The Department of Natural Resources manages this land as a state park.

Maps: Maps are available at the Unicoi State Park office. Ask for the Unicoi Mountain Bike Trail Map.

Finding the trail: A parking lot above the library can be used, provided there's not something big going on in Helen (such as its annual Oktoberfest), and you get there early enough. Otherwise, head up to the park and, well, park. The trail goes behind the library headed south first, then east up the mountain.

Sources of additional information:

Unicoi State Park and Lodge
Highway 356
Helen, GA 30545
(706) 878-2201; reservations: 878-2824

National Off-Road Bicycle Association
One Olympic Plaza
Colorado Springs, CO 80909
(719) 578-4717

Alpine Helen Convention and Visitors Bureau
City Hall Building
Chattahoochee Street
Helen, GA 30545
(706) 878-2181

Notes on the trail: Riding on this trail requires following directional signs. Blazes show the different loops. The current hiking trail from the lodge to Helen is blazed with green and is off-limits to bikers. For those young and aspiring NORBA racers, 5 laps around the 7.4-mile course makes up the pros' mileage. Once around will be enough for me.

The folks at Unicoi have been responsible for putting in this many-featured trail. It was nice to see the care and thought they put into protecting the low-lying areas by placing culverts and plastic echo-stones where necessary to control the erosion. Sections have been hand-built while others have been created by using a narrow dozer. Other measures, like planting creeping red fescue, have been used to enhance the already spectacular scenery and to ensure this trail lasts a long time under reasonable conditions.

Afterword

Land-Use Controversy

A few years ago I wrote a long piece on this issue for *Sierra* magazine that entailed calling literally dozens of government land managers, game wardens, mountain bikers, and local officials to get a feeling for how riders were being welcomed on the trails. All that I've seen personally since, and heard from my authors, indicates there hasn't been much change. We're still considered the new kid on the block. We have less of a right to the trails than equestrians and hikers, and we're excluded from many areas, including:

a) wilderness areas
b) national parks (except on roads, and those paths specifically marked "bike path")
c) national monuments (except on roads open to the public)
d) most state parks and monuments (except on roads, and those paths specifically marked "bike path")
e) an increasing number of urban and county parks, especially in California (except on roads, and those paths specifically marked "bike path")

Frankly, I have little difficulty with these exclusions and would, in fact, restrict our presence from some trails I've ridden (one time) due to the environmental damage and chance of blindsiding the many walkers and hikers I met up with along the way. But these are my personal views. The author of this volume and mountain bikers as a group may hold different opinions.

You can do your part in keeping us from being excluded from even more trails by riding responsibly. Many local and national off-road bicycle organizations have been formed with exactly this in mind, and one of the largest—the National Off-Road Bicycle Association (NORBA)—offers the following code of behavior for mountain bikers:

1. I will yield the right of way to other nonmotorized recreationists. I realize that people judge all cyclists by my actions.
2. I will slow down and use caution when approaching or overtaking another cyclist and will make my presence known well in advance.

3. I will maintain control of my speed at all times and will approach turns in anticipation of someone around the bend.
4. I will stay on designated trails to avoid trampling native vegetation and minimize potential erosion to trails by not using muddy trails or short-cutting switchbacks.
5. I will not disturb wildlife or livestock.
6. I will not litter. I will pack out what I pack in, and pack out more than my share whenever possible.
7. I will respect public and private property, including trail use signs and no trespassing signs, and I will leave gates as I have found them.
8. I will always be self-sufficient and my destination and travel speed will be determined by my ability, my equipment, the terrain, the present and potential weather conditions.
9. I will not travel solo when bikepacking in remote areas. I will leave word of my destination and when I plan to return.
10. I will observe the practice of minimum impact bicycling by "taking only pictures and memories and leaving only waffle prints."
11. I will always wear a helmet whenever I ride.

Now, I have a problem with some of these—number nine, for instance. The most enjoyable mountain biking I've ever done has been solo. And as for leaving word of destination and time of return, I've enjoyed living in such a way as to say, "I'm off to pedal Colorado. See you in the fall." Of course it's senseless to take needless risks, and I plan a ride and pack my gear with this in mind. But for me number nine smacks too much of the "never-out-of-touch" mentality. And getting away from civilization, deep into the wild, is, for many people, what mountain biking's all about.

All in all, however, NORBA's is a good list, and surely we mountain bikers would be liked more, and excluded less, if we followed the suggestions. But let me offer a "code of ethics" I much prefer, one given to cyclists by Utah's Wasatch-Cache National Forest office.

Study a Forest Map Before You Ride
Currently, bicycles are permitted on roads and developed trails within the Wasatch-Cache National Forest except in designated Wilderness. If your route crosses private land, it is your responsibility to obtain right of way permission from the landowner.

Keep Groups Small
Riding in large groups degrades the outdoor experience for others, can disturb wildlife, and usually leads to greater resource damage.

Avoid Riding on Wet Trails
Bicycle tires leave ruts in wet trails. These ruts concentrate runoff and accelerate erosion. Postponing a ride when the trails are wet will preserve the trails for future use.

Stay on Roads and Trails
Riding cross-country destroys vegetation and damages the soil.

Always Yield to Others
Trails are shared by hikers, horses, and bicycles. Move off the trail to allow horses to pass and stop to allow hikers adequate room to share the trail. Simply yelling "Bicycle!" is not acceptable.

Control Your Speed
Excessive speed endangers yourself and other forest users.

Avoid Wheel Lock-up and Spin-out
Steep terrain is especially vulnerable to trail wear. Locking brakes on steep descents or when stopping needlessly damages trails. If a slope is steep enough to require locking wheels and skidding, dismount and walk your bicycle. Likewise, if an ascent is so steep your rear wheel slips and spins, dismount and walk your bicycle.

Protect Waterbars and Switchbacks
Waterbars, the rock and log drains built to direct water off trails, protect trails from erosion. When you encounter a waterbar, ride directly over the top or dismount and walk your bicycle. Riding around the ends of waterbars destroys them and speeds erosion. Skidding around switchback corners shortens trail life. Slow down for switchback corners and keep your wheels rolling.

If You Abuse It, You Lose It
Mountain bikers are relative newcomers to the forest and must prove themselves responsible trail users. By following the guidelines above, and by participating in trail maintenance service projects, bicyclists can help avoid closures which would prevent them from using trails.

I've never seen a better trail-etiquette list for mountain bikers. So have fun. Be careful. And don't screw things up for the next rider.

Dennis Coello
Series Editor

Glossary

This short list of terms does not contain all the words used by mountain bike enthusiasts when discussing their sport. But it should serve as an introduction to the lingo you'll hear on the trails.

ATB   all-terrain bike; this, like "fat-tire bike," is another name for a mountain bike

ATV   all-terrain vehicle; this usually refers to the loud, fume-spewing three- or four-wheeled motorized vehicles you will not enjoy meeting on the trail—except, of course, if you crash and have to hitch a ride out on one

bladed   refers to a dirt road which has been smoothed out by the use of a wide blade on earth-moving equipment; "blading" gets rid of the teeth-chattering, much-cursed washboards found on so many dirt roads after heavy vehicle use

blaze   a mark on a tree made by chipping away a piece of the bark, usually done to designate a trail; such trails are sometimes described as "blazed"

blind corner   a curve in the road or trail that conceals bikers, hikers, equestrians, and other traffic

BLM   Bureau of Land Management, an agency of the federal government

buffed   used to describe a very smooth trail

catching air taking a jump in such a way that both wheels of the bike are off the ground at the same time

clean   while this may describe what you and your bike *won't* be after following many trials, the term is most often used as a verb to denote the action of pedaling a tough section of trail successfully

combination this type of route may combine two or more configurations; for example, a point-to-point route may integrate a scenic loop or out-and-back spur midway through the ride;

likewise, an out-and-back may have a loop at its farthest point (this configuration looks like a cherry with a stem attached; the stem is the out-and-back, the fruit is the terminus loop); or a loop route may have multiple out-and-back spurs and/or loops to the side; mileage for a combination route is for the total distance to complete the ride

dab   touching the ground with a foot or hand

deadfall   a tangled mass of fallen trees or branches

diversion ditch   a usually narrow, shallow ditch dug across or around a trail; funneling the water in this manner keeps it from destroying the trail

double-track   the dual tracks made by a jeep or other vehicle, with grass or weeds or rocks between; mountain bikers can ride in either of the tracks, but you will of course find that whichever one you choose, and no matter how many times you change back and forth, the other track will appear to offer smoother travel

dugway   a steep, unpaved, switchbacked descent

endo   flipping end over end

feathering   using a light touch on the brake lever, hitting it lightly many times rather than very hard or locking the brake

four-wheel-drive   this refers to any vehicle with drive-wheel capability on all four wheels (a jeep, for instance, has four-wheel drive as compared with a two-wheel-drive passenger car), or to a rough road or trail that requires four-wheel-drive capability (or a one-wheel-drive mountain bike!) to negotiate it

game trail   the usually narrow trail made by deer, elk, or other game

gated   everyone knows what a gate is, and how many variations exist upon this theme; well, if a trail is described as "gated" it simply has a gate across it; don't forget that the rule is if you find a gate closed, close it behind you; if you find one open, leave it that way

Giardia   shorthand for *Giardia lamblia,* and known as the "backpacker's bane" until we mountain bikers expropriated it; this is a waterborne parasite that begins its life cycle when swallowed, and one to four weeks later has its host (you) bloated, vomiting, shivering with chills, and living in the bathroom; the disease can be avoided by "treating" (purifying) the water you acquire along the trail (see "Hitting the Trail" in the Introduction)

gnarly	a term thankfully used less and less these days, it refers to tough trails
hammer	to ride very hard
hardpack	a trail in which the dirt surface is packed down hard; such trails make for good and fast riding, and very painful landings; bikers most often use "hardpack" as both a noun and adjective, and "hard-packed" as an adjective only (the grammar lesson will help when diagramming sentences in camp)
hike-a-bike	what you do when the road or trail becomes too steep or rough to remain in the saddle
jeep road, jeep trail	a rough road or trail passable only with four-wheel-drive capability (or a horse or mountain bike)
kamikaze	while this once referred primarily to those Japanese fliers who quaffed a glass of sake, then flew off as human bombs in suicide missions against U.S. naval vessels, it has more recently been applied to the idiot mountain bikers who, far less honorably, scream down hiking trails, endangering the physical and mental safety of the walking, biking, and equestrian traffic they meet; deck guns were necessary to stop the Japanese kamikaze pilots, but a bike pump or walking staff in the spokes is sufficient for the current-day kamikazes who threaten to get us all kicked off the trails
loop	this route configuration is characterized by riding from the designated trailhead to a distant point, then returning to the trailhead via a different route (or simply continuing on the same in a circle route) without doubling back; you always move forward across new terrain, but return to the starting point when finished; mileage is for the entire loop from the trailhead back to trailhead
multi-purpose	a BLM designation of land which is open to many uses; mountain biking is allowed
ORV	a motorized off-road vehicle
out-and-back	a ride where you will return on the same trail you pedaled out; while this might sound far more boring than a loop route, many trails look very different when pedaled in the opposite direction; unless otherwise noted, mileage figures are the *total* distance out *and* back
pack stock	horses, mules, llamas, et cetera, carrying provisions along the trails . . . and unfortunately leaving a trail of their own behind

point-to-point	a vehicle shuttle (or similar assistance) is required for this type of route, which is ridden from the designated trailhead to a distant location, or endpoint, where the route ends; total mileage is for the one-way trip from the trailhead to endpoint
portage	to carry your bike on your person
pummy	volcanic activity in the Pacific Northwest and elsewhere produces soil with a high content of pumice; trails through such soil often become thick with dust, but this is light in consistency and can usually be pedaled; remember, however, to pedal carefully, for this dust obscures whatever might lurk below
quads	bikers use this term to refer both to the extensor muscle in the front of the thigh (which is separated into four parts) and to USGS maps; the expression "Nice quads!" refers always to the former, however, except in those instances when the speaker is an engineer
runoff	rainwater or snowmelt
scree	an accumulation of loose stones or rocky debris lying on a slope or at the base of a hill or cliff
signed	a "signed" trail has signs in place of blazes
single-track	a single, narrow path through grass or brush or over rocky terrain, often created by deer, elk, or backpackers; single-track riding is some of the best fun around
slickrock	the rock-hard, compacted sandstone that is *great* to ride and even prettier to look at; you'll appreciate it even more if you think of it as a petrified sand dune or seabed, and if the rider before you hasn't left tire marks (from unnecessary skidding) or granola bar wrappers behind
snowmelt	runoff produced by the melting of snow
snowpack	unmelted snow accumulated over weeks or months of winter—or over years in high-mountain terrain
spur	a road or trail that intersects the main trail you're following
switchback	a zigzagging road or trail designed to assist in traversing steep terrain: mountain bikers should *not* skid through switchbacks

technical	terrain that is difficult to ride due not to its grade (steepness) but to its obstacles—rocks, logs, ledges, loose soil . . .
topo	short for topographical map, the kind that shows both linear distance *and* elevation gain and loss; "topo" is pronounced with both vowels long
trashed	a trail that has been destroyed (same term used no matter what has destroyed it . . . cattle, horses, or even mountain bikers riding when the ground was too wet)
two-wheel-drive	this refers to any vehicle with drive-wheel capability on only two wheels (a passenger car, for instance, has two-wheel-drive); a two-wheel-drive road is a road or trail easily traveled by an ordinary car
water bar	an earth, rock, or wooden structure that funnels water off trails to reduce erosion
washboarded	a road that is surfaced with many ridges spaced closely together, like the ripples on a washboard; these make for very rough riding, and even worse driving in a car or jeep
whoop-de-doo	closely spaced dips or undulations in a trail; these are often encountered in areas traveled heavily by ORVs
wilderness area	land that is officially set aside by the federal government to remain *natural*—pure, pristine, and untrammeled by any vehicle, including mountain bikes; though mountain bikes had not been born in 1964 (when the United States Congress passed the Wilderness Act, establishing the National Wilderness Preservation system), they are considered a "form of mechanical transport" and are thereby excluded; in short, stay out
wind chill	a reference to the wind's cooling effect upon exposed flesh; for example, if the temperature is 10 degrees Fahrenheit and the wind is blowing at 20 miles per hour, the wind-chill (that is, the actual temperature to which your skin reacts) is *minus* 32 degrees; if you are riding in wet conditions things are even worse, for the wind-chill would then be *minus 74 degrees!*
windfall	anything (trees, limbs, brush, fellow bikers) blown down by the wind

STEVE JONES grew up thinking the whole country eats grits for breakfast. It wasn't until after a move from Marietta, Georgia, to Pennsyl-vania, followed by a stint in the Navy, that he figured out cuisine is as varied as facial expressions. After receiving B.A. and M.A. degrees in English, Steve taught high school for 13 years before stomping off the chalk dust from his feet to become a writer. In addition to this—his first book—his stories have appeared in *Natural History, Georgia Journal,* and *Dirt Rag* magazines. He is currently writing a biography on Vernon Medders, trainer and handler of bloodhounds. Besides mountain biking, Steve finds time to hike, camp, canoe, sail, coach his son's soccer team, and raise fox terriers and raspberries.

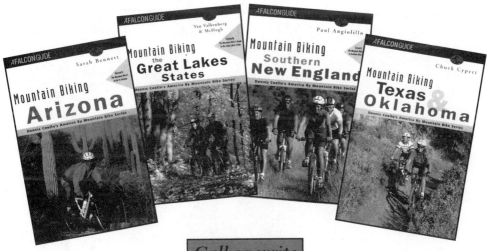